THE TOP 10

OF EVERYTHING

2006

THE TOP 10

OF EVERYTHING

2006

The Ultimate Book of Lists

RUSSELL ASH

A Dorling Kindersley Book

LONDON, NEW YORK, MUNICH, MELBOURNE, DELHI

Senior Editor Dawn Henderson
DTP Designer Adam Walker
Production Controller Shane Higgins

Managing Editor Julie Oughton
Managing Art Editor Heather McCarry
Category Publisher Stephanie Jackson

Produced for Dorling Kindersley by
The Bridgewater Book Company,
The Old Candlemakers, West Street,
Lewes, East Sussex BN7 2NZ

Project Editor Emily Casey Bailey
Project Designer Lisa McCormick
Designer Bernard Higton
Picture Research Vanessa Fletcher

Author's Project Manager Aylla Macphail

Published in Great Britain in 2005 by
Dorling Kindersley Limited, 80 Strand,
London WC2R 0RL

A Penguin Company

2 4 6 8 10 9 7 5 3 1

This edition produced for The Book People Ltd,
Hall Wood Avenue, Haydock, St Helens, WA11 9UL

ISBN 14053 1068 5

Reproduction by ImageScanhouse Global
Services, Malaysia

Printed and bound by Toppan, China

See our complete catalogue at
www.dk.com

Contents

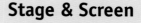

3

The Human World

4

Town & Country

5

Culture & Learning

8

Commercial World

9

Transport & Tourism

10

Sport

Introduction

The Top 10 of Everything has been published annually since 1989, so this is the 17th edition. When I began compiling it, I set myself the task of ensuring that every featured Top 10 list was definitive. In most instances, that means quantifiable, hence the Top 10 films, for example, are generally ranked according to how much each has earned internationally. No lists are subjective, so it is not a book of "bests" except those that are measurably bestsellers, while "worsts" in such categories as murders and disasters are similarly quantified, usually by numbers of victims. Alongside these lists are a variety of "firsts" or "latests" that recognize the pioneers and the most recent achievers in various fields of endeavour.

THE PACE OF CHANGE

This new collection of Top 10 lists features the latest updates of established favourites alongside hundreds of entirely new lists. They range from the most expensive pop lyrics, the countries with most executions, the fastest-growing cities and the biggest beer drinkers to the world's longest-running shows, the richest Russians, the top video games, and the most successful skateboarders. Since the last edition many momentous events have occurred, including the tragedy of the worst-ever tsunami. After a post-Cold War lull, military spending is escalating again, while in the realm of entertainment we have had the first-ever animated film (*Shrek 2*) to earn more than $900 million and the first documentary (*Fahrenheit 9/11*) to make over $200 million worldwide. The inexorable rise of DVD – sales of which can now outstrip box office earnings – continues, and record charts now take account of the new phenomenon of legal downloading.

FACTS AND FIGURES

In every instance, the figures are the latest available, although we are occasionally thwarted when new figures have not been released in time, or where a sporting season is still in progress as we go to press. Where

SPECIAL FEATURES

- Completely redesigned in an exciting and user-friendly style

- Top 10 Close-ups feature major single lists, ranging from the most valuable comics to medal-winning countries at the summer Olympics

- FirstFacts and FastFacts throughout – from the first billionaire to the largest whale ever measured

- Further Information – invaluable website links on Top 10 topics

certain figures differ from those published elsewhere, the discrepancy may derive from varying methods of measurement and definitions (in measuring a skyscraper, for example, do you include or exclude a building's spires, and what are the precise boundaries of a city?). Some disagreements may arise from the immense difficulty of accurately calculating certain statistics (how many Muslims are there in the world, and how many people in the USA are called "Smith"?). Figures for country and city populations are based on the latest available census, with estimates for increases where officially available, while in most instances "countries" should be taken as meaning "countries, colonies, and dependant territories".

THANKS FOR EVERYTHING

The question most commonly asked of authors of fiction is "Where do you get your ideas?" The question I hear most frequently is "Where do you get your information?" It comes from a huge variety of sources, from organizations, commercial companies and research bodies, specialized and often obscure publications, and, especially, a network of individuals around the world who have shared their knowledge of subjects from birds to bridges. As always, I acknowledge their invaluable contribution (see page 255 for full list of credits), as well as the many people who have been involved with the book at all stages of its development over its 17-year history.

CONTACT ME

Your comments, corrections, and suggestions for new lists are always welcome. Contact me via the publishers or visit my website:
http://www.top10ofeverything.com

Russell Ash

Chapter

12345

top 10 largest bodies in the Solar System: page 16

The Universe & The Earth

top 10 longest spacewalks: page 19

Elements

top 10 **LIGHTEST** SOLID ELEMENTS

	ELEMENT	DISCOVERER / COUNTRY	YEAR DISCOVERED	DENSITY*
1	Lithium	Johan August Arfvedson, Sweden	1817	0.533
2	Potassium	Sir Humphry Davy, UK	1807	0.859
3	Sodium	Sir Humphry Davy	1807	0.969
4	Calcium	Sir Humphry Davy	1808	1.526
5	Rubidium	Robert Wilhelm Bunsen/ Gustav Kirchoff, Germany	1861	1.534
6	Magnesium	Sir Humphry Davy	1808#	1.737
7	Phosphorus	Hennig Brandt, Germany	1669	1.825
8	Beryllium	Friedrich Wöhler, Germany/ Antoine-Alexandré Brutus Bussy, France	1828†	1.846
9	Caesium	Robert Wilhelm Bunsen/ Gustav Kirchoff	1860	1.896
10	Sulphur	–	Prehistoric	2.070

* g per cm³ at 20°C

\# Recognized by Joseph Black, 1755, but not isolated

† Recognized by Nicholas Vauquelin, 1797, but not isolated

Osmium, the heaviest element, is over 42 times heavier than lithium, the lightest solid. Lithium, a metal, is not only extremely light, but also so soft that it can be easily cut with a knife. It is half as heavy as water, and lighter even than certain types of wood. Lithium is used in the aerospace industry to make alloys and in the air filtration systems in spacecraft, while the hydrogen in hydrogen bombs is a compound of lithium – lithium hydride. The "dilithium crystals" employed in the warp drives of starships in *Star Trek* are, however, pure fiction.

⊃ Lighter than air
Although the commonest and lightest of all elements, hydrogen is too explosive to use in balloons. In consequence, hot air balloons dominate the sport, with helium reserved for wealthy purists.

top 10 **MOST COMMON** ELEMENTS IN THE UNIVERSE

ELEMENT / PARTS PER MILLION*

1 **Hydrogen** 750,000   2 **Helium** 230,000

3 **Oxygen** 10,000   4 **Carbon** 5,000   5 **Neon** 1,300

6 **Iron** 1,100   7 **Nitrogen** 1,000   8 **Silicon** 700

9 **Magnesium** 600   10 **Sulphur** 500

* mg per kg

top 10 ELEMENTS WITH THE **HIGHEST** BOILING POINT

ELEMENT	BOILING POINT (°C)	(°F)
1 Rhenium	5,596	10,105
2 Tungsten	5,555	10,031
3 Tantalum	5,458	9,856
4 Osmium	5,012	9,054
5 Thorium	4,820	8,708
6 Niobium	4,744	8,571
7 Molybdenum	4,639	8,382
8 Hafnium	4,603	8,317
9 Iridium	4,428	8,002
10 Zirconium	4,409	7,968

Source: WebElements

top 10 ELEMENTS WITH THE **LOWEST** BOILING POINT

ELEMENT	BOILING POINT (°C)	(°F)
1 Helium	-268.93	-452.07
2 Hydrogen	-252.87	-423.17
3 Neon	-246.08	-410.94
4 Nitrogen	-195.79	-320.42
5 Flourine	-188.12	-306.62
6 Argon	-185.80	-302.40
7 Oxygen	-182.90	-297.20
8 Krypton	-153.22	-243.80
9 Xenon	-108.00	-162.00
10 Radon	-61.70	-79.10

Source: WebElements

← High light
Familiar as the filament in incandescent light bulbs, tungsten's high melting point and hardness also makes it valuable for drills and cutting tools.

→ Low melting mercury
Although mercury is the only metal that is liquid at room temperature, below its melting point it becomes solid and can be bent like steel.

top 10 ELEMENTS WITH THE **HIGHEST** MELTING POINTS

ELEMENT	MELTING POINT (°C)	(°F)
1 Carbon	3,527	6,381
2 Tungsten	3,422	6,192
3 Rhenium	3,186	5,767
4 Osmium	3,033	5,491
5 Tantalum	3,017	5,463
6 Molybdenum	2,623	4,753
7 Niobium	2,477	4,491
8 Iridium	2,466	4,471
9 Ruthenium	2,334	4,233
10 Hafnium	2,233	4,051

Other elements that melt at high temperatures include chromium (1,907°C/3,465°F), iron (1,538°C/2,800°F), and gold (1,064°C/1,947°F). For comparison, the surface of the Sun attains 5,330°C (9,626°F).

top 10 ELEMENTS WITH THE **LOWEST** MELTING POINTS*

ELEMENT	MELTING POINT (°C)	(°F)
1 Mercury	−38.8	−37.8
2 Bromine	−7.3	19.0
3 Francium	27.0	80.6
4 Caesium	28.4	83.1
5 Gallium	29.7	85.5
6 Rubidium	39.3	103.7
7 Phosphorus	44.2	111.6
8 Potassium	63.4	146.1
9 Sodium	97.7	207.9
10 Iodine	113.7	236.7

* Non-gaseous only

Among other familiar elements that melt at relatively low temperatures are tin (231.9°C/449.4°F) and lead (327.5°C/621.5°F).

Stars & Comets

the 10 **MOST RECENT** OBSERVATIONS OF HALLEY'S COMET

1 1986 The Japanese *Suisei* probe passed within 151,000 km (93,827 miles) of its 15-km (9-mile) nucleus on 8 March 1986, revealing a whirling nucleus within a hydrogen cloud emitting 20–50 tonnes of water per second. The Soviet probes *Vega 1* and *Vega 2* passed within 8,890 km (5,524 miles) and 8,030 km (4,990 miles) respectively. The European Space Agency's *Giotto* passed as close as 596 km (370 miles) on 14 March. All were heavily battered by dust particles, and it was concluded that Halley's Comet is composed of dust bonded by water and carbon dioxide ice.

2 1910 Predictions of disaster were widely published, with many people convinced that the world would come to an end. Mark Twain, who had been born at the time of the 1835 appearance and believed that his fate was linked to that of the comet, died when it reappeared this year.

3 1835 Widely observed, but noticeably dimmer than in 1759.

4 1759 The comet's first return, as predicted by Halley, and thus proving his calculations correct.

5 1682 Observed in Africa and China, and extensively in Europe, where it was observed from 5 to 19 September by Edmond Halley, who predicted its return.

6 1607 Seen extensively in China, Japan, Korea, and Europe, described by German astronomer Joannes Kepler and its position accurately measured by amateur Welsh astronomer Thomas Harriot.

7 1531 Observed in China, Japan, and Korea, and in Europe from 13 to 23 August by Peter Appian, German geographer and astronomer, who noted that comets' tails point away from the Sun.

8 1456 Observed in China, Japan, and Korea, and by the Turkish army that was threatening to invade Europe. When the Turks were defeated by Papal forces, the comet was seen as a portent of victory.

9 1378 Observed in China, Japan, Korea, and Europe.

10 1301 Seen in Iceland, parts of Europe, China, Japan, and Korea.

⊗ Early warning
The appearance of Halley's Comet in 1066, shown here in the Bayeux Tapestry, was seen as a portent of King Harold's defeat by William the Conqueror.

top 10 COMETS COMING **CLOSEST** TO THE EARTH

	COMET	DATE*	(AU#)	DISTANCE (KM)	(MILES)
1	Comet of 1491	20 Feb 1491	0.0094	1,406,220	873,784
2	Lexell	1 July 1770	0.0151	2,258,928	1,403,633
3	Tempel-Tuttle	26 Oct 1366	0.0229	3,425,791	2,128,688
4	IRAS-Araki-Alcock	11 May 1983	0.0313	4,682,413	2,909,516
5	Halley	10 Apr 837	0.0334	4,996,569	3,104,724
6	Biela	9 Dec 1805	0.0366	5,475,282	3,402,182
7	Grischow	8 Feb 1743	0.0390	5,834,317	3,625,276
8	Pons-Winnecke	26 June 1927	0.0394	5,894,156	3,662,458
9	Comet of 1014	24 Feb 1014	0.0407	6,088,633	3,783,301
10	La Hire	20 Apr 1702	0.0437	6,537,427	4,062,168

* Of closest approach to the Earth

Astronomical Units: 1 AU = mean distance from the Earth to the Sun (149,597,870 km/92,955,793 miles)

◐ **Last sighting**
Halley's Comet's 76-year orbit means it was last seen in 1986 and is scheduled to reappear in 2061.

top 10 GALAXIES **NEAREST** TO THE EARTH

	GALAXY	DISCOVERED	APPROXIMATE DIAMETER*	DISTANCE#
1	Sagittarius Dwarf	1994	10,000	82,000
2	Large Magellanic Cloud	Prehist.	30,000	160,000
3	Small Magellanic Cloud	Prehist.	16,000	190,000
4	= Draco Dwarf	1954	3,000	205,000
	= Ursa Minor Dwarf	1954	2,000	205,000
6	Sculptor Dwarf	1937	3,000	254,000
7	Sextans Dwarf	1990	4,000	258,000
8	Carina Dwarf	1977	2,000	330,000
9	Fornax Dwarf	1938	6,000	450,000
10	Leo II	1950	3,000	660,000

* In light years

From the Earth in light years

Source: Peter Bond, Royal Astronomical Society

These galaxies are members of the so-called "Local Group", although with such vast distances, "local" is clearly a relative term. As our solar system and the Earth are at the outer edge of the Milky Way, this galaxy is excluded. Over the next hundred million years, the Sagittarius Dwarf – our nearest neighbouring galaxy – will be progressively absorbed into the Milky Way.

top 10 **BRIGHTEST** STARS*

	STAR	CONSTELLATION	DISTANCE#	APPARENT MAGNITUDE
1	Sirius	Canis Major	8.65	-1.46
2	Canopus	Carina	313	-0.62
3	Alpha Centauri	Centaurus	4.35	-0.27
4	Arcturus	Boötes	36	-0.04
5	Vega	Lyra	25	+0.03
6	Capella	Auriga	42	+0.08
7	Rigel	Orion	773	+0.18
8	Procyon	Canis Minor	11.4	+0.38
9	Achernar	Eridanus	144	+0.46
10	Beta Centauri	Centaurus	525	+0.61

* Excluding the Sun

From the Earth in light years

Source: Peter Bond, Royal Astronomical Society

This Top 10 is based on apparent visual magnitude as viewed from the Earth – the lower the number, the brighter the star. At its brightest, the star Betelgeuse is brighter than some of these, but its variability means that its average brightness disqualifies it from the Top 10. The absolute magnitude of Cygnus OB2 No. 12, discovered in 1992, may make it the brightest star in the galaxy, but it is 5,900 light years away.

Planets, Moons & Asteroids

⊖ Over the moon
Named after its discoverer, the *Huygens* probe
reached Saturn's moon Titan (top) on 14 January 2005.
With a diameter of 5,150 km (3,200 miles), Titan is larger
than both our own Moon (3,475 km/2,159 miles) and the
planet Pluto (2,390 km/1,485 miles).

top 10 BODIES* FARTHEST FROM THE SUN

BODY	AVERAGE DISTANCE FROM THE SUN (KM)	(MILES)
1 Pluto	5,914,000,000	3,675,000,000
2 Neptune	4,497,000,000	2,794,000,000
3 Uranus	2,871,000,000	1,784,000,000
4 Chiron	2,800,000,000	1,740,000,000
5 Saturn	1,427,000,000	887,000,000
6 Jupiter	778,300,000	483,600,000
7 Mars	227,900,000	141,600,000
8 Earth	149,597,870	92,955,793
9 Venus	108,200,000	67,200,000
10 Mercury	57,900,000	36,000,000

* In the Solar System, excluding satellites and asteroids

the 10 FIRST PLANETARY MOONS TO BE DISCOVERED

MOON	PLANET	DISCOVERER / COUNTRY	YEAR
1 Moon	Earth	–	Ancient
2 Io	Jupiter	Galileo Galilei, Italy	1610
3 Europa	Jupiter	Galileo Galilei	1610
4 Ganymede	Jupiter	Galileo Galilei	1610
5 Callisto	Jupiter	Galileo Galilei	1610
6 Titan	Saturn	Christian Huygens, Netherlands	1655
7 Iapetus	Saturn	Giovanni Cassini, Italy/France	1671
8 Rhea	Saturn	Giovanni Cassini	1672
9 Tethys	Saturn	Giovanni Cassini	1684
10 Dione	Saturn	Giovanni Cassini	1684

While the Earth's moon has been observed since ancient times,
it was not until the development of the telescope that Galileo
was able to discover (on 7 January 1610) the first moons of
another planet. These, which are Jupiter's four largest, were
named by German astronomer Simon Marius and are known
as the Galileans.

top 10 LARGEST ASTEROIDS

NAME	YEAR DISCOVERED	DIAMETER (KM)	(MILES)
1 Ceres	1801	914	568
2 Pallas	1802	524	325
3 Vesta	1807	502	312
4 Hygeia	1849	430	267
5 Davida	1903	338	210
6 Interamnia	1910	334	207
7 Europa	1858	312	194
8 Eunomia	1851	272	169
9 Sylvia	1866	270	168
10 Psyche	1852	264	164

Asteroids, sometimes known as "minor planets", are fragments
of rock orbiting between Mars and Jupiter. The orbits of over
96,000 have been calculated and some 12,000 officially named.
Each of the four Beatles has an asteroid named after them, as
do the members of the Monty Python team and James Bond.
The first and largest to be discovered was Ceres, which was
found by Giuseppe Piazzi (1746–1826), director of the
observatory in Palermo, Sicily, on New Year's Day, 1801.

top 10 OBJECTS COMING CLOSEST TO THE EARTH

	NAME / DESIGNATION	DUE DATE	DISTANCE* (KM)	DISTANCE* (MILES)
1	**2004 MX2**	17 July 2050	6,000	3,700
2	**2003 MH4**	12 June 2132	15,000	9,300
3	**2004 KH17**	11 June 2099	75,000	46,600
4	**2004 KH17**	10 June 2187	120,000	74,600
5	**2000 WO107**	2 Dec 2169	135,000	83,900
6	= **2004 KH17**	11 June 2090	150,000	93,200
	= **2000 EH26**	21 Apr 2106	150,000	93,200
8	= **2004 KH17**	10 June 2096	165,000	102,500
	= **2000 TU28**	16 Apr 2051	165,000	102,500
10	**2000 QK130**	15 Mar 2089	180,000	111,800

* Minimum possible distance from the Earth

Source: NASA

It is widely accepted that an asteroid impact with Earth some 65 million years ago was responsible for the extinction of the dinosaurs. It is believed that there are up to 2,000 "Near-Earth Objects" (mostly asteroids and comets) over one kilometre (0.62 mile) in diameter, and many thousands of smaller ones, that approach Earth's orbit and could potentially impact with our planet, with those listed here predicted to make the closest approaches. Asteroids approaching Earth are divided into three groups: Apollos (orbit-crossers), Amors (those that approach but do not cross) and Atens (within our orbit). The "Doomsday Scenario" of an asteroid's colliding with Earth, as presented by such films as *Armageddon* (1998), would probably involve an Apollo.

⊙ Collision course?
Small meteoroids usually break up on contact with the atmosphere, but an asteroid over 50 m (164 ft) in diameter could cause a catastrophe on Earth.

top 10 LARGEST BODIES
IN THE SOLAR SYSTEM

BODY / MAXIMUM DIAMETER (KM / MILES)

1 Sun 1,392,140 km / 865,036 miles

2 Jupiter 142,984 km / 88,846 miles

3 Saturn 120,536 km / 74,898 miles

10 Titan 5,150 km / 3,200 miles

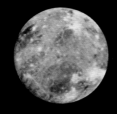

9 Ganymede 5,269 km / 3,274 miles

Most of the planets are visible
with the naked eye and have
been observed since ancient
times. The exceptions are Uranus,
discovered on 13 March 1781 by
British astronomer Sir William
Herschel; Neptune, found by
German astronomer Johann Galle
on 23 September 1846 (Galle was led
to his discovery by the independent
calculations of French astronomer
Urbain Leverrier and British
mathematician John Adams);
and – outside the Top 10 –
Pluto, located using
photographic techniques
by American astronomer Clyde
Tombaugh. Pluto's discovery was
announced on 13 March 1930; its
diameter is uncertain, but is thought
to be approximately 2,302 km
(1,430 miles). Mercury, also outside
the Top 10, has a diameter of
4,880 km (3,032 miles). Ganymede
is the largest of Jupiter's 63 satellites,
and Titan the largest of Saturn's 34.

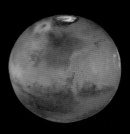

8 Mars 6,794 km / 4,222 miles

7 Venus 12,103 km / 7,520 miles

6 Earth 12,756 km / 7,926 miles

5 Neptune 49,532 km / 30,778 miles

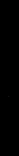

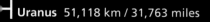

4 Uranus 51,118 km / 31,763 miles

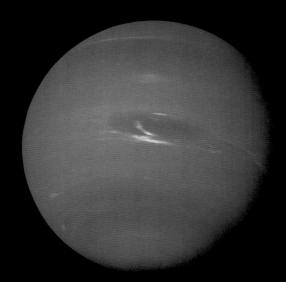

Astronauts & Cosmonauts

top 10 YOUNGEST ASTRONAUTS AND COSMONAUTS*

	ASTRONAUT OR COSMONAUT / COUNTRY#	FIRST FLIGHT	AGE (YRS	MTHS	DAYS)
1	Gherman S. Titov	6 Aug 1961	25	10	25
2	Valentina V. Tereshkova	16 June 1963	26	3	10
3	Boris B. Yegorov	15 Oct 1964	26	10	19
4	Yuri A. Gagarin	12 Apr 1961	27	1	3
5	Helen P. Sharman, UK	18 May 1991	27	11	19
6	Mark R. Shuttleworth, South Africa	25 Apr 2002	28	7	7
7	Dumitru D. Prunariu, Romania	14 May 1981	28	7	24
8	Valery F. Bykovsky	14 June 1963	28	10	19
9	Salman Abdel Aziz Al-Saud, Saudi Arabia	17 June 1985	28	11	20
10	Vladimir Remek, Czechoslovakia	2 Mar 1978	29	5	6

* To 1 Jan 2005

All Soviet, unless otherwise stated

⏻ Blast off
In the 24-year history of the Shuttle programme, 113 Space Shuttle launches have achieved a cumulative total of 1,031 days in space.

top 10 COUNTRIES WITH THE MOST EXPERIENCE OF SPACEFLIGHT

	COUNTRY	ASTRONAUTS	TOTAL DURATION OF MISSIONS* (DAYS	HRS	MINS	SECS)
1	USSR/Russia	97	16,858	17	8	24
2	USA	275	9,380	10	4	48
3	France	9	384	23	38	0
4	Kazakhstan	2	349	14	59	3
5	Germany	10	309	17	8	56
6	Canada	8	122	13	30	58
7	Japan	5	88	6	0	40
8	Italy	4	76	6	34	9
9	Switzerland	1	42	12	5	32
10	South Africa	1	24	22	28	22
	UK	1	7	21	13	45

* To 24 Oct 2004 landing of Soyuz TMA-4

The USSR, and now Russia, has clocked up its considerable lead on the rest of the world (with 60.2 per cent of the total time spent by humans in space) largely through the long-duration stays of its cosmonauts on board the Mir space station.

top 10 LONGEST SPACE SHUTTLE FLIGHTS*

	FLIGHT	DATES	DURATION (DAYS	HRS	MINS	SECS)
1	STS-80 Columbia	19 Nov–7 Dec 1996	17	8	53	18
2	STS-78 Columbia	20 June–7 July 1996	16	21	48	30
3	STS-67 Endeavor	2–18 Mar 1995	16	15	9	46
4	STS-107 Columbia#	16 Jan–1 Feb 2003	15	22	20	0
5	STS-73 Columbia	20 Oct–5 Nov 1995	15	21	53	16
6	STS-90 Columbia	17 Apr–3 May 1998	15	21	15	58
7	STS-75 Columbia	22 Feb–9 Mar 1996	15	17	41	25
8	STS-94 Columbia	1–17 July 1997	15	16	46	1
9	STS-87 Atlantis	25 Sept–6 Oct 1997	15	16	35	1
10	STS-65 Columbia	8–23 July 1994	14	17	55	0

* To 1 Jan 2005   # Destroyed on re-entry

The abbreviation STS (Space Transportation System) has been used throughout the Shuttle programme. The first nine flights were simply numbered STS-1 (12–14 April 1981) to STS-9. Thereafter a more complex system was employed: the first of the double-digit numbers shows the fiscal year (1 October–30 September) in which the launch took place; the number 1 indicates that it was made from the Kennedy Space Center, 2 from Vandenberg Air Force Base, and the letter the order in which the flights were scheduled, starting with A (although this does not necessarily show the actual sequence in which the mission occurred, due to occasional delays). The ill-fated STS-51-L *Challenger* was the last to be so numbered; all subsequent launches have reverted to the original system of STS + number alone and assigned sequentially to each mission, but the flights do not follow this order precisely.

Spacewalk
US astronaut Mark C. Lee uses a jetpack to conduct a free spacewalk from *Discovery* (1994); those who performed the longest duration EVAs have all been tethered to Shuttles.

top 10 LONGEST SPACEWALKS*

ASTRONAUTS#	SPACECRAFT	DATE	DURATION (HRS:MINS)
1 James Voss, Susan Helms	STS-102/ISS†	10–11 Mar 2001	8:56
2 Thomas D. Akers, Richard J. Hieb, Pierre J. Thuot	STS-49	13 May 1992	8:29
3 John M. Grunsfeld, Steven L. Smith	STS-103	22 Dec 1999	8:15
4 C. Michael Foale, Claude Nicollier	STS-103	23 Dec 1999	8:10
5 John M. Grunsfeld, Steven L. Smith	STS-103	24 Dec 1999	8:08
6 Daniel T. Barry, Tamara E. Jernigan	STS-96/ISS	29 May 1999	7:55
7 Jeffrey A. Hoffman, F. Story Musgrave	STS-61	4 Dec 1993	7:54
8 Steven S. Smith, Rex J. Walheim	STS-110/ISS	11 Apr 2002	7:48
9 Thomas D. Akers, Kathryn C. Thornton	STS-49	14 May 1992	7:44
10 Takao Doi, Winston E. Scott	STS-87	24 Nov 1997	7:43

* To 1 Jan 2005   # All USA exc. C. M. Foale who has dual citizenship with UK   † International Space Station

All of these EVAs (Extra Vehicular Activities) were from NASA Space Shuttles, most of them concerned with capture or repairs to satellites and other equipment, including the Hubble space telescope, and from the International Space Station. The longest EVA on the Moon lasted 7 hours 37 minutes. It was conducted by Eugene A. Cernan (Commander) and Harrison H. Schmitt (Lunar Module Pilot) on 12 December 1972 during Apollo 17's 75-hour stay on the lunar surface – the last occasion on which humans set foot on the Moon.

Oceans & Seas

top 10 LARGEST OCEANS AND SEAS

OCEAN OR SEA	APPROXIMATE AREA* (SQ KM)	(SQ MILES)
1 Pacific Ocean	166,242,500	64,186,600
2 Atlantic Ocean	86,557,800	33,420,160
3 Indian Ocean	73,427,800	28,350,640
4 Arctic Ocean	13,223,800	5,105,740
5 South China Sea	2,974,600	1,148,499
6 Caribbean Sea	2,515,900	971,400
7 Mediterranean Sea	2,510,000	969,120
8 Bering Sea	2,261,100	873,020
9 Sea of Okhotsk	1,527,570	589,800
10 Gulf of Mexico	1,507,600	582,100

* Excluding tributary seas

Geographers' opinions vary as to whether certain bodies of water are regarded as seas in their own right or as parts of a larger ocean. For example, the Coral, Weddell, and Tasman seas would be eligible for this list, but most authorities consider them part of the Pacific Ocean, whereas the Bering Sea is more commonly identified as an independent sea.

top 10 SMALLEST SEAS

SEA* / OCEAN	APPROXIMATE AREA (SQ KM)	(SQ MILES)
1 Gulf of California, Pacific Ocean	153,070	59,100
2 Persian Gulf, Indian Ocean	230,000	88,800
3 Yellow Sea, Pacific Ocean	293,960	113,500
4 Baltic Sea, Atlantic Ocean	382,000	147,500
5 North Sea, Atlantic Ocean	427,090	164,900
6 Red Sea, Indian Ocean	452,990	174,900
7 Black Sea, Atlantic Ocean	507,900	196,100
8 Andaman Sea, Indian Ocean	564,880	218,100
9 East China Sea, Pacific Ocean	664,590	256,600
10 Hudson Bay, Atlantic Ocean	730,120	281,900

* Excludes landlocked seas

top 10 COUNTRIES WITH THE LARGEST AREAS OF CORAL REEF

COUNTRY	REEF AREA (SQ KM)	(SQ MILES)	PERCENTAGE OF WORLD TOTAL
1 Indonesia	51,020	19,699	17.95
2 Australia	48,960	18,903	17.22
3 The Philippines	25,060	9,675	8.81
4 French overseas territories*	14,280	5,513	5.02
5 Papua New Guinea	13,840	5,343	4.87
6 Fiji	10,020	3,868	3.52
7 Maldives	8,920	3,444	3.14
8 Saudi Arabia	6,660	2,571	2.34
9 Marshall Islands	6,110	2,359	2.15
10 India	5,790	2,235	2.04
World total (including those not in Top 10)	*284,300*	*109,768*	*100.00*

* Clipperton, French Polynesia, Guadeloupe, Martinique, Mayotte, New Caledonia, Réunion, and Wallis and Futuna Islands

Source: *World Atlas of Coral Reefs*

⊕ Coral reef residents
The world's coral reefs support a diverse range of life, including many exotic fish, in a delicately balanced ecosystem that is vulnerable to outside influences.

Coral reefs thrive in shallow and clear waters and the sea temperatures found in the tropics. Among the richest of the world's ecosystems, they are extremely vulnerable to human intervention, with over-fishing, pollution, and the consequences of global warming presenting the biggest threats to their existence.

top 10 SHALLOWEST OCEANS AND SEAS

OCEAN OR SEA* / LOCATION	AVERAGE DEPTH (M)	(FT)
1 **Yellow Sea**, Pacific Ocean	36.8	121
2 **Baltic Sea**, Atlantic Ocean	54.8	180
3 **Hudson Bay**, Atlantic Ocean	92.9	305
4 **North Sea**, Atlantic Ocean	93.8	308
5 **Persian Gulf**, Indian Ocean	99.9	328
6 **East China Sea**, Indian Ocean	188.9	620
7 **Red Sea**, Indian Ocean	537.6	1,764
8 **Gulf of California**, Pacific Ocean	723.9	2,375
9 **Sea of Okhotsk**, Pacific Ocean	972.9	3,192
10 **Arctic Ocean**	1,038.4	3,407

* Excludes landlocked seas

With a maximum depth of 152 m (500 ft), the Yellow Sea will probably not remain on the Top 10 list of shallowest oceans and seas forever – it is likely that environmental changes in the next few millennia will result in the total disappearance of the sea.

Shallow yellow The Yellow sea between Korea and China gets its distinctive colour from the sand particles carried into it from the Yellow River (Huang He), its shallowness causing them to be dispersed slowly.

top 10 DEEPEST OCEANS AND SEAS

OCEAN OR SEA	GREATEST DEPTH (M)	(FT)	AVERAGE DEPTH (M)	(FT)
1 **Pacific Ocean**	10,924	35,837	4,028	13,215
2 **Indian Ocean**	7,455	24,460	3,963	13,002
3 **Atlantic Ocean**	9,219	30,246	3,926	12,880
4 **Caribbean Sea**	6,946	22,788	2,647	8,685
5 **South China Sea**	5,016	16,456	1,652	5,419
6 **Bering Sea**	4,773	15,659	1,547	5,075
7 **Gulf of Mexico**	3,787	12,425	1,486	4,874
8 **Mediterranean Sea**	4,632	15,197	1,429	4,688
9 **Japan Sea**	3,742	12,276	1,350	4,429
10 **Arctic Ocean**	5,625	18,456	1,205	3,953

The deepest point in the deepest ocean is the Marianas Trench in the Pacific, at a depth of 10,924 m (35,837 ft) according to a recent survey. However, the slightly lesser depth of 10,916 m (35,814 ft) was recorded on 23 January 1960 by Jacques Piccard (Switzerland) and Donald Walsh (USA) in their 17.7-m (58-ft) long bathyscaphe *Trieste 2* during the deepest-ever ocean descent. Whichever is correct, it is close to 11 km (6.8 miles) down, or almost 29 times the height of the Empire State Building.

First Fact The first craft capable of exploring the world's deepest oceans was the bathyscaphe (from the Greek words for "depth" and "ship") invented by Auguste Piccard (Switzerland, 1884–62). The holder of the world balloon altitude record, he adapted design elements from his balloon gondola to the bathyscaphe, taking it down to record depths. Its successor *Trieste 2* was the craft in which his son Jacques set the unbeatable depth record in 1960. In 1999 Auguste's grandson Bertrand Piccard took part in the first balloon circumnavigation of the globe.

Rivers & Lakes

top 10 GREATEST RIVER SYSTEMS*

RIVER SYSTEM	CONTINENT	AVERAGE DISCHARGE AT MOUTH (CU M / SEC)
1 **Amazon**	South America	180,000
2 **Congo (Zaïre)**	Africa	42,000
3 **Yangtze (Chang Jiang)**	Asia	35,000
4 **Orinoco**	South America	28,000
5 **Brahmaputra (Tsangpo)**	Asia	20,000
6 **Yenisei/Angara**	Asia	19,600
7 **Río de la Plata/Paraná/ Uruguay**	South America	19,500
8 **Mississippi/Missouri**	North America	17,545
9 **Lena**	Asia	16,400
10 **Mekong**	Asia	15,900

* Based on rate of discharge at mouth

Source: River Systems of the World

top 10 LONGEST RIVER SYSTEMS

RIVER SYSTEM	CONTINENT	APPROXIMATE LENGTH (KM)	(MILES)
1 **Nile**	Africa	6,695	4,160
2 **Amazon**	South America	6,448	4,007
3 **Yangtze (Chang Jiang)**	Asia	6,378	3,964
4 **Mississippi/Missouri**	North America	6,228	3,870
5 **Ob'**	Asia	5,570	3,460
6 **Yenisei/Angara**	Asia	5,550	3,448
7 **Huang He (Yellow)**	Asia	5,464	3,395
8 **Río de la Plata/ Paraná/Uruguay**	South America	4,700	2,920
9 **Amur**	Asia	4,415	2,744
10 **Lena**	Asia	4,400	2,734

The source of the Nile was discovered in 1858 when British explorer John Hanning Speke reached lake Victoria Nyanza, in what is now Burundi. It was not until 1953 that the source of the Amazon was identified as a stream called Huarco, which flows from the Misuie glacier in the Peruvian Andes mountains.

top 10 LAKES WITH THE GREATEST VOLUME OF WATER

LAKE / LOCATION	VOLUME (CU KM)	(CU MILES)
1 **Caspian Sea**, Azerbaijan/Iran/ Kazakhstan/Russia/Turkmenistan	78,707	18,882
2 **Baikal**, Russia	22,995	5,517
3 **Tanganyika**, Burundi/Tanzania/ Dem. Rep. of Congo/Zambia	18,304	4,391
4 **Superior**, Canada/USA	12,174	2,921
5 **Michigan/Huron**, Canada/US	8,449	2,642
6 **Nyasa (Malawi)**, Malawi/ Mozambique/Tanzania	7,775	1,865
7 **Victoria**, Kenya/Tanzania/Uganda	2,518	604
8 **Great Bear**, Canada	2,292	550
9 **Great Slave**, Canada	2,258	542
10 **Issyk Kul**, Kyrgyzstan	1,725	420

The Caspian Sea is the world's largest inland sea or lake, containing some 40 per cent of all the planet's surface water and receiving more water than any other landlocked body of water – an average of 340 cu km (82 cu miles) per annum, which is causing a steady rise in sea level. This environmental change, along with pollution and the overfishing of the Caspian's famed sturgeon population, is among the many threats to its future.

➲ Great lake

Once called the Hyrcanian Ocean, the Caspian Sea, seen here from space, is a saltwater lake that has been landlocked for over five million years. It is fed by the Volga (top left) and other rivers.

top 10 LARGEST LAKES

LAKE / LOCATION	APPROXIMATE AREA (SQ KM)	(SQ MILES)
1 Caspian Sea Azerbaijan/Iran/Kazakhstan/ Russia/Turkmenistan	371,000	143,000
2 Michigan/Huron* Canada/USA	117,436	45,342
3 Superior Canada/USA	82,103	31,700
4 Victoria Kenya/Tanzania/Uganda	69,485	26,828
5 Tanganyika Burundi/Tanzania/Dem. Rep. of Congo/Zambia	32,893	12,700
6 Baikal Russia	31,500	12,162
7 Great Bear Canada	31,328	12,096
8 Malawi (Nyasa) Tanzania/Malawi/Mozambique	28,880	11,150
9 Great Slave Canada	28,568	11,030
10 Lake Erie Canada/USA	25,667	9,910

* Now considered two lobes of the same lake

Lake Michigan/Huron is the world's largest freshwater lake. Lake Baikal (or Baykal) in Siberia, with a depth of as much as 1.74 km (1.08 miles) in parts, is the world's deepest. As recently as 1960, the Aral Sea (Kazakhstan/Uzbekistan), with an area, including lake islands, of some 68,300 sq km (26,371 sq miles) was the fourth largest lake in the world, but as a result of the diverting of rivers for irrigation, it has dropped to 17,158 sq km (6,625 sq miles).

Fast Fact Sealed 4,000 m (13,124 ft) beneath the Antarctic, Lake Vostok may be one of the largest lakes on Earth. Despite its location, it is liquid, rather than frozen. It covers an area of some 14,000 sq km (5,405 sq miles) and has a volume of 5,400 cu km (1,295 cu miles). Discovered in 1996 through radar observations from space, it has not been investigated because drilling through the ice into the lake may force it to gush to the surface, contaminating water that has

top 10 DEEPEST LAKES

LAKE / LOCATION	GREATEST DEPTH (M)	(FT)
10 Hornindals Norway	514	1,686
9 Toba Sumatra, Indonesia	529	1,736
8 Crater Oregon, USA	589	1,932
7 Matana Sulawesi, Indonesia	590	1,936
6 Great Slave Canada	614	2,015
5 Issyk-kul Kyrgyzstan	668	2,191
4 Malawi Malawi/Mozambique/Tanzania	706	2,316
3 Caspian Sea Azerbaijan/Iran/Kazakhstan/ Russia/Turkmenistan	1,025	3,363
2 Tanganyika Burundi/Tanzania/ Dem. Rep. of Congo/ Zambia	1,471	4,825
1 Baikal Russia	1,741	5,712

Islands

top 10 SMALLEST ISLAND COUNTRIES

	COUNTRY / LOCATION	AREA (SQ KM)	(SQ MILES)
1	**Nauru**, Pacific Ocean	21	8
2	**Tuvalu**, Pacific Ocean	26	10
3	**Marshall Islands**, Pacific Ocean	181	70
4	**Maldives**, Indian Ocean	300	116
5	**Malta**, Mediterranean Sea	321	124
6	= **Grenada**, Caribbean Sea	339	131
	= **St. Vincent and the Grenadines**, Caribbean Sea	339	131
8	**St. Kitts and Nevis**, Caribbean Sea	360	139
9	**Barbados**, Caribbean Sea	430	166
10	**Antigua and Barbuda**, Caribbean Sea	440	170

Source: US Census Bureau, International Data Base

Marshall Islands
One of the world's smallest island countries, the Marshall Islands – a group of 34 coral atolls and islands – has been an independent country since 1986.

top 10 LARGEST LAKE ISLANDS

	ISLAND / LAKE / LOCATION	AREA (SQ KM)	(SQ MILES)
1	**Manitoulin** Huron, Ontario, Canada	2,766	1,068
2	**René-Lavasseur** Manicouagan Reservoir, Quebec, Canada	2,020	780
3	**Olkhon** Baikal, Russia	730	282
4	**Samosir** Toba, Sumatra, Indonesia	630	243
5	**Isle Royale** Superior, Michigan, USA	541	209
6	**Ukerewe** Victoria, Tanzania	530	205
7	**St. Joseph** Huron, Ontario, Canada	365	141
8	**Drummond** Huron, Michigan, USA	347	134
9	**Idjwi** Kivu, Dem. Rep. of Congo	285	110
10	**Ometepe** Nicaragua, Nicaragua	276	107

top 10 LARGEST ISLANDS

	ISLAND / LOCATION	AREA* (SQ KM)	(SQ MILES)
1	**Greenland (Kalaatdlit Nunaat)**, North Atlantic	2,175,600	840,004
2	**New Guinea**, Southwest Pacific	785,753	303,381
3	**Borneo**, West mid-Pacific	748,168	288,869
4	**Madagascar**, Indian Ocean	587,713	226,917
5	**Baffin Island**, North Atlantic	503,944	194,574
6	**Sumatra**, Northeast Indian Ocean	443,065	171,068
7	**Great Britain**, off coast of Northwest Europe	229,957	88,787
8	**Honshu**, Sea of Japan	225,800	87,182
9	**Victoria Island**, Arctic Ocean	220,548	85,154
10	**Ellesmere Island**, Arctic Ocean	183,964	71,029

* Mainlands, including areas of inland water, but excluding offshore islands

Not all islands are surrounded by sea: many sizeable islands are situated in lakes. Vozrozhdeniya Island, Uzbekistan, previously 2nd in this list with an area of roughly 2,300 sq km (900 sq miles), has grown as the Aral Sea contracts, and has now linked up with the surrounding land to become a peninsula. There are even larger islands in freshwater river outlets, including Marajó in the mouth of the Amazon, Brazil (48,000 sq km/18,533 sq miles), and Bananal in the River Araguaia, Brazil (20,000 sq km/7,722 sq miles).

Australia is regarded as a continental land mass rather than an island; otherwise it would rank first, at 7,618,493 sq km (2,941,517 sq miles), or 35 times the size of Great Britain. The largest US island is Hawaii, which measures 10,456 sq km (4,037 sq miles), and the largest off mainland USA is Kodiak, Alaska, at 9,510 sq km (3,672 sq miles).

top 10 MOST ISOLATED ISLANDS

ISLAND / LOCATION / ISOLATION INDEX

The United Nations' isolation index is calculated by adding together the square roots of the distances to the nearest island, group of islands, and continent. The higher the number, the more remote the island.

Source: United Nations

Gough Island, South Atlantic, Isolation index: 125

=9

Bouvet Island, South Atlantic, Isolation index: 125

Far away
The United Nations' isolation index identifies these islands as the most remote on the planet.

Palmyra Island, Central Pacific, Isolation index: 125

=9

Kiritimati, Line Islands, Central Pacific, Isolation index: 129

3

Jarvis Island, Central Pacific, Isolation index:128

4

=5

Kosrae, Micronesia, Pacific, Isolation index: 126

Starbuck, Line Islands, Central Pacific, Isolation index: 126

=5 **Malden**, Line Islands, Central Pacific, Isolation index: 126

Vostok, Line Islands, Central Pacific, Isolation index: 126

Easter Island, South Pacific, Isolation index: 149

2

1

Rapa Iti, Tubuai Islands, South Pacific, Isolation index: 130

◐ **Solitary sentinels**
The most isolated place on Earth, Easter Island is "guarded" by more than 600 curious statues or *moai*, some over 9.8 m (32 ft) high and weighing 91.5 tonnes (90 tons).

Mountains & Other Land Features

top 10 **LARGEST** METEORITE CRATERS

	CRATER / LOCATION	DIAMETER (KM)	(MILES)
1	**Vredefort**, South Africa	300	186
2	**Sudbury**, Ontario, Canada	250	155
3	**Chicxulub**, Yucatan, Mexico	170	107
4 =	**Manicougan**, Canada	100	62
=	**Popigai**, Russia	100	62
6	**Acraman**, Australia	90	56
7	**Chesapeake Bay**, Virginia, USA	85	53
8	**Puchezh-Katunki**, Russia	80	50
9	**Morokweng**, South Africa	70	43
10	**Kara**, Russia	65	40

Source: Canada Geological Survey, Continental Geoscience Division

Unlike on the Solar System's other planets and moons, many astroblemes (collision sites) on the Earth have been weathered over time and obscured. Thus, one of the ongoing debates in geology is whether or not certain crater-like structures are of meteoric origin or are the remnants of long-extinct volcanoes. The Vredefort Ring, for example, long thought to be meteoric, was declared in 1963 to be volcanic, but has since been claimed as a definite meteor crater, as are all the giant meteorite craters in the Top 10 (along with 106 others) by the International Union of Geological Sciences Commission on Comparative Planetology.

top 10 **DEEPEST** DEPRESSIONS

	DEPRESSION / LOCATION	MAXIMUM DEPTH BELOW SEA LEVEL (M)	(FT)
1	**Dead Sea**, Israel/Jordan	400	1,312
2	**Lake Assal**, Djibouti	156	511
3	**Turfan Depression**, China	154	505
4	**Qattâra Depression**, Egypt	133	436
5	**Mangyshlak Peninsula**, Kazakhstan	132	433
6	**Danakil Depression**, Ethiopia	117	383
7	**Death Valley**, USA	86	282
8	**Salton Sink**, USA	72	235
9	**Zapadny Chink Ustyurta**, Kazakhstan	70	230
10	**Prikaspiyskaya Nizmennost**, Kazakhstan/Russia	67	220

The shore of the Dead Sea is the lowest exposed ground below sea level, but the bed of the sea actually reaches 728 m (2,388 ft) below sea level, and that of Lake Baikal, Russia, attains 1,485 m (4,872 ft) below sea level. Much of Antarctica is below sea level (some as low as 2,538 m/8,326 ft) – but the land there is covered by an ice cap that averages 2,100 m (6,890 ft) in depth. The lowest points on continents outside those appearing in the Top 10 include South America's Peninsula Valdés, Argentina (40 m/131 ft below sea level), Europe's Caspian Sea shore (28 m/92 ft), and Australia's Lake Eyre (12 m/52 ft).

top 10 **LONGEST** CAVES

CAVE / LOCATION / TOTAL KNOWN LENGTH (KM / MILES)

The world's longest cave systems compared with the as-the-crow-flies 370-km (230-mile) distance between London and Paris.

SCALE | 100 KM / 64 MILES | 200 KM / 128 MILES | 300 KM / 192 MILES

10 Ozernaja, Ukrainskaja, Ukraine, 122 km / 76 miles

9 Sistema Ox Bel Ha, Quintana Roo, Mexico, 133 km / 83 miles

8 Siebenhengste-hohgant, Bern, Switzerland, 149 km / 92 miles

7 Fisher Ridge System, Kentucky, USA, 172 km / 107 miles

6 Wind Cave, South Dakota, USA, 182 km / 113 miles

5 Lechuguilla Cave, New Mexico, USA, 183 km / 114 miles

4 Hölloch, Schwyz, Switzerland, 189 km / 117 miles

3 Jewel Cave, South Dakota, USA, 207 km / 129 mil

2 Optimisticeskaja, Ukrainskaja, Ukraine, 214

Source: Bob Gulden

The longest-known cave system in the UK is Ease Gill in West Yorkshire at 70,500 m (231,300 ft).

top 10 HIGHEST MOUNTAINS

	MOUNTAIN / LOCATION	FIRST ASCENT	TEAM NATIONALITY	HEIGHT* (M)	HEIGHT* (FT)
1	**Everest** Nepal/China	29 May 1953	British/ New Zealand	8,850	29,035
2	**K2 (Chogori)** Pakistan/China	31 July 1954	Italian	8,607	28,238
3	**Kangchenjunga** Nepal/India	25 May 1955	British	8,598	28,208
4	**Lhotse** Nepal/China	18 May 1956	Swiss	8,511	27,923
5	**Makalu I** Nepal/China	15 May 1955	French	8,481	27,824
6	**Lhotse Shar II** Nepal/China	12 May 1970	Austrian	8,383	27,504
7	**Dhaulagiri I** Nepal	13 May 1960	Swiss/ Austrian	8,172	26,810
8	**Manaslu I (Kutang I)** Nepal	9 May 1956	Japanese	8,156	26,760
9	**Cho Oyu** Nepal	19 Oct 1954	Austrian	8,153	26,750
10	**Nanga Parbat (Diamir)** Kashmir	3 July 1953	German/ Austrian	8,126	26,660

* Height of principal peak; lower peaks of the same mountain are excluded

top 10 MOST ACTIVE VOLCANOES*

	VOLCANO / LOCATION	CONTINUOUSLY ACTIVE SINCE
1	**Mount Etna**, Italy	c. 1500 BC
2	**Stromboli**, Italy	c. 4
3	**Yasur**, Vanuatu	c. 1204
4	**Piton de la Fournaise**, Reunion	1920
5	**Santa Maria**, Guatemala	1922
6	**Dukono**, Indonesia	1933
7	**Sangay**, Ecuador	1934
8	**Ambrym**, Vanuatu	1935
9	**Suwanose-jima**, Japan	1949
10	**Tinakula**, Solomon Islands	1951

* Based on years of continuous eruption

Source: John Seach, www.volcanolive.com

Sicily's 3,350-m (10,991-ft) Mount Etna may have been erupting for more than half a million years, with occasional dormant periods. Continuous activity has been recorded for the past 3,500 years, the eruption of 1843 killing 56, with a further nine in 1979 and two in 1987.

400 KM / 256 MILES

Edouard-Alfred Martel

Edouard-Alfred Martel (1859–1938), a French lawyer, invented the science of speleology (cave exploration). From 1888 onwards he explored numerous caves in Europe – many for the first time – discovering underground lakes and streams and developing some of the first caving equipment, including portable ladders and collapsible canoes. In 1889 he became the first to enter the spectacular Gouffre de Padirac, France, and in 1898 established it as France's first cave open to the public.

➲ **Cave man**
In an illustration by Lucien Rudeaux, Martel is shown during the first exploration of Britain's largest cavern, Gaping Gill, Yorkshire, 1895.

1 Mammoth Cave System, Kentucky, USA, 579 km / 360 miles

World Weather

top 10 COLDEST PLACES – EXTREMES

	LOCATION*	LOWEST RECORDED TEMPERATURE (°C)	(°F)
1	**Vostok**#, Antarctica	-89.2	-128.6
2	**Sovietskaya**#, Antarctica	-86.7	-124.1
3	**Oymyakon**, Russia	-71.2	-96.2
4	**Verkhoyansk**, Russia	-69.8	-93.6
5	**Northice**#, Greenland	-66.0	-87.0
6	**Eismitte**#, Greenland	-64.9	-85.0
7	= **Snag**, Yukon, Canada	-63.0	-81.4
8	= **Bulunkul Lake**, Tajikistan	-63.0	-81.4
9	**Mayo**, Yukon, Canada	-62.2	-80.0
10	**Prospect Creek**, Alaska, USA	-62.1	-79.8

* Maximum of two places per country listed

Present or former scientific research base

Source: Philip Eden/Roland Bert

Vostok, a Russian research station, recorded the lowest temperature on Earth on 21 July 1983, and – though unofficial – an even colder one of -91°C (-132°F) in 1997. It is situated at an altitude of 3,420 m (11,220 ft) and is susceptible to katabatic (downhill) winds that can reach up to 322 km/h (200 mph).

top 10 DULLEST PLACES*

	LOCATION#	PERCENTAGE OF MAXIMUM POSSIBLE SUNSHINE	AVERAGE ANNUAL HOURS OF SUNSHINE
1	**Ben Nevis**, Scotland	16	736
2	**Hoyvik**, Faeroes, Denmark	19	902
3	**Maam**, Ireland	19	929
4	**Prince Rupert**, British Columbia, Canada	20	955
5	**Riksgransen**, Sweden	20	965
6	**Akureyri**, Iceland	20	973
7	**Raufarhöfn**, Iceland	21	995
8	**Nanortalik**, Greenland	22	1,000
9	**Dalwhinnie**, Scotland	22	1,032
10	**Karasjok**, Norway	23	1,090

* Lowest yearly sunshine total, averaged over a long period of years

Maximum of two places per country listed

Source: Philip Eden

The least sunny places on Earth tend to be in northern latitudes and at elevations that make them susceptible to cloud cover. As a result, Ben Nevis receives about one-sixth of the total sunshine hours of the world's desert areas.

top 10 PLACES WITH THE HEAVIEST DAILY DOWNPOURS*

LOCATION# / HIGHEST RAINFALL IN 24 HOURS (MM / IN)

1 Chilaos, Réunion 1,870 mm / 73.6 in
2 Baguio, Philippines 1,168 mm / 46.0 in
3 Alvin, Texas, USA 1,092 mm / 43.0 in
4 Cherrapunji, India 1,041 mm / 41.0 in
5 Smithport, Pennsylvania, USA 1,013 mm / 39.9 in
6 Crohamhurst, Australia 907 mm / 35.7 in
7 Finch-Hatton, Australia 879 mm / 34.6 in
8 Suva, Fiji 673 mm / 26.5 in
9 Cayenne, French Guyana 597 mm / 23.5 in
10 Aitutaki, Cook Islands 572 mm / 22.5 in

* Based on limited data
# Maximum of two places per country listed
Source: Philip Eden

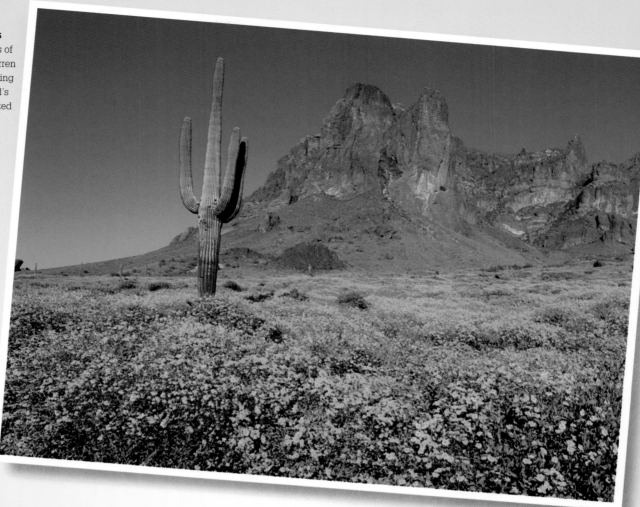

Desert blooms
At certain times of the year, the barren desert surrounding Yuma, the world's sunniest inhabited place, supports a profusion of wild flowers.

top 10 **HOTTEST** PLACES – EXTREMES

	LOCATION*	HIGHEST RECORDED TEMPERATURE (°C)	(°F)
1	**Al'Azīzīyah**, Libya	58.0	136.4
2	**Greenland Ranch**, Death Valley, USA	56.7	134.0
3	=**Ghudamis**, Libya	55.0	131.0
	=**Kebili**, Tunisia	55.0	131.0
5	**Tombouctou**, Mali	54.5	130.1
6	=**Araouane**, Mali	54.4	130.0
	=**Mammoth Tank**#, California, USA	54.4	130.0
8	**Tirat Tavi**, Israel	54.0	129.0
9	**Ahwāz**, Iran	53.5	128.3
10	**Agha Jārī**, Iran	53.3	128.0

* Maximum of two places per country listed
# Former weather station
Source: Philip Eden/Roland Bert

top 10 **SUNNIEST** PLACES*

	LOCATION#	PERCENTAGE OF MAXIMUM POSSIBLE SUNSHINE	AVERAGE ANNUAL HOURS OF SUNSHINE
1	**Yuma**, Arizona, USA	91	4,127
2	**Phoenix**, Arizona, USA	90	4,041
3	**Wadi Halfa**, Sudan	89	3,964
4	**Bordj Omar Driss**, Algeria	88	3,899
5	**Keetmanshoop**, Namibia	88	3,876
6	**Aoulef**, Algeria	86	3,784
7	**Upington**, South Africa	86	3,766
8	**Atbara**, Sudan	85	3,739
9	**Mariental**, Namibia	84	3,707
10	**Bilma**, Niger	84	3,699

* Highest yearly sunshine total, averaged over a long period of years
# Maximum of two places per country listed
Source: Philip Eden

Natural Disasters

the 10 WORST AVALANCHES AND LANDSLIDES*

LOCATION / INCIDENT / DATE / ESTIMATED NO. KILLED

1 **Alps, Italy**
Avalanche, Oct 218 BC
18,000

2 **Yungay, Peru**
Landslide, 31 May 1970
17,500

3 **Alps, Italy**
Avalanche, 13 Dec 1916
10,000

4 **Huarás, Peru**
Avalanche, 13 Dec 1941
5,000

5 **Nevada Huascaran, Peru**
Avalanche, 10 Jan 1962
3,500

6 **Chiavenna, Italy**
Landslide, 4 Sept 1618
2,427

7 **Plurs, Switzerland**
Avalanche, 4 Sept 1618
1,496

8 **Goldau Valley, Switzerland**
Landslide, 2 Sept 1806
800

9 **Medellin, Colombia**
Landslide, 27 Sept 1987
683

10 **Chungar, Peru**
Avalanche, 19 Mar 1971
600

* Excluding those where most deaths resulted from flooding, earthquakes, volcanoes, etc., associated with landslides

the 10 WORST HURRICANES, TYPHOONS, AND CYCLONES

LOCATION / DATE / ESTIMATED NO. KILLED

1 **East Pakistan (Bangladesh)**
13 Nov 1970
500,000–1,000,000

2 **Bengal, India**
7 Oct 1737
>300,000

3 **Haiphong, Vietnam**
1881
300,000

4 **Bengal, India**
31 Oct 1876
200,000

5 **Bombay, India**
6 June 1882
>100,000

6 **Southern Japan**
23 Aug 1281
68,000

7 **Northeast China**
2–3 Aug 1922
60,000

8 **Calcutta, India**
5 Oct 1864
50,000–70,000

9 **Bengal, India**
15–16 Oct 1942
40,000

10 **East Pakistan (Bangladesh))**
May–June 1965
35,000–40,000

the 10 COSTLIEST HURRICANES TO STRIKE THE US

HURRICANE / YEAR / COST OF DAMAGE*

1 **"Great Miami"**
1926
$83,814,000,000

2 **Andrew**
1992
$44,878,000,000

3 **North Texas**
1900
$36,096,000,000

4 **North Texas**
1915
$30,585,000,000

5 **New England**
1938
$22,549,000,000

6 **Southwest Florida**
1944
$22,070,000,000

7 **Southeast Florida/ Lake Okeechobee**
1928
$18,708,000,000

8 **Betsy**
1965
$16,863,000,000

9 **Donna**
1960
$16,339,000,000

10 **Camille**
1969
$14,870,000,000

* Adjusted to 2003 dollars

Source: Atlantic Oceanographic and Meteorological Laboratory/National Oceanic and Atmospheric Administration

⊖ Eye of the storm
A cyclone seen from space: the size and power of these and related meteorological phenomena cause loss of life and property on an often massive scale.

the 10 WORST EARTHQUAKES

1 **Near East/Mediterranean**
20 May 1202
1,100,000

2 **Shenshi, China**
2 Feb 1556
820,000

3 **Calcutta, India**
11 Oct 1737
300,000

4 **Antioch, Syria**
20 May AD 526
250,000

5 **Tangshan, China**
28 July 1976
242,419

6 **Nanshan, China**
22 May 1927
200,000

7 **Yeddo, Japan**
30 Dec 1703
190,000

8 **Kansu, China**
16 Dec 1920
180,000

9 **Messina, Italy**
28 Dec 1908
160,000

10 **Tokyo/Yokohama, Japan**
1 Sept 1923
142,807

There are some discrepancies between the "official" death tolls in many of the world's worst earthquakes and the estimates of other authorities. For example, 750,000 is sometimes quoted for the Tang-shan earthquake of 1976, and totals of 58,000–250,000 are given for the quake that devastated Messina in 1908. Several other earthquakes in China and Turkey resulted in deaths of 100,000 or more, and more recently an Armenian quake (7 Dec 1988) and an Irananian one (21 June 1990) caused more than 55,000/50,000 deaths respectively.

✿ Killer wave

Familiar from the images of Japanese artist Hokusai, tsunamis can reach great heights. One caused by an earthquake in Lituya Bay, Alaska, on 9 July 1958, travelled at 160 km/h (100 mph) and surged to 524 m (1,720 ft), but only two people were killed.

the 10 WORST TSUNAMIS

1 Southeast Asia, 26 Dec 2004, **287,534**

2 Krakatoa, Sumatra/Java*, 27 Aug 1883, **36,380**

3 Sanriku, Japan, 15 June 1896, **28,000**

4 Agadir, Morocco#, 29 Feb 1960, **12,000**

5 Lisbon, Portugal, 1 Nov 1755, **10,000**

6 Papua New Guinea, 18 July 1998, **8,000**

7 Chile/Pacific islands/Japan, 22 May 1960, **5,700**

8 Philippines, 17 Aug 1976, **5,000**

9 Hyuga to Izu, Japan, 28 Oct 1707, **4,900**

10 Sanriku, Japan, 3 Mar 1933, **3,000**

* Combined effect of volcanic eruption and tsunamis

Combined effect of earthquake and tsunamis

Tsunamis (from the Japanese *tsu*, meaning "port", and *nami*, meaning "wave"), are powerful waves caused by undersea disturbances such as earthquakes or volcanic eruptions. They are often mistakenly called tidal waves, which are a different phenomenon. Tsunamis can be so intense that they frequently cross entire oceans, devastating islands and coastal regions in their paths. Triggered by a massive undersea earthquake in the Indian Ocean, the 2004 tsunami was exceptionally powerful and destructive. It devastated coastal settlements in low-lying areas of Indonesia, Sri Lanka, Thailand, and other countries as far away as Africa, resulting in loss of life on an unprecedented scale.

Chapter

12**2**3456

top 10 heaviest flighted birds: page 38

top 10 fastest mammals: page 37

top 10 deadliest spiders: page 41

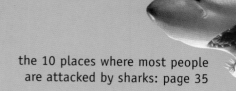

the 10 places where most people are attacked by sharks: page 35

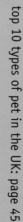

top 10 types of pet in the UK: page 45

Life on Earth

Aquatic Animals

top 10 **HEAVIEST** MARINE MAMMALS

MAMMAL / SCIENTIFIC NAME	LENGTH (M)	(FT)	WEIGHT (TONNES)
1 Blue whale, *Balaenoptera musculus*	33.5	110.0	137.0
2 Bowhead whale (Greenland right), *Balaena mysticetus*	20.0	65.0	86.0
3 Northern right whale (black right), *Balaena glacialis*	18.6	60.0	77.7
4 Fin whale (common rorqual), *Balaenoptera physalus*	25.0	82.0	63.4
5 Sperm whale, *Physeter catodon*	18.0	59.0	43.7
6 Grey whale, *Eschrichtius robustus*	14.0	46.0	34.9
7 Humpback whale, *Megaptera novaeangliae*	15.0	49.2	34.6
8 Sei whale, *Balaenoptera borealis*	18.5	60.0	29.4
9 Bryde's whale, *Balaenoptera edeni*	14.6	47.9	20.0
10 Baird's whale, *Berardius bairdii*	5.5	18.0	12.1

Source: Lucy T. Verma

Probably the largest animal that ever lived, the blue whale dwarfs even the other whales listed here – all but one of which far outweigh the biggest land animal, the elephant. The elephant seal, with a weight of 3.5 tonnes (3.4 tons), is the largest marine mammal that is not a whale.

FastFact
No blue whale has ever been weighed intact, and size estimates come from measurements of specimens that have been killed and cut up by whalers. Based on this method, the largest was a 27.6-m (90-ft 6-in) female weighing up to 190 tonnes (186 tons) caught by the Russian *Slava* whaling fleet off South Georgia on 20 March 1947. It produced 66 tonnes (65 tons) of meat, 30 tonnes (29.5 tons) of blubber; its skeleton alone weighed 26 tonnes (25.5 tons), and its tongue 4.3 tonnes (4.2 tons).

Big blue
The blue whale is longer than and weighs four times as much as a Boeing 737 aircraft.

Designed for speed
The skeleton of a sailfish tailfin. Its powerful structure and the streamlined shape of its body are perfectly designed to enable the sailfish to travel in water at speeds faster than a cheetah can attain on land.

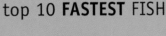

top 10 **FASTEST** FISH

FISH / SCIENTIFIC NAME	MAXIMUM RECORDED SPEED (KM/H)	(MPH)
1 Sailfish, *Istiophorus platypterus*	112	69
2 Striped marlin, *Tetrapturus audax*	80	50
3 Wahoo (peto, jack mackerel), *Acanthocybium solandri*	77	48
4 Southern bluefin tuna, *Thunnus maccoyii*	76	47
5 Yellowfin tuna, *Thunnus albacares*	74	46
6 Blue shark, *Prionace glauca*	69	43
7 = Bonefish, *Albula vulpes*	64	40
= Swordfish, *Xiphias gladius*	64	40
9 Tarpon (ox-eye herring), *Megalops cyprinoides*	56	35
10 Tiger shark, *Galeocerdo cuvier*	53	33

Source: Lucy T. Verma

Flying fish are excluded: they have a top speed in the water of only 37 km/h (23 mph), but airborne they can reach 56 km/h (35 mph). Many sharks qualify for the list, but only two are listed here to prevent the list becoming overly shark-infested.

the 10 PLACES WHERE **MOST PEOPLE** ARE ATTACKED BY SHARKS

	LOCATION	FATAL ATTACKS	LAST FATAL ATTACK	TOTAL ATTACKS*		LOCATION	FATAL ATTACKS	LAST FATAL ATTACK	TOTAL ATTACKS*
1	USA (excluding Hawaii)	39	2004	761	6	Papua New Guinea	25	2000	48
2	Australia	134	2004	294	7	New Zealand	9	1968	45
3	South Africa	41	2004	204	8	Mexico	20	1997	35
4	Hawaii	15	2004	100	9	Iran	8	1985	23
5	Brazil	20	2004	85	10	The Bahamas	1	1968	22

* Confirmed unprovoked attacks, including non-fatal

Source: International Shark Attack File/American Elasmobranch Society/Florida Museum of Natural History

The International Shark Attack File monitors worldwide incidents, a total of 1,969 of which have been recorded since the 16th century. The 1990s had the highest attack total (514) of any decade, while 61 unprovoked attacks were recorded in 2004 alone. This upward trend is believed to reflect the growth in the numbers of people encountering them rather than an increase in the aggressive behaviour of sharks.

➲ Jaws of death
Led by the great white, shark attacks worldwide have increased as the amount of time humans spend in the water has increased.

top 10 **HEAVIEST** SPECIES OF SALTWATER FISH CAUGHT

SPECIES / SCIENTIFIC NAME	ANGLER / LOCATION / DATE	WEIGHT (KG / G)		(LB / OZ)	
1 Great white shark, *Carcharodon carcharias*	Alfred Dean, Ceduna, South Australia, 21 Apr 1959	1,208	380	2,664	0
2 Tiger shark, *Galeocerdo cuvier*	Kevin James Clapson, Ulladulla, Australia, 28 Mar 2004	810	0	1,785	11
3 Greenland shark, *Somniosus microcephalus*	Terje Nordtvedt, Trondheimsfjord, Norway, 18 Oct 1987	775	0	1,708	9
4 Black marlin, *Istiompax marlina*	Alfred C. Glassell, Jr., Cabo Blanco, Peru, 4 Aug 1953	707	610	1,560	0
5 Bluefin tuna, *Thunnus thynnus*	Ken Fraser, Aulds Cove, Nova Scotia, Canada, 26 Oct 1979	678	580	1,496	0
6 Atlantic blue marlin, *Makaira nigricans*	Paulo Amorim, Vitoria, Brazil 29 Feb 1992	636	0	1,402	2
7 Pacific blue marlin, *Makaira nigricans*	Jay W. de Beaubien, Kaaiwi Point, Kona, 31 May 1982	624	140	1,376	0
8 Shortfin mako shark, *Isurus oxyrinchus*	Luke Sweeney, Chatham, Massachusetts, USA, 21 July 2001	553	840	1,221	0
9 Sixgilled shark, *Hexanchus griseus*	Clemens Rump, Ascension Island, 21 Nov 2002	588	760	1,298	0
10 Swordfish, *Xiphias gladius*	Louis Marron, Iquique, Chile, 7 May 1953	536	150	1,182	0

Source: International Game Fish Association, World Record Game Fishes, 2005

Land Animals

top 10 FASTEST-GESTATING MAMMALS

	MAMMAL* / SCIENTIFIC NAME	AVERAGE GESTATION (DAYS)
1	**Short-nosed bandicoot**, *Isoodon obesulus*	12
2	**Black-shouldered opossum**, *Caluromysiops irrupta*	12–14
3 =	**Long-nosed bandicoot**, *Perameles nasuta*	12.5
=	**Narrow-footed marsupial mouse (striped face dunnart)**, *Sminthopsis macroura*	12.5
5	**Virginia (common) opossum**, *Didelphis virginiana*	12.5–13
6	**Common (northern common) cuscus**, *Phalanger orientalis*	13
7	**Dusky (montane) shrew**, *Sorex monticolus*	13–28
8	**Raffray's bandicoot**, *Peroryctes rafrayana*	15
9	**Mountain (short-eared) brushtail possum (bobuc)**, *Trichosurus caninus*	15–17
10	**Western quoll (chuditch, Western native cat)**, *Dasyurus geoffroii*	16–23

* One example per genus listed

top 10 WILD MAMMALS WITH THE LARGEST LITTERS

	MAMMAL / SCIENTIFIC NAME	AVERAGE LITTER
1	**Common tenrec**, *Tenrec ecaudatus*	25
2	**Virginia (common) opossum**, *Didelphis virginiana*	21
3	**Southern (black-eared) opossum** *Didelphis marsupialis*	10
4 =	**Ermine**, *Mustela erminea*	9
=	**Prairie vole**, *Microtus ochrogaster*	9
=	**Syrian (golden) hamster**, *Mesocricetus auratus*	9
7	**African hunting dog**, *Lycaon pictus*	8.8
8 =	**Dhole (Indian wild dog)**, *Cuon alpinus*	8
=	**Pygmy opossum**, *Marmosa robinsoni*	8
=	**South American mouse opossum**, *Gracilinanus agilis*	8

⬅ Playing possum

The Virginia opossum, North America's only marsupial, has a short gestation period and produces large litters. After birth, the young transfer to a pouch and later cling to the mother's back for several months.

Nature appears to confer on most mammals a lifetime's supply of approximately 800 million heartbeats. Small creatures such as shrews have a remarkably fast heart rate of 900–1,400 beats a minute. They thus "use up" their heartbeats and so have an average lifespan of less than two years. The shrew's metabolism also demands that it feeds constantly to survive: it seldom sleeps and can die of starvation if it does not eat for a few hours.

top 10 LIGHTEST TERRESTRIAL MAMMALS

MAMMAL* / SCIENTIFIC NAME	LENGTH (MM)	LENGTH (IN)	WEIGHT# (G)	WEIGHT# (OZ)
1 **Pygmy shrew**, *Sorex hoyi*	46–100	1.8–3.9	2.1–18	0.07–0.63
2 **Pygmy shrew**, *Suncus etruscus*	35–48	1.4–1.9	2.5	0.22
3 **African pygmy mouse**, *Mus minutoides*	45–82	1.8–3.2	2.5–12.0	0.09–0.42
4 **Desert shrew**, *Notiosorex crawfordi*	48–69	1.9–2.7	3.0–5.0	0.1–0.17
5 **Forest musk shrew**, *Sylvisorex* sp.	45–100	1.8–3.9	3.0–12.0	0.1–0.42
6 **White-toothed shrew**, *Crocidura suaveolens*	40–100	1.6–3.9	3.0–13.0	0.1–0.46
7 **Asiatic shrew**, *Soriculus salenskii*	44–99	1.7–3.9	5.0–6.0	0.17–0.21
8 **Delany's swamp mouse**, *Delanymys brooksi*	50–63	1.9–2.5	5.2–6.5	0.18–0.23
9 **Birch mouse**, *Sicista* sp.	50–90	1.9–3.5	6.0–14	0.21–0.49
10 **Pygmy mouse**, *Baiomys* sp.	50–81	1.9–3.2	7.0–8.0	0.24–0.59

* Lightest species per genus

\# Ranked by lightest in range; some jerboas are smaller, but no precise weights have yet been recorded

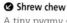

🕑 Shrew chew

A tiny pygmy shrew, the smallest of all land mammals, makes a meal of a worm many times its own length.

top 10 FASTEST MAMMALS

Along with its relatively slow rivals, the cheetah can deliver its astonishing maximum speed over only relatively short distances. For comparison, the human male 100 m record (Tim Montgomery, USA, 2002) stands at 9.78 seconds, equivalent to a speed of 37 km/h (23 mph), so all the mammals in the Top 10, and several others, are capable of outrunning a man. If a human ran the 100 m at the cheetah's speed, the record would fall to 3 seconds.

MAMMAL* / SCIENTIFIC NAME / MAXIMUM RECORDED SPEED (KM/H / MPH)

1 **Cheetah**, *Acinonyx jubatus*, 114 km/h / 71 mph

2 **Pronghorn antelope**, *Antilocapra americana*, 95 km/h / 57 mph

=3 **Blue wildebeest (brindled gnu)**, *Connochaetes taurinus*) / **Lion**, *Panthera leo* / **Springbok**, *Antidorcas marsupialis*, 80 km/h / 50 mph

=6 **Brown hare**, *Lepus capensis* / **Red fox**, *Vulpes vulpes*, 77 km/h / 48 mph

=8 **Grant's gazelle**, *Gazella granti* / **Thomson's gazelle**, *Gazella thomsonii*, 76 km/h / 47 mph

10 **Horse**, *Equus caballus* 72 km/h / 45 mph

⊕ Flying start

The cheetah's metabolism, extended claws, and body structure are perfectly adapted to enable it to achieve phenomenal acceleration and bursts of speed. As it runs, all four legs leave the ground for as much as half the distance it travels.

* Of those species for which data available at time of collection

Birds

top 10 FASTEST BIRDS

BIRD* / SCIENTIFIC NAME		MAXIMUM RECORDED SPEED (KM/H)	(MPH)
1	**Common eider**, *Somateria mollissima*	76	47
2	**Bewick's swan**, *Cygnus columbianus*	72	44
3 =	**Barnacle goose**, *Branta leucopsis*	68	42
=	**Common crane**, *Grus grus*	68	42
5	**Mallard**, *Anas platyrhynchos*	65	40
6 =	**Red-throated diver**, *Gavia stellata*	61	38
=	**Wood pigeon**, *Columba palumbus*	61	38
8	**Oystercatcher**, *Haematopus ostralegus*	58	36
9 =	**Ring-necked pheasant**, *Phasianus colchichus*	54	33
=	**White-fronted goose**, *Anser albifrons*	54	33

* By species

Source: Chris Mead

⊕ Heaviest and fastest
The mute swan ranks as the heaviest flighted bird and can live for over 20 years. Mute swans usually mate for life and breed in the same place year after year.

Recent research reveals that, contrary to popular belief, swifts are not fast fliers, just very efficient with long thin wings like gliders and low wing-loading. Fast fliers generally have high wing-loading and fast wing beats. The fastest swimming birds are penguins, which can achieve speeds of 35 km/h (21 mph). The fasting running bird is the ostrich, which can reach a speed of 72 km/h (44 mph), and maintain it for 20 minutes – ostrich racing with human jockeys or drawing chariots is pursued in South Africa and other countries.

top 10 HEAVIEST FLIGHTED BIRDS

BIRD* / SCIENTIFIC NAME		WINGSPAN (CM)	(IN)	WEIGHT (KG)	(LB / OZ)	
1	**Mute swan**, *Cygnus olor*	238	93	22.50	49	6
2	**Kori bustard**, *Ardeotis kori*	270	106	19.00	41	8
3 =	**Andean condor**, *Vultur gryphus*	320	126	15.00	33	1
=	**Great white pelican**, *Pelecanus onocrotalus*	360	141	15.00	33	1
5	**European black vulture**, *Aegypius monachus*	295	116	12.50	27	5
6	**Sarus crane**, *Grus antigone*	280	110	12.24	26	9
7	**Himalayan griffon (vulture)**, *Gyps himalayensis*	310	122	12.00	26	5
8	**Wandering albatross**, *Diomedea exulans*	350	137	11.30	24	9
9	**Steller's sea eagle**, *Haliaeetus pelagicus*	265	104	9.00	19	8
10	**Marabou stork**, *Leptoptilos crumeniferus*	287	113	8.90	19	6

* By species

Source: Chris Mead

First Fact
The first observation of migrating birds in the New World was made by the sailors of Christopher Columbus's ships, the *Niña*, *Pinta*, and *Santa Maria*. On 7 October 1492 they encountered huge flocks of migrating (and now extinct) Eskimo curlews and American golden plovers, some of which landed on deck. Realizing that these were land birds, *Pinta* captain Martín Alonso Pinzón urged the fleet to turn its course to the southwest, the direction the birds were flying. As a result, Columbus made landfall on San Salvador, rather than mainland America.

top 10 LONGEST BIRD MIGRATIONS

BIRD* / SCIENTIFIC NAME	APPROXIMATE DISTANCE (KM)	(MILES)
1 **Pectoral sandpiper**, *Calidris melanotos*	19,000#	11,806
2 **Wheatear**, *Oenanthe oenanthe*	18,000	11,184
3 **Slender-billed shearwater**, *Puffinus tenuirostris*	17,500#	10,874
4 **Ruff**, *Philomachus pugnax*	16,600	10,314
5 **Willow warbler**, *Phylloscopus trochilus*	16,300	10,128
6 **Arctic tern**, *Sterna paradisaea*	16,200	10,066
7 **Arctic skua**, *Stercorarius parasiticus*	15,600	9,693
8 **Swainson's hawk**, *Buteo swainsoni*	15,200	9,445
9 **Knot**, *Calidris canutus*	15,000	9,320
10 **Swallow**, *Hirundo rustica*	14,900	9,258

* By species

Thought to be only half of the path taken during a whole year

Source: Chris Mead

This list is of the likely extremes for a normal migrant. All migrant birds fly far longer than is indicated by the direct route. Many species fly all year, except when they come to land to breed, or, in the case of seabirds, to rest on the sea. Such species include the albatross, petrel, tern, and some types of swift and house martin. The annual distance covered by these birds may range from 150,000 km (93,206 miles) to almost 300,000 km (186,413 miles).

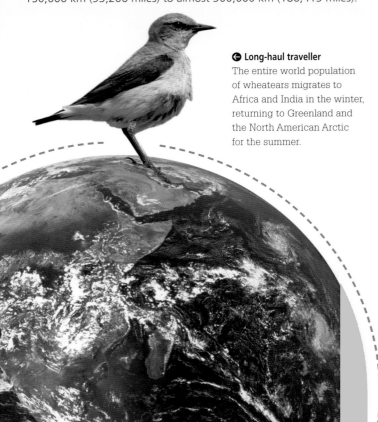

Long-haul traveller
The entire world population of wheatears migrates to Africa and India in the winter, returning to Greenland and the North American Arctic for the summer.

Big bird
The ostrich, a native of Africa (but with an introduced population in Australia), is the heaviest and tallest of all living birds. It also has the longest legs and is capable of outrunning a racehorse.

TOP 10 HEAVIEST FLIGHTLESS BIRDS

BIRD* / SCIENTIFIC NAME	WEIGHT (KG)	(LB	/ OZ)
1 **Ostrich (male)**, *Struthio camelus*	156.0	343	9
2 **Northern cassowary**, *Casuarius unappendiculatus*	58.0	127	9
3 **Emu (female)**, *Dromaius novaehollandiae*	55.0	121	6
4 **Emperor penguin (female)**, *Aptenodytes forsteri*	46.0	101	4
5 **Greater rhea**, *Rhea americana*	25.0	55	2
6 **Flightless steamer (duck)**, *Tachyeres brachypterus*	6.2	13	7
7 **Flightless cormorant**, *Nannopterum harrisi*	4.5	9	15
8 **Kiwi (female)**, *Apteryx haastii*	3.8	8	4
9 **Takahe (rail)**, *Porphyrio mantelli*	3.2	7	2
10 **Kakapo (parrot)**, *Strigops habroptilus*	3.2	7	1

* By species

Source: Chris Mead

Insects & Spiders

top 10 SMALLEST BUTTERFLIES

BUTTERFLY / SCIENTIFIC NAME	AVERAGE WINGSPAN (MM)	(IN)
1 Dwarf blue, *Brephidium barberae*	14	0.55
2 Western pygmy blue, *Brephidium exilis*	15	0.62
3 Western square-dotted blue, *Euphilotes battoides*	17	0.66
4 Pallid dotted-blue, *Euphilotes pallescens*	18	0.70
5 = Bernardino dotted-blue, *Euphilotes bernardino*	19	0.74
= Cyna blue, *Zizula cyna*	19	0.74
= Intermediate dotted-blue, *Euphilotes intermedia*	19	0.74
= Little metalmark, *Calephelis virginiensis*	19	0.74
= Rita dotted-blue, *Euphilotes rita*	19	0.74
= Small dotted-blue, *Philotiella speciosa*	19	0.74
= Telea hairstreak, *Chlorostrymon teleai*	19	0.74

top 10 LARGEST BUTTERFLIES

BUTTERFLY / SCIENTIFIC NAME	AVERAGE WINGSPAN (MM)	(IN)
1 Queen Alexandra's birdwing, *Ornithoptera alexandrae*	280	11.0
2 African giant swallowtail, *Papilio antimachus*	230	9.1
3 Goliath birdwing, *Ornithoptera goliath*	210	8.3
4 = Buru opalescent birdwing, *Troides prattorum*	200	7.9
= *Trogonoptera trojana*	200	7.9
= *Troides hypolitus*	200	7.9
7 = Chimaera birdwing, *Ornithoptera chimaera*	190	7.5
= *Ornithoptera lydius*	190	7.5
= *Troides magellanus*	190	7.5
= *Troides miranda*	190	7.5

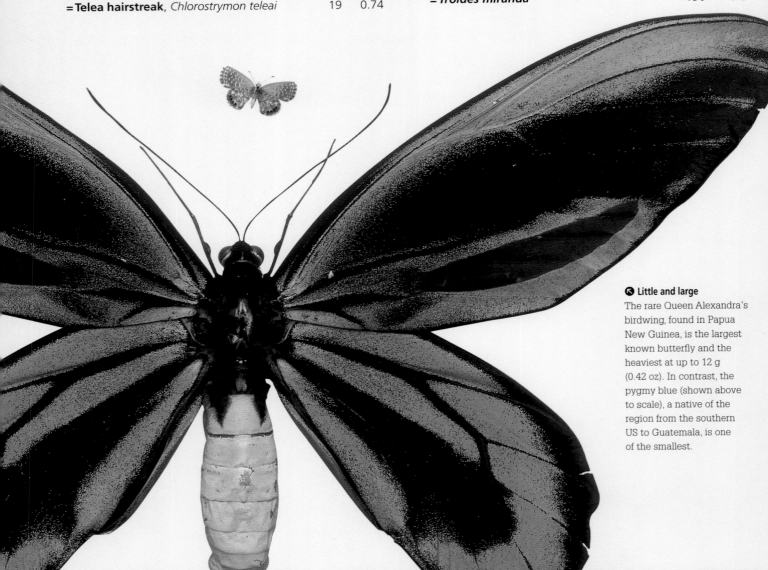

◉ Little and large
The rare Queen Alexandra's birdwing, found in Papua New Guinea, is the largest known butterfly and the heaviest at up to 12 g (0.42 oz). In contrast, the pygmy blue (shown above to scale), a native of the region from the southern US to Guatemala, is one of the smallest.

top 10 **FASTEST** INSECT FLYERS

INSECT* / SCIENTIFIC NAME	MAXIMUM RECORDED SPEED (KM/H)	(MPH)
1 Hawkmoth, *Sphingidae*	53.6	33.3
2 = Deer bot fly, *Cephenemyia pratti*	48.0	30.0
= West Indian butterfly, *Nymphalidae prepona*	48.0	30.0
4 Deer bot fly, *Chrysops*	40.0	25.0
5 West Indian butterfly, *Hesperiidae* sp.	30.0	18.6
6 Lesser Emperor dragonfly, *Anax parthenope*	28.6	17.8
7 = Dragonfly, *Aeschna*	25.2	15.6
= Hornet, *Vespa*	25.2	15.6
9 = Honey bee, *Apis millefera*	22.4	13.9
= Horsefly, *Tabanus bovinus*	22.4	13.9

* By species; of those for which data are available

Few accurate assessments of insect flying speed have ever been attempted, and this Top 10 represents only the results of the handful of scientific studies that are widely recognized by entomologists. Some experts have also suggested that the male horsefly (*Hybomitra linei wrighti*) is capable of travelling at 145 km/h (90 mph) when in pursuit of a female, while there are exceptional one-off examples such as that of a dragonfly allegedly recorded by Dr. R.J. Tilyard as flying at a speed of 98 km/h (61 mph). Many so-called records are clearly flawed, however: in 1917, for example, Charles Townsend estimated the flying speed of the deer bot fly at an unbelievable 1,317 km/h (818 mph). If true, it would have broken the sound barrier!

⊕ **Evil bunch**
The deadly and aggressive Brazilian wandering spider is also known as the banana spider because it frequently stows away on fruit boats.

top 10 **DEADLIEST** SPIDERS

SPIDER / SCIENTIFIC NAME / RANGE

1 **Banana spider**, *Phoneutria nigriventer*, Central and South America

2 **Sydney funnel web**, *Atrax robustus*, Australia

3 **Wolf spider**, *Lycosa raptoria/erythrognatha*, Central and South America

4 **Black widow**, *Latrodectus* sp., Widespread

5 **Violin spider/Recluse spider**, *Loxesceles reclusa*, Widespread

6 **Sac spider**, *Cheiracanthium punctorium*, Central Europe

7 **Tarantula**, *Eurypelma rubropilosum*, Neotropics

8 **Tarantula**, *Acanthoscurria atrox*, Neotropics

9 **Tarantula**, *Lasiodora klugi*, Neotropics

10 **Tarantula**, *Pamphobeteus species*, Neotropics

This list ranks spiders according to their "lethal potential" – their venom yield divided by their venom potency. The banana spider, for example, yields 6 mg of venom, with 1 mg the estimated lethal dose in man. However, few spiders are capable of killing humans – there were just 14 recorded deaths caused by black widows in the USA in the whole of the 19th century. Their venom yield is relatively low compared with that of the most dangerous snakes – the tarantula, for example, produces 1.5 mg of venom, but its lethal dose for an adult human is 12 mg. Originally applied to the wolf spider, the name tarantula is confusingly used for various members of the *Theraphosidae* family and *Lycos tarantula*, the spider once believed to cause the disease tarantism.

top 10 HEAVIEST TERRESTRIAL MAMMALS

MAMMAL* / SCIENTIFIC NAME	LENGTH (M)	(FT)	WEIGHT (KG)	(LB)
1 African elephant *Loxodonta africana*	7.5	24.6	7,500	16,534
2 Hippopotamus *Hippopotamus amphibius*	5.0	16.4	4,500	9,920
3 White rhinoceros *Ceratotherium simum*	4.2	13.7	3,600	7,937
4 Giraffe *Giraffa camelopardalis*	4.7	15.4	1,930	4,255
5 American buffalo *Bison bison*	3.5	11.4	1,000	2,205
6 Moose *Alces alces*	3.1	10.1	825	1,820
7 Grizzly bear *Ursus arctos*	3.0	9.8	780	1,720
8 Arabian camel (dromedary) *Camelus dromedarius*	3.4	11.3	690	1,521
9 Siberian tiger *Panthera tigris altaica*	3.3	10.8	360	793
10 Gorilla *Gorilla gorilla gorilla*	2.0	6.5	275	606

* Heaviest species per genus

This Top 10 list excludes domesticated cattle and horses. It also avoids comparing close kin such as the African and Indian elephants, highlighting instead the "sumo stars" within distinctive large mammal groups such as the bears, big cats, primates, and bovines (ox-like mammals).

⟵ The heavy brigade

The elephant, hippopotamus, and rhinoceros head the list of the heaviest land mammals while the gorilla is the heaviest primate, and thus humans' closest super-sized relative. The widespread use of "Jumbo"– originally the name of a huge elephant – to describe oversized objects, and the iconic image of King Kong as a giant gorilla, underline our respect for nature's heavyweights.

2

3

Perfect Pets

top 10 PET BIRD POPULATIONS

COUNTRY	ESTIMATED PET BIRD POPULATION, 2003*
1 China	72,547,000
2 USA	29,000,000
3 Japan	21,250,000
4 Brazil	17,500,000
5 Italy	13,000,000
6 Spain	7,873,000
7 Australia	7,500,000
8 France	6,450,000
9 Germany	4,700,000
10 UK	3,020,000

* In those countries for which data available

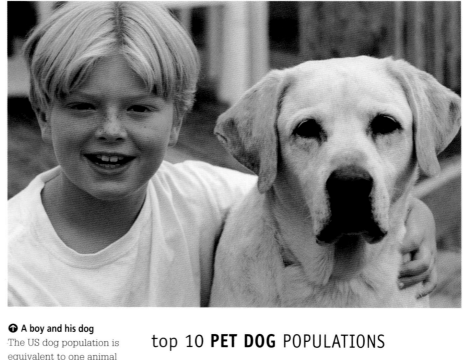

⊕ Birds of a feather
Cagebirds have been kept as pets worldwide since ancient times.

⊕ A boy and his dog
The US dog population is equivalent to one animal for every 4.8 humans.

top 10 PET DOG POPULATIONS

COUNTRY / ESIMATED PET DOG POPULATION, 2003*

1 **USA** 61,340,000

2 **Brazil** 27,000,000

3 **China** 23,366,000

4 **Mexico** 16,111,000

5 **Japan** 9,523,000

6 **France** 8,100,000

7 **Poland** 7,525,000

8 **Italy** 6,950,000

9 **UK** 6,500,000

10 **Germany** 4,800,000

* In those countries for which data available
Source: Euromonitor

Dog ownership in the USA has become increasingly humanized: not only are dogs given human names and often considered as "one of the family", but a huge industry has grown up to cater for their nutrition and welfare to a standard that rivals that of many people. Second only to the USA for its dog population, dogs have become Brazil's most popular pets, accounting for almost 43 per cent of the country's total pet population and – despite economic hardship – 77 per cent of pet food sales, while pet megastores, dog gyms, and massage parlours have been established in major cities.

top 10 PET CAT POPULATIONS

	COUNTRY	ESTIMATED PET CAT POPULATION, 2003*
1	USA	78,350,000
2	China	54,161,000
3	Brazil	11,000,000
4	France	9,800,000
5	UK	7,700,000
6	Italy	7,500,000
7	Japan	7,119,000
8	Germany	7,100,000
9	Canada	6,961,000
10	Mexico	6,101,000

* In those countries for which data available

Source: Euromonitor

Estimates of the numbers of domestic cats in the 20 leading cat-owning countries show a total population of 216,132,000, with the biggest increase in Mexico (up 31.2 per cent since 1998), and the greatest decline in Australia (down 16.4 per cent).

⊕ Goldfish
Bred in the Far East for 3,000 years, goldfish have been popular in the West since the late 17th century.

top 10 TYPES OF PET IN THE UK*

	PET	PERCENTAGE OF ANIMAL-OWNING HOUSEHOLDS, 2003
1	Cat	24.4
2	Dog	20.9
3	Goldfish	8.6
4	Pond fish	6.2
5	Rabbit	4.6
6	Tropical fish	3.6
7	Caged birds (excluding budgerigars)	3.4
8	Hamster	3.2
9	Budgerigar	3.0
10	Guinea pig	2.9

* Ranked by pet ownership

Source: Pet Food Manufacturers' Association

An estimated 52.7 per cent of households in the UK own a pet. Cat ownership has risen to overtake that of dogs, while more exotic animals have steadily gained ground.

top 10 CATS' NAMES IN THE UK

GIRLS		BOYS
Lucy	1	Charlie
Poppy	2	Sammy
Cleo	3	Billy
Holly	4	Oscar
Daisy	5	Oliver
Molly	6	Ben
Tabitha	7	Smokie
Misty	8	Tigger
Amber	9	Sooty
Chloe	10	Leo

Source: Feline Advisory Bureau/Felix

Gone are the traditional Puss and Tiddles of yesteryear: today's cats receive human names to an even greater extent than dogs – three-quarters of the 20 most common cats' names are also found in the Top 20 babies' names.

Livestock & Crops

top 10 TYPES OF **LIVESTOCK**

ANIMAL / WORLD STOCKS, 2004*

1 Chickens 16,194,925,000 **2 Cattle** 1,334,501,290 **3 Sheep** 1,038,765,370 **4 Ducks** 1,019,479,000 **5 Pigs** 951,771,892
6 Goats 780,099,948 **7 Rabbits** 511,591,000 **8 Turkeys** 276,225,000 **9 Geese** 262,232,000 **10 Buffaloes** 172,719,487

* Provisional figures

Source: Food and Agriculture Organization of the United Nations

First Fact

The auroch is the ancestor of all European breeds of cattle. Aurochs are depicted in cave paintings and their remains show that they were bigger than today's cattle, with longer horns. Roman writers, including Julius Caesar, described Gaulish auroch hunts. As a result of over-hunting, aurochs died out in Britain in the Bronze Age and in France by the 16th century, but continued to roam elsewhere in Europe. Although their hunting was restricted to royalty, poaching caused a further decline until only a small herd survived in Poland's Jaktorów Forest. The last cow died there in 1627 and the aurochs became extinct.

top 10 **CHICKEN** COUNTRIES

	COUNTRY	CHICKENS, 2004*
1	China	3,974,748,000
2	USA	1,970,000,000
3	Indonesia	1,200,000,000
4	Brazil	1,100,000,000
5	Mexico	540,000,000
6	India	425,000,000
7	Russia	340,000,000
8	Japan	286,000,000
9	Iran	280,000,000
10	Turkey	250,000,000
	World	*16,194,925,000*
	UK	*170,000,000*

* Provisional figures

Source: Food and Agriculture Organization of the United Nations

top 10 **SHEEP** COUNTRIES

	COUNTRY	SHEEP, 2004*
1	China	157,330,415
2	Australia	94,500,000
3	India	62,500,000
4	Iran	54,000,000
5	Sudan	47,000,000
6	New Zealand	40,065,000
7	UK	35,500,000
8	South Africa	29,100,000
9	Turkey	25,000,000
10	Pakistan	24,700,000
	World	*1,038,765,370*

* Provisional figures

Source: Food and Agriculture Organization of the United Nations

➲ Watermelons

Watermelons were recorded in Egypt 5,000 years ago and introduced into North America in 1629. Although now cultivated worldwide, some 73 per cent of the world's watermelons are grown in China where they are an important part of national cuisine and culture, often presented as gifts and decoratively carved like Halloween pumpkins in the West.

top 10 **PIG** COUNTRIES

	COUNTRY	PIGS, 2004*
1	China	472,895,791
2	USA	60,388,700
3	Brazil	33,000,000
4	Germany	26,495,000
5	Spain	23,990,000
6	Vietnam	23,500,000
7	=Mexico	18,100,000
	=Poland	18,100,000
9	Russia	15,979,600
10	France	15,189,000
	World	*909,486,000*
	UK	*5,038,000*

* Provisional figures

Source: Food and Agricultural Organization of the United Nations

The distribution of the world's pig population is determined by cultural, religious, and dietary factors – with the result that there is a disproportionate concentration of pigs in those countries that do not have such prohibitions.

top 10 **VEGETABLE** CROPS

	CROP*	PRODUCTION, 2004# (TONNES)
1	Sugar cane	1,318,178,070
2	Potatoes	328,865,936
3	Sugar beets	237,857,862
4	Soybeans	206,409,525
5	Sweet potatoes	127,535,008
6	Cabbages	68,389,593
7	Onions (dry)	53,591,283
8	Yams	40,654,872
9	Cucumbers/gherkins	40,190,104
10	Aubergines	29,903,983

* Excluding cereals
# Provisional figures

Source: Food and Agriculture Organization of the United Nations

This includes only vegetables grown for human and animal consumption. Among non-food vegetable crops, cotton has a total annual production approaching 70 million tonnes, while rubber, tobacco, jute, and other fibres are also economically significant.

top 10 **FRUIT** CROPS

	CROP	PRODUCTION, 2004* (TONNES)
1	Tomatoes	115,950,851
2	Watermelons	93,481,266
3	Bananas	70,629,047
4	Grapes	65,486,235
5	Oranges	63,039,736
6	Apples	59,059,142
7	Coconuts	53,473,584
8	Plantains	32,668,323
9	Cantaloupes and other melons	27,371,268
10	Mangoes	26,286,255

* Provisional figures

Source: Food and Agriculture Organization of the United Nations

Over 500 million tonnes of fruit are grown worldwide every year. The status of the tomato is controversial: botanically, it is a fruit, but – based on its use in cooking – for legal and import duty purposes, some countries consider it a vegetable.

Tree Tops

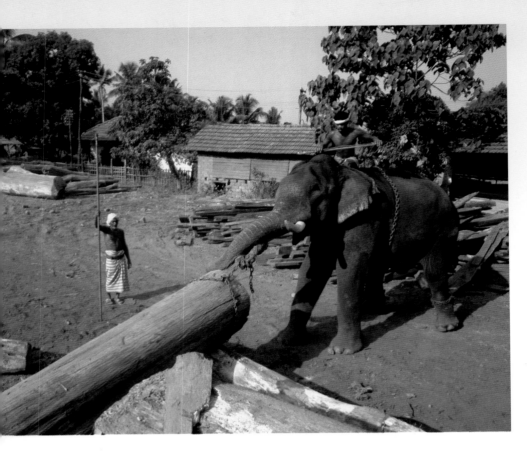

top 10 **MOST FORESTED** COUNTRIES

COUNTRY	PERCENTAGE OF FOREST COVER, 2000
1 Surinam	90.5
2 Solomon Islands	88.8
3 Gabon	84.7
4 Brunei	83.9
5 Guyana	78.5
6 Palau	76.1
7 Finland	72.0
8 North Korea	68.2
9 Papua New Guinea	67.6
10 Seychelles	66.7
UK	*11.6*

Source: Food and Agriculture Organization of the United Nations, *State of the World's Forests*, 2005

These are the 10 countries with the greatest area of forest and woodland as a percentage of their total land area. With increasing deforestation, the world average has fallen from about 32 per cent in 1972 to its present 29.6 per cent. The least forested large countries in the world are the desert lands of the Middle East and North Africa, such as Oman, which has none, and Egypt and Qatar, each with just 0.1 per cent.

top 10 **TIMBER-PRODUCING** COUNTRIES

COUNTRY	ROUNDWOOD PRODUCTION, 2003 (CU M)	(CU FT)
1 USA	448,058,992	15,823,055,440
2 India	321,027,107	11,336,966,340
3 China	286,106,512	10,103,757,060
4 Brazil	238,536,476	8,423,836,933
5 Canada	194,726,500	6,876,702,088
6 Russia	168,500,000	5,950,521,895
7 Indonesia	112,004,236	3,955,392,633
8 Ethiopia	94,061,392	3,321,747,018
9 Dem. Rep. of Congo	72,170,264	2,548,669,057
10 Nigeria	69,867,216	2,467,337,677
UK	*7,835,000*	*276,690,439*
World total	*3,342,245,450*	*118,030,295,100*

Source: Food and Agriculture Organization of the United Nations

If all the world's annual timber production were made into 30 x 2.5 cm planks, laid end to end they would stretch 100 times round the world at the Equator.

↟ Tree trunk
Although elephants are still used in the Indian logging industry, forestry has increasingly become a highly mechanized business and is an important component of the economies of many developing countries.

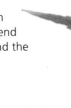

top 10 MOST COMMON TREES IN THE UK

	TREE	PERCENTAGE OF TOTAL FOREST AREA
1	Sitka spruce	29
2	Scots pine	10
3	Oak	9
4	Birch	7
5	Lodgepole pine	6
6 =	Ash	5
=	Japanese/hybrid larch	5
8	Beech	4
9 =	Norway spruce	3
=	Sycamore	3

Source: Forestry Commission

Seven per cent of the UK's forested areas is classified as mixed broadleaves and one per cent as mixed conifers.

top 10 TALLEST TREES IN THE UK*

	TREE	LOCATION	HEIGHT (M)	(FT)
1	Douglas fir#	Dunans Estate, Argyll and Bute, Scotland	62	203
2	Grand fir	Ardkinglas Woodland Garden, Argyll and Bute, Scotland	61	200
3	Sitka spruce	Randolph's Leap, Moray, Scotland	58	190
4	Giant sequoia#	Benmore Botanical Garden, Argyll and Bute, Scotland	53	174
5 =	Norway spruce	Reelig Glen Wood, Moniack, Highland, Scotland	52	171
=	Noble fir	Ardkinglas Woodland Garden, Argyll and Bute, Scotland	52	171
7	Western hemlock	Benmore Botanical Garden, Argyll and Bute, Scotland	51	167
8	European silver fir	Benmore Botanical Garden, Argyll and Bute, Scotland	50	164
9	Nordmann fir	Cragside, Northumberland	48	157
10	Coastal redwood	Bodnant Garden, Colwyn Bay, Conwy, Wales	47	154

* The tallest known example of each of the 10 tallest species

Further examples of the same species match this height

Source: The Tree Register of the British Isles

Although America's record Giant sequoia is taller at 83.5 m (274 ft), Britain's tallest is remarkable as it is only one of a row of 48 laid out in an avenue over 300 m (984 ft) long. They were planted in 1863 by the American owner of the Benmore Estate, Piers Patrick.

the 10 countries suffering the greatest aircraft losses in World War II: page 74

Chapter

2 3 4 5 6

the 10 US presidents with the greatest number of popular votes: page 67

the 10 worst gun massacres: page 73

top 10 longest reigning monarchs: page 68

89101

The Human World

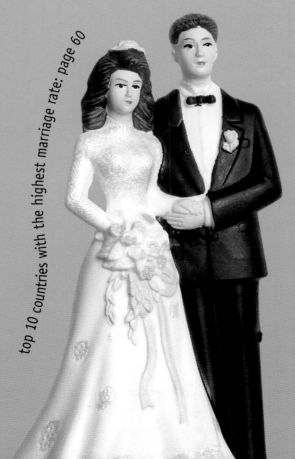

top 10 countries with the highest marriage rate: page 60

Human Body

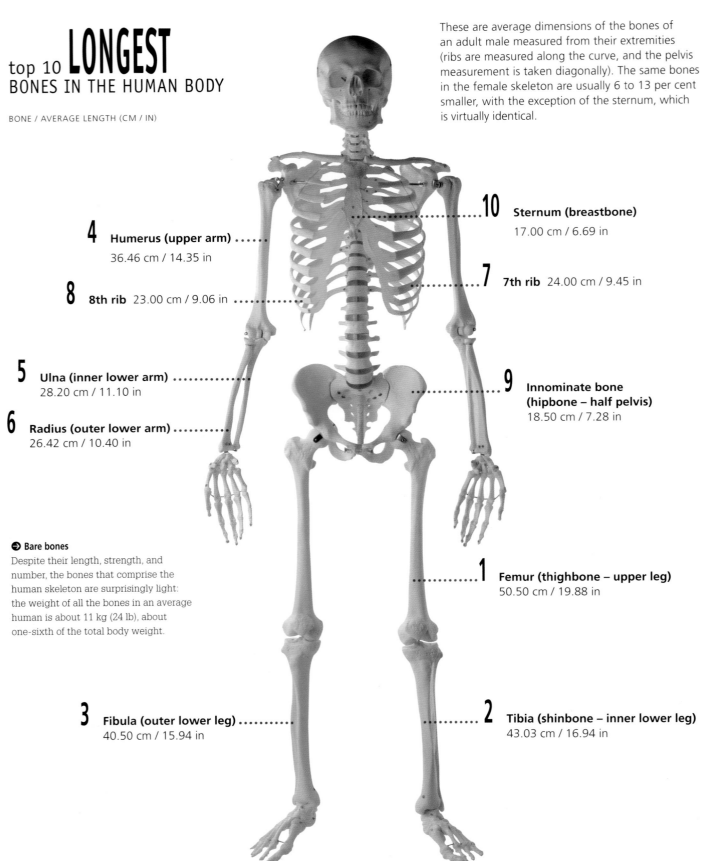

top 10 LONGEST
BONES IN THE HUMAN BODY

BONE / AVERAGE LENGTH (CM / IN)

These are average dimensions of the bones of an adult male measured from their extremities (ribs are measured along the curve, and the pelvis measurement is taken diagonally). The same bones in the female skeleton are usually 6 to 13 per cent smaller, with the exception of the sternum, which is virtually identical.

10 Sternum (breastbone)
17.00 cm / 6.69 in

4 Humerus (upper arm)
36.46 cm / 14.35 in

7 7th rib 24.00 cm / 9.45 in

8 8th rib 23.00 cm / 9.06 in

5 Ulna (inner lower arm)
28.20 cm / 11.10 in

9 Innominate bone (hipbone – half pelvis)
18.50 cm / 7.28 in

6 Radius (outer lower arm)
26.42 cm / 10.40 in

➲ Bare bones
Despite their length, strength, and number, the bones that comprise the human skeleton are surprisingly light: the weight of all the bones in an average human is about 11 kg (24 lb), about one-sixth of the total body weight.

1 Femur (thighbone – upper leg)
50.50 cm / 19.88 in

3 Fibula (outer lower leg)
40.50 cm / 15.94 in

2 Tibia (shinbone – inner lower leg)
43.03 cm / 16.94 in

top 10 COUNTRIES IN EUROPE WITH THE **MOST OBESE** PEOPLE

COUNTRY	PERCENTAGE OF OBESE ADULTS*	
	(MEN)	(WOMEN)
1 Russia	10.8	27.9
2 Czech Republic	16.3	20.2
3 England	17.0	20.0
4 Germany	17.2	19.3
5 Finland	19.0	19.0
6 Belgium	12.1	18.4
7 Scotland	15.9	17.3
8 Spain	11.5	15.2
9 Sweden	10.0	11.9
10 France	9.6	10.5

* In those countries and latest year for which data available; ranked by percentage of obese women

Source: International Obesity Task Force (IOTF)

top 10 **LARGEST** HUMAN ORGANS

ORGAN		AVERAGE WEIGHT	
		(G)	(OZ)
1 Skin		10,886	384.0
2 Liver		1,560	55.0
3 Brain	male	1,408	49.7
	female	1,263	44.6
4 Lungs	total	1,090	38.5
	right	*580*	*20.5*
	left	*510*	*18.0*
5 Heart	male	315	11.1
	female	265	9.3
6 Kidneys	total	290	10.2
	right	*140*	*4.9*
	left	*150*	*5.3*
7 Spleen		170	6.0
8 Pancreas		98	3.5
9 Thyroid		35	1.2
10 Prostate	male only	20	0.7

This list is based on average immediate post-mortem weights, as recorded by St. Bartholemew's Hospital, London, UK, and other sources during a 10-year period. Various instances of organs far in excess of the average have been recorded, including male brains of over 2 kg (4.4 lb).

top 10 **COSMETIC SURGERY** PROCEDURES

PROCEDURE*

1 **Body reshaping by liposuction/liposculpture**
2 **Nose reshaping** (rhinoplasty)
3 **Upper or lower eye bag removal** (blepharoplasty)
4 **Face lift**
5 **Breast augmentation**
6 **Breast reduction**
7 **Ear reshaping** (otoplasty)
8 **Laser treatment for the removal of lines and wrinkles**
9 **Laser treatment for snoring problems**
10 **Varicose veins/thread vein removal**

* Based on latest data available

Plastic surgery to rebuild damaged parts of the human body was performed in India in ancient times. It was later developed to aid disfigured service personnel during World War I, and in recent times has spawned cosmetic surgery techniques, whereby individuals elect to have various parts of their bodies reshaped in the interests of aesthetic appeal.

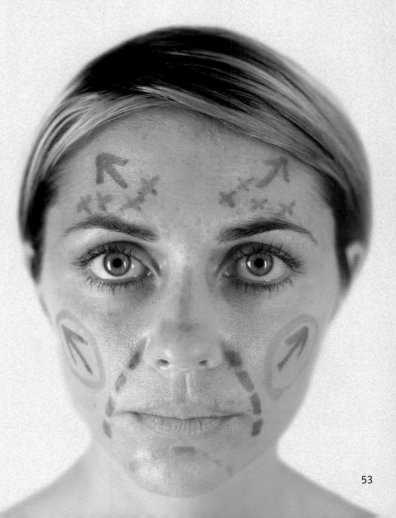

➔ Face value
Once the preserve of the wealthy and celebrities, cosmetic surgery has become a global industry valued at over $20 billion.

Disease & Illness

the 10 WORST EPIDEMICS

	EPIDEMIC / LOCATION	DATE	ESTIMATED NO. OF DEATHS
1	**Black Death** Europe/Asia	1347–80s	75,000,000
2	**AIDS** Worldwide	1981–	27,800,000*
3	**Influenza** Worldwide	1918–20	21,640,000
4	**Bubonic plague** India	1896–1948	12,000,000
5	**Typhus** Eastern Europe	1914–15	3,000,000
6	=**"Plague of Justinian"** Europe/Asia	541–90	millions[#]
	=**Cholera** Europe	1826–37	millions[#]
	=**Cholera** Worldwide	1846–60	millions[#]
	=**Cholera** Worldwide	1893–94	millions[#]
10	**Smallpox** Mexico	1530–45	>1,000,000

* Up to 2005

[#] No precise figures available

Precise figures for deaths during the disruptions of epidemics are inevitably unreliable, but the Black Death or bubonic plague – which was probably transmitted by fleas from infected rats – swept across Asia and Europe in the 14th century, destroying entire populations, including more than half the inhabitants of London, some 25 million in Europe, and 50 million in Asia.

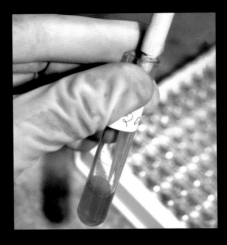

⊙ AIDS test
It is commonly accepted that AIDS (Acquired Immunodeficiency Syndrome) results from the HIV (Human Immunodeficiency Virus) infection. In the past 25 years it has become one of the biggest killers worldwide, with total deaths second only to those of the Black Death and still gaining.

the 10 MOST COMMON CAUSES OF DEATH BY INFECTIOUS AND PARASITIC DISEASES

	CAUSE	APPROXIMATE NO. OF DEATHS, 2002
1	**Lower respiratory infections**	3,884,000
2	**HIV/AIDS**	2,777,000
3	**Diarrhoeal diseases**	1,798,000
4	**Tuberculosis**	1,566,000
5	**Malaria**	1,272,000
6	**Measles**	611,000
7	**Whooping cough** (pertussis)	294,000
8	**Neonatal tetanus**	214,000
9	**Meningitis**	173,000
10	**Syphilis**	157,000

Source: World Health Organization, *World Health Report 2004*

In 2002, infectious and parasitic diseases accounted for some 10,904,000 of the 57,029,000 deaths worldwide. After declining, certain childhood diseases, including measles and whooping cough, showed an increase in this year.

the 10 COUNTRIES WITH THE **MOST** CASES OF **MALARIA**

	COUNTRY	MALARIA CASES PER 100,000 PEOPLE*, 2000
1	Guinea	75,386
2	Botswana	48,704
3	Burundi	48,098
4	Zambia	34,204
5	Malawi	25,948
6	Mozambique	18,115
7	Gambia	17,340
8	Ghana	15,344
9	Solomon Islands	15,172
10	Yemen	15,160

* Data refers to malaria cases reported to the World Health Organization (WHO) and may represent only a fraction of the true number in a country

Source: United Nations, *Human Development Report 2004*

the 10 COUNTRIES WITH THE **MOST** DEATHS FROM **CANCER**

	COUNTRY	DEATH RATE PER 100,000* (FEMALE)	(MALE)
1	Hungary	269.1	386.7
2	Croatia	216.9	330.9
3	Italy	227.8	328.0
4	Belgium	227.1	323.2
5	Czech Republic	243.1	321.8
6	France	187.9	303.2
7	Spain	168.7	298.5
8	Estonia	213.3	297.6
9	Denmark	283.2	296.9
10	Japan	181.4	291.3
	UK	*246.6*	*279.2*

* Ranked by incidence in male population, in latest year for which data available

Source: International Agency for Research on Cancer at http://www-dep.iarc.fr

Cancer has become the leading cause of death in many Western countries, with such factors as diet, obesity, and smoking cited among those that predispose individuals to its various forms. Improved methods of treatment, however, mean that in many cases a cancer diagnosis no longer connotes a death sentence.

⊖ **Small but deadly**
The anopheles mosquito carries the parasite that causes malaria, a disease of tropical countries and one of the world's foremost killers.

⬆ **Bad habit**
The world's annual consumption of 5.5 trillion cigarettes affects the health of one in six of its inhabitants.

the 10 COUNTRIES WITH THE **MOST** DEATHS FROM **HEART DISEASE**

	COUNTRY	DEATH RATE PER 100,000*
1	Ukraine	935.8
2	Bulgaria	887.8
3	Russia	746.6
4	Latvia	734.7
5	Estonia	715.6
6	Romania	701.6
7	Hungary	687.1
8	Moldova	632.0
9	Croatia	609.6
10	Czech Republic	566.5
	UK	*426.2*

* In those countries/latest year for which data available

Source: United Nations

High-risk factors including diet and smoking have contributed to the former Soviet states having rates of coronary heart disease that are seven or eight times greater than those of France and Italy.

Birth & Death

the 10 COUNTRIES WITH THE **HIGHEST BIRTH RATE**

	COUNTRY	EST. BIRTH RATE, 2006*
1	Niger	47.64
2	Uganda	47.35
3	Afghanistan	46.60
4	Mali	46.18
5	Chad	45.41
6	Somalia	45.13
7	Angola	44.18
8	Dem. Rep. of Congo	43.97
9	Burkina Faso	43.83
10	Liberia	43.55
	UK	*10.71*
	World	*20.10*

* The estimated number of live births per 1,000 people in the population

Source: US Census Bureau, International Data Base

The countries with the highest birth rates are among the poorest countries in the world. In these countries, people often deliberately have large families so that the children can help to earn income for the family when they are older. The 10 countries with the highest birth rate therefore correspond very closely with the 10 countries with the highest fertility rate – the average number of children born to each woman in the country.

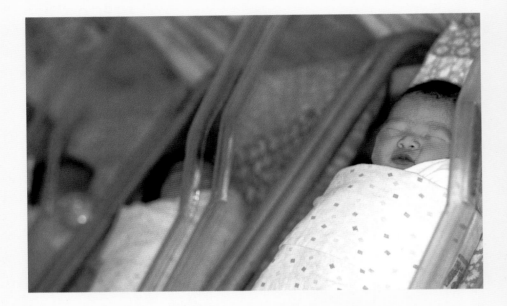

the 10 COUNTRIES WITH THE **LOWEST BIRTH RATE**

	COUNTRY	EST. BIRTH RATE, 2006*
1	Hong Kong	7.29
2	Germany	8.25
3	Andorra	8.71
4	Italy	8.72
5	Austria	8.74
6	Lithuania	8.75
7	Slovenia	8.98
8	Czech Republic	9.02
9	Latvia	9.24
10	Monaco	9.19

* The estimated number of live births per 1,000 people in the population

Source: US Census Bureau, International Data Base

Improvements in birth control, the cost of raising children, and the decision of many to limit the size of their families are among a range of reasons why the birth rate in many countries has steadily declined in modern times: in 2003, the US birth rate was reported as having fallen to the lowest ever recorded, at 13.9 per 1,000. If counted as an independent country, the Vatican – with a birth rate of zero – would head this list.

➊ New arrivals

For many reasons, including the cost of bringing up children and the effect on the ability of mothers to continue to work, the fertility rate of most developed countries is considerably lower than that of the less developed regions of the world.

top 10 COUNTRIES WITH THE **MOST BIRTHS**

	COUNTRY	EST. BIRTHS, 2006
1	India	24,108,697
2	China	17,410,152
3	Nigeria	5,331,353
4	Indonesia	4,992,509
5	Pakistan	4,930,998
6	Bangladesh	4,391,487
7	USA	4,220,001
8	Brazil	3,114,575
9	Ethiopia	2,840,068
10	Dem. Rep. of Congo	2,721,565
	UK	*649,124*
	World	*130,712,621*

Source: US Census Bureau, International Data Base

As India's birth rate is maintained and China's subject to curbs, the population of India is set to overtake that of China by 2030.

top 10 YEARS WITH THE MOST BIRTHS IN THE UK

YEAR	BIRTHS
1920	1,194,068
1903	1,183,627
1904	1,181,770
1902	1,174,639
1908	1,173,759
1906	1,170,622
1905	1,163,535
1899	1,163,279
1901	1,162,975
1900	1,159,922

The total number of births in the UK more than doubled in the 19th century. High figures were also experienced in the early years of the 20th century, with an all-time peak in 1920, the so-called post-World War I "bulge". This was paralleled in 1947 by a post-World War II surge from 703,858 (1941) to 1,025,000.

⊕ Africa's tragedy

The world's highest death rates are suffered disproportionately in African countries, where the AIDS epidemic in particular has more than doubled the rates recorded in the 1990s.

top 10 COUNTRIES WITH THE LOWEST DEATH RATE

COUNTRY	EST. DEATH RATE, 2006*
1 Kuwait	2.41
2 Saudi Arabia	2.58
3 Jordan	2.65
4 Brunei	3.45
5 Libya	3.48
6 Oman	3.81
7 Solomon Islands	3.92
8 Bahrain	4.14
9 Ecuador	4.23
10 Costa Rica	4.36

* The estimated number of deaths per 1,000 people in the population

Source: US Census Bureau, International Data Base

The crude death rate is derived by dividing the total number of deaths in a given year by the total population and multiplying by 1,000. These tend to mean that countries with young populations have low death rates and older populations high rates, so statisticians also use age-standardized death rates, which factor in the age structure.

the 10 COUNTRIES WITH THE HIGHEST DEATH RATE

	COUNTRY	EST. DEATH RATE, 2006*
1	Botswana	29.50
2	Angola	26.04
3	Swaziland	25.88
4	Lesotho	25.17
5	Zimbabwe	25.16
6	Malawi	23.30
7	South Africa	22.00
8	Mozambique	21.35
9	Niger	21.21
10	Sierra Leone	20.56
	UK	10.13
	World	8.80

* The estimated number of deaths per 1,000 people in the population

Source: US Census Bureau, International Data Base

All 10 of the countries with the highest death rate are in sub-Saharan Africa. A decade ago, South Africa had a rate of just 9.8, but the AIDS toll has severely affected the demographic pattern, with a high proportion of young people falling victim. The societies affected by this imbalance and its repercussions face decades of hardship.

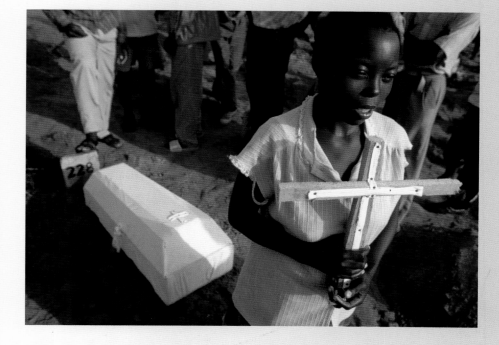

Lifespans

top 10 COUNTRIES WITH THE **HIGHEST** LIFE EXPECTANCY

	COUNTRY	LIFE EXPECTANCY AT BIRTH, 2006
1	Andorra	83.51
2 =	San Marino	81.71
=	Singapore	81.71
4	Hong Kong	81.59
5	Japan	81.25
6 =	Sweden	80.51
=	Switzerland	80.51
8	Australia	80.50
9	Iceland	80.31
10	Canada	80.22
	UK	*78.54*
	World	*64.60*

Source: US Census Bureau, International Data Base

the 10 COUNTRIES WITH THE **LOWEST** LIFE EXPECTANCY

	COUNTRY	LIFE EXPECTANCY AT BIRTH, 2006
1	Botswana	33.74
2	Swaziland	35.12
3	Zimbabwe	36.26
4	Angola	36.32
5	Lesotho	36.65
6	Malawi	36.96
7	Mozambique	39.82
8	Zambia	40.03
9	Central African Republic	41.03
10	Niger	42.02

Source: US Census Bureau, International Data Base

● Brief lives

The average life expectancies of many African countries are worse than those of Europe over 100 years ago, and less than half those of most developed countries today.

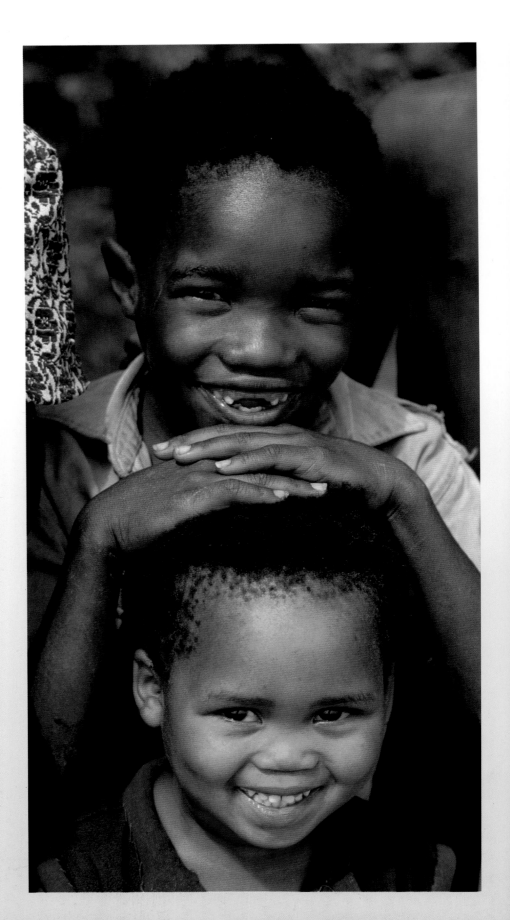

the 10 COUNTRIES WITH THE **SMALLEST DISPARITY** BETWEEN MALE AND FEMALE LIFE EXPECTANCIES

	COUNTRY	ESTIMATED LIFE EXPECTANCY, 2006 (MALE)	(FEMALE)	GAP*
1	Bangladesh	62.47	62.45	0.02
2	Lesotho	36.80	36.50	0.30
3	Botswana	33.90	33.56	0.34
4	Afghanistan	43.16	43.53	0.37
5	Bhutan	55.02	54.53	0.49
6	Nepal	60.43	59.91	0.52
7	Malawi	36.69	37.23	0.54
8	=Niger	42.29	41.74	0.55
	=Zambia	39.76	40.31	0.55
10	Mozambique	39.53	40.13	0.60
	UK	*76.09*	*81.13*	*5.24*

* Number of years by which male and female life expectancies differ

Source: US Census Bureau, International Data Base

➜ Sex equality
Except in a few cases, female life expectancy exceeds that of male, but Bangladesh is unusual in that its inhabitants can expect virtually identical lifespans.

the 10 COUNTRIES WHERE **MALE LIFE EXPECTANCY MOST EXCEEDS** FEMALE LIFE EXPECTANCY

COUNTRY	ESTIMATED LIFE EXPECTANCY, 2006 (MALE)	(FEMALE)	GAP*
1 Swaziland	36.51	33.69	2.82
2 Namibia	44.46	42.29	2.17
3 Kenya	49.78	48.07	1.71
4 Zimbabwe	39.76	40.31	1.20
5 South Africa	43.25	42.19	1.06
6 Martinique	79.50	78.85	0.65
7 Niger	42.29	41.74	0.55
8 Nepal	60.43	59.91	0.52
9 Bhutan	55.02	54.53	0.49
10 Botswana	33.90	33.56	0.34

* Number of years by which male life expectancy exceeds female life expectancy

Source: US Census Bureau, International Data Base

the 10 COUNTRIES WHERE **FEMALE LIFE EXPECTANCY MOST EXCEEDS** MALE LIFE EXPECTANCY

COUNTRY	ESTIMATED LIFE EXPECTANCY, 2006 (MALE)	(FEMALE)	GAP*
1 Russia	60.45	74.10	13.65
2 Belarus	63.47	74.98	11.51
3 Estonia	66.58	77.83	11.25
4 Kazakhstan	61.56	72.52	10.96
5 Seychelles	66.69	77.63	10.94
6 Latvia	66.08	76.85	10.77
7 Ukraine	61.92	72.68	10.76
8 Lithuania	69.20	79.49	10.29
9 Hungary	68.45	77.14	8.69
10 Azerbaijan	59.78	68.13	8.35

* Number of years by which female life expectancy exceeds male life expectancy

Source: US Census Bureau, International Data Base

Marriage & Divorce

top 10 COUNTRIES WITH THE HIGHEST MARRIAGE RATE

COUNTRY / MARRIAGES PER 1,000 PER ANNUM*

1 **China** 35.9

2 **Cyprus** 13.4

3 **Barbados** 13.1

4 **Liechtenstein** 12.6

5 **Jamaica** 10.4

6 **Ethiopia** 10.2

7 **Fiji** 10.1

8 **Seychelles** 9.7

9 **Bangladesh** 9.5

10 **Jordan** 9.1

UK 5.1

* In those countries/latest year for which data available

Source: United Nations

High marriage rates may be distorted by the numbers of visitors to a country. Jamaica, for example, has a low marriage rate among Jamaican nationals but a high number of visitors who marry on the island and spend their honeymoon there. The highest marriage rates in the world are actually recorded in places that are not independent countries. Gibraltar, for example, a British dependency, has a marriage rate of 24.9 per 1,000.

⬆ **Afghan teen bride**
A young woman prepares for marriage in Afghanistan, where local tradition determines that many girls wed at an age when those in developed countries are still at school.

top 10 COUNTRIES WHERE WOMEN MARRY THE YOUNGEST

	COUNTRY	AVERAGE AGE AT FIRST MARRIAGE
1	**Dem. Rep. of Congo**	16.6
2	**Niger**	17.6
3	**=Afghanistan**	17.8
	=São Tomé and Príncipe	17.8
5	**=Chad**	18.0
	=Mozambique	18.0
7	**Bangladesh**	18.1
8	**Uganda**	18.2
9	**=Congo**	18.4
	=Mali	18.4

Source: United Nations

top 10 COUNTRIES WHERE MEN MARRY THE YOUNGEST

	COUNTRY	AVERAGE AGE AT FIRST MARRIAGE
1	**Nepal**	22.0
2	**San Marino**	22.2
3	**Uganda**	22.5
4	**Mozambique**	22.6
5	**São Tomé and Príncipe**	23.0
6	**Tajikistan**	23.1
7	**Maldives**	23.2
8	**Uzbekistan**	23.3
9	**=Cuba**	23.5
	=Malawi	23.5

Source: United Nations

the 10 COUNTRIES WITH THE LOWEST MARRIAGE RATE

	COUNTRY	MARRIAGES PER 1,000 PER ANNUM*
1	El Salvador	2.1
2	Peru	2.4
3	United Arab Emirates	2.5
4	Georgia	2.7
5	Dominican Republic	2.9
6 =	Andorra	3.2
=	Armenia	3.2
=	Saudi Arabia	3.2
9	Venezuela	3.3
10 =	Panama	3.4
=	Qatar	3.4

* In those countries/latest year for which data available

Source: United Nations

the 10 COUNTRIES WITH THE HIGHEST DIVORCE RATE

	COUNTRY	DIVORCE RATE PER 1,000*
1	Russia	5.30
2	Belarus	4.35
3	USA	4.19
4	Ukraine	3.70
5	Aruba	3.61
6	Cuba	3.32
7 =	Estonia	3.17
=	Lithuania	3.17
9	Czech Republic	3.09
10	Belgium	2.85
	UK	*2.58*

* In those countries/latest year for which data available

Source: United Nations

top 10 COUNTRIES WITH THE LOWEST DIVORCE RATE

	COUNTRY	DIVORCE RATE PER 1,000
1	Guatemala	0.12
2	Mongolia	0.21
3	Libya	0.3
4	Georgia	0.40
5 =	Chile	0.42
=	El Salvador	0.42
7	Jamaica	0.44
8	Armenia	0.47
9	Turkey	0.49
10	Bosnia & Herzegovina	0.54

* In those countries/latest year for which data available

Source: United Nations

The countries that figure among those with the lowest rates represent a range of cultures and religions, which either condone or condemn divorce to varying extents, thus affecting its prevalence or otherwise. In Libya, for example, it has long been relatively easy for men to divorce women, but not the other way round, while in many countries the status of a divorced woman is extremely low and her withdrawal from a marriage ends her economic support. In Jamaica, partners often separate without the formality of divorce.

First Fact The first divorce in the New World was granted on 5 January 1643 by the Colony of the Massachusetts Bay to Anne Clarke, wife of Denis Clarke, who had deserted her. The court record declared that, "She is garunted to bee divorced." By 1975, the number of divorces in the USA had exceeded one million a year, a level it has maintained ever since.

⊙ D-I-V-O-R-C-E
Once unmentionable, prohibited, or rare, divorce is now so common in many countries that almost half of all marriages end in divorce.

Name Game

top 10 FIRST NAMES IN ENGLAND & WALES

GIRLS		BOYS	
(2004)	(2003)	(2004)	(2003)
1 Emily	Emily	Jack	Jack
2 Ellie	Ellie	Joshua	Joshua
3 Jessica	Chloe	Thomas	Thomas
4 Sophie	Jessica	James	James
5 Chloe	Sophie	Daniel	Daniel
6 Lucy	Megan	Samuel	Oliver
7 Olivia	Lucy	Oliver	Benjamin
8 Charlotte	Olivia	William	Samuel
9 Katie	Charlotte	Benjamin	William
10 Megan	Hannah	Joseph	Joseph

Source: Office for National Statistics

top 10 FIRST NAMES IN AUSTRALIA*

GIRLS		BOYS	
(2004)	(2000–2003)	(2004)	(2000–2003)
1 Emily	Emily	Jack	Jack
2 Olivia	Jessica	Joshua	Joshua
3 Chloe	Olivia	Lachlan	Lachlan
4 Jessica	Sarah	Thomas	Thomas
5 Charlotte	Georgia	William	Daniel
6 Ella	Isabella	James	James
7 Isabella	Chloe	Ethan	William
8 Sophie	Hannah	Samuel	Benjamin
9 Emma	Emma	Daniel	Nicholas
10 Grace	Sophie	Benjamin	Matthew

* Based on figures from New South Wales and Victoria

Source: New South Wales Registry of Births, Deaths and Marriages in Australia/Victorian Registry of Births, Deaths and Marriages in Australia

◄ Jack Black
Born Thomas Black in 1969, when Thomas was one of the USA's most popular names, comedy actor Jack Black adopted the name Jack, currently both England and Australia's most popular boy's name.

➔ Olivia Newton-John
Born in 1948 when the name Olivia was distinctly unfashionable, British-born Australian actress Olivia Newton-John's first name now ranks among the favourites in English-speaking countries.

top 10 FIRST NAMES IN THE US

GIRLS		BOYS	
(2003)	(2002)	(2003)	(2002)
1 Emily	Emily	Jacob	Jacob
2 Emma	Madison	Michael	Michael
3 Madison	Hannah	Joshua	Joshua
4 Hannah	Emma	Matthew	Matthew
5 Olivia	Alexis	Andrew	Ethan
6 Abigail	Ashley	Joseph	Joseph
7 Alexis	Abigail	Ethan	Andrew
8 Ashley	Sarah	Daniel	Christopher
9 Elizabeth	Samantha	Christopher	Daniel
10 Samantha	Olivia	Anthony	Nicholas

Source: Social Security Administration

These rankings are based on a cross-country sampling of US Social Security Number applications. They indicate that within the Top 10 in the course of a single year the name Olivia gained the greatest popularity, rising from 10th to 5th place.

top 10 SURNAMES IN THE UK

	SURNAME	NUMBER
1	Smith	652,563
2	Jones	538,874
3	Williams	380,379
4	Taylor	306,296
5	Brown	291,872
6	Davies*	279,647
7	Evans	225,580
8	Thomas	202,773
9	Wilson	201,224
10	Johnson	193,260

* There are also 97,349 people bearing the surname Davis

This survey of British surnames is based on an analysis of 54.4 million appearing in the British electoral rolls – hence enumerating only those aged over 18 and eligible to vote. Some 12 people out of every thousand in the UK are now called Smith, compared with 14.55 per thousand of names appearing in a sample from the 1851 Census.

top 10 SURNAMES IN THE US

	NAME	PERCENTAGE OF ALL US NAMES
1	Smith	1.006
2	Johnson	0.810
3	Williams	0.699
4 =	Brown	0.621
=	Jones	0.621
6	Davis	0.480
7	Miller	0.424
8	Wilson	0.339
9	Moore	0.312
10 =	Anderson	0.311
=	Taylor	0.311
=	Thomas	0.311

The Top 10 US surnames together make up over six per cent of the entire US population – in other words, one American in every 16 bears one of these names. Extending the list, some 28 different names comprise 10 per cent of the whole population.

First Fact The longest sustained popularity of any female first name in England and Wales, the USA, and Australia was that of Mary. It was the most common name among the first settlers in America in the 17th century and up to 1962, when it lost out to Lisa. In post-Reformation England Mary was briefly unfashionable for its Catholic associations, but was the No. 1 female name from 1700 until about 1924, when it was overtaken by Margaret, and in Australia throughout the 19th century, and up to 1970, when it was replaced at the top spot by Jennifer.

Accident & Injury

the 10 MOST COMMON ACCIDENTS IN UK HOMES

ACCIDENT / NO. OF ACCIDENTS, 2002*

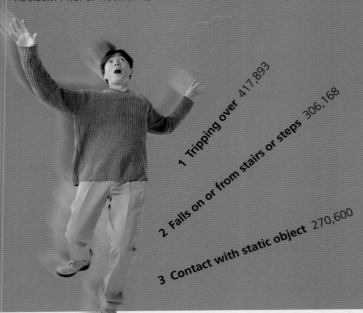

1 Tripping over 417,893

2 Falls on or from stairs or steps 306,168

3 Contact with static object 270,600

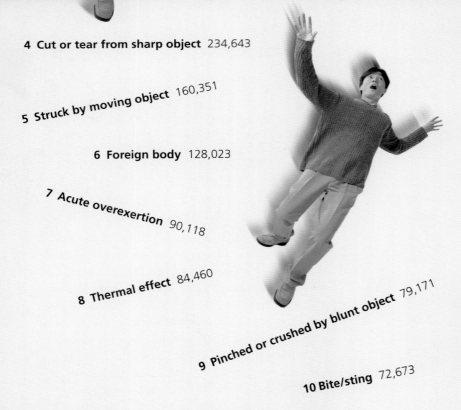

4 Cut or tear from sharp object 234,643

5 Struck by moving object 160,351

6 Foreign body 128,023

7 Acute overexertion 90,118

8 Thermal effect 84,460

9 Pinched or crushed by blunt object 79,171

10 Bite/sting 72,673

* National estimates based on actual Home Accident Surveillance System figures for sample population

the 10 MOST COMMON CAUSES OF INJURY AT WORK IN THE UK

CAUSE OF INJURY	NONFATAL INJURIES, 2003–04*	
	(MAJOR)	(TOTAL)#
1 Handling, lifting, or carrying	4,324	52,422
2 Slip, trip, or fall on same level	11,269	30,499
3 Struck by moving (including flying/falling) object	4,013	14,780
4 Struck against fixed or stationary object	1,261	6,010
5 Acts of violence	985	5,389
6 Fall from height	3,884	5,021
7 Contact with moving machinery	1,475	3,899
8 Exposure to or contact with a harmful substance	850	3,353
9 Struck by moving vehicle	810	1,975
10 Animal	252	851

* Provisional figures; employees only

Includes all injuries resulting in over 3 days away from work

Source: Health and Safety Executive

⬆ **Accidents will happen**
Unintentional injuries result in large numbers of visits to doctors and hospital emergency departments.

the 10 MOST COMMON ACCIDENTAL CAUSES OF DEATH AT WORK IN THE UK

	CAUSE OF DEATH	FATALITIES, 2003–04*
1	Fall from height	67
2	Struck by moving vehicle	44
3	Struck by moving (including flying/falling) object	29
4	Drowning or asphyxiation	21
5	Contact with electricity	13
6	Contact with moving machinery	11
7	Trapped by something collapsing/overturning	7
8 =	Exposure to or contact with a harmful substance	6
=	Struck against fixed or stationary object	6
10	Slip, trip, or fall on same level	4
	Total (all causes)	*235*

* Provisional figures; includes employees and self-employed

Source: Health and Safety Executive

Although still among the lowest rates in Europe, fatal injuries in the UK increased in this period to a rate equivalent to 0.81 per 100,000 workers. Half of all fatalities occurred in construction, agriculture, forestry, and fisheries, including the drowning in February 2004 of 21 people harvesting cockles in Morecambe Bay.

⬆ **Danger, men at work**
Some 30 per cent of all work fatalities in the UK occur in the construction industry, with agriculture, forestry, and fisheries accounting for a further 19 per cent.

the 10 MOST ACCIDENT-PRONE COUNTRIES

	COUNTRY	ACCIDENT DEATH RATE PER 100,000*
1	Estonia	102.8
2	Latvia	101.4
3	Russia	100.2
4	Ukraine	83.0
5	Lithuania	75.2
6	Hungary	58.6
7	Moldova	56.7
8 =	Finland	52.8
=	France	52.8
10	Belarus	51.7
	UK	*21.4*

* In those countries/latest year for which data available

Source: *UN Demographic Yearbook*

the 10 TYPES OF SPORTS EQUIPMENT MOST FREQUENTLY INVOLVED IN ACCIDENTS IN THE UK

	SPORTS EQUIPMENT	ACCIDENTS, 2002*
1	Football/basketball	191,387
2	Skateboard/snakeboard	34,379
3	Rugby-shape ball	25,933
4	Cricket ball	17,118
5	Netball	13,612
6	Hockey stick	10,578
7	Rollerblade/in-line skates	10,394
8	Gymnasium mat	10,230
9	Ice rink	9,963
10	Ice skates	9,041

* National estimates based on actual Leisure Accident Surveillance System figures for sample population

Rulers & Leaders

top 10 **IN LINE** TO THE BRITISH THRONE

HRH The Prince of Wales

(Prince Charles Philip
Arthur George)
b. 14 November 1948

then his elder son:

HRH The Duke of York

(Prince Andrew Albert
Christian Edward)
b. 19 February 1960

then his elder daughter:

HRH Prince Edward

(Prince Edward Antony
Richard Louis)
b. 10 March 1964

then his daughter:

HRH The Princess Royal

(Princess Anne Elizabeth
Alice Louise)
b. 15 August 1950

then her son:

**HRH Prince William
of Wales**

(Prince William Arthur
Philip Louis)
b. 21 June 1982

then his younger brother:

**HRH Princess Beatrice
of York**

(Princess Beatrice
Elizabeth Mary)
b. 8 August 1988

then her younger sister:

**Lady Louise Alice
Elizabeth Mary
Mountbatten Windsor**

b. 8 November 2003

then her aunt:
HRH The Princess Royal

**Master Peter Mark
Andrew Phillips**

b. 15 November 1977

**HRH Prince Henry
of Wales**

(Prince Henry Charles
Albert David)
b. 15 September 1984

then his uncle:
HRH The Duke of York

**HRH Princess Eugenie
of York**

(Princess Eugenie
Victoria Helena)
b. 23 March 1990

then her uncle:
HRH Prince Edward

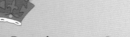 **Prime time**

The daughter of Jawaharal
Nehru, India's first prime
minister following the country's
independence, Indira Gandhi
became the world's second
female prime minister. Both
she and her son Rajiv, who
succeeded her to the office,
were assassinated.

The birth in 1988 of Princess Beatrice altered the order of
succession, ousting David Albert Charles Armstrong-Jones,
Viscount Linley (the son of Princess Margaret), from the
No. 10 position. The birth of her sister, Princess Eugenie,
in 1990 evicted HRH Princess Margaret (the sister of the
Queen), who died in 2002. The recent birth of Lady Louise
Windsor means that Zara Phillips (the daughter of Princess
Anne) has fallen out of the Top 10.

→ **Presidential popularity**
Father and son George H. W. and George W. Bush rank alongside each other for popular votes received in their first elections, with George W. achieving a record number in his 2004 re-election.

top 10 LONGEST-SERVING PRESIDENTS TODAY

	PRESIDENT	COUNTRY	TOOK OFFICE
1	General Gnassingbé Eyadéma	Togo	14 Apr 1967
2	El Hadj Omar Bongo	Gabon	2 Dec 1967
3	Colonel Mu'ammar Gadhafi*	Libya	1 Sept 1969
4	Zayid ibn Sultan al-Nuhayyan	United Arab Emirates	2 Dec 1971
5	Fidel Castro	Cuba	2 Nov 1976
6	Ali Abdullah Saleh	Yemen	17 July 1978
7	Maumoon Abdul Gayoom	Maldives	11 Nov 1978
8	Teodoro Obiang Nguema Mbasogo	Equatorial Guinea	3 Aug 1979
9	José Eduardo Dos Santos	Angola	21 Sept 1979
10	Hosni Mubarak	Egypt	6 Oct 1981

* Since a reorganization in 1979, Colonel Gadhafi has held no formal position, but continues to rule under the ceremonial title of "Leader of the Revolution"

All the presidents in this list have been in power for more than 20 – some for over 30 – years. Fidel Castro was prime minister of Cuba from February 1959. As he was also chief of the army, and there was no opposition party, he effectively ruled as dictator from then, but he was not technically president until the Cuban constitution was revised in 1976. Similarly, Robert Mugabe has ruled Zimbabwe since 18 April 1980, but only became president in 1987 (prior to this he held the title of prime minister).

the 10 US PRESIDENTS WITH THE GREATEST NUMBER OF POPULAR VOTES

	PRESIDENT	YEAR	VOTES
1	George W. Bush	2004	59,459,765
2	Ronald W. Reagan	1984	54,281,858
3	George W. Bush	2000	50,459,211
4	George H. W. Bush	1988	48,881,221
5	William J. Clinton	1996	47,401,185
6	Richard M. Nixon	1972	47,165,234
7	William J. Clinton	1992	44,908,254
8	Ronald W. Reagan	1980	43,899,248
9	Lyndon B. Johnson	1964	43,126,506
10	James E. Carter	1976	40,828,929

The American electorate's popular vote is actually cast for electors of each state's Electoral College, who in turn vote for the President. The candidate with the greatest popular vote can fail to win the Electoral College vote and thus lose the election.

the 10 FIRST FEMALE PRIME MINISTERS AND PRESIDENTS

	PRIME MINISTER OR PRESIDENT	COUNTRY	FIRST PERIOD IN OFFICE
1	Sirimavo Bandaranaike (PM)	Sri Lanka	July 1960–Mar 1965
2	Indira Gandhi (PM)	India	Jan 1966–Mar 1977
3	Golda Meir (PM)	Israel	Mar 1969–June 1974
4	Maria Estela Perón (President)	Argentina	July 1974–Mar 1976
5	Elisabeth Domitien (PM)	Central African Republic	Jan 1975–Apr 1976
6	Margaret Thatcher (PM)	UK	May 1979–Nov 1990
7	Dr. Maria Lurdes Pintasilgo (PM)	Portugal	Aug 1979–Jan 1980
8	Mary Eugenia Charles (PM)	Dominica	July 1980–June 1995
9	Vigdís Finnbogadóttir (President)	Iceland	Aug 1980–Aug 1996
10	Gro Harlem Brundtland (PM)	Norway	Feb–Oct 1981

First Fact

Following the assassination of her husband Solomon West Ridgeway Dias Bandaranaike, Sirimavo Ratwatte Dias Bandaranaike (1916–2000) took over as leader of the Ceylon (later Sri Lanka) Freedom Party, won the election and thereby became the world's first female prime minister. She was to serve in this office three times (1960–65, 1970–77, and 1994–2000), while her daughter Chandrika Kumaratunga became the country's first female president in 1994.

top 10 **LONGEST REIGNING MONARCHS**

	MONARCH	COUNTRY	REIGN	AGE AT ACCESSION	REIGN (YEARS)
1	King Louis XIV	France	1643–1715	5	72
2	King John II	Liechtenstein	1858–1929	18	71
3	Emperor Franz-Josef	Austria-Hungary	1848–1916	18	67
4	Queen Victoria	UK	1837–1901	18	63
5	Emperor Hirohito	Japan	1926–89	25	62
6	Emperor K'ang Hsi	China	1661–1722	7	61
7	King Sobhuza II*	Swaziland	1921–82	22	60#
8	Emperor Ch'ien Lung	China	1735–96	25	60#
9	King Christian IV	Denmark	1588–1648	11	59#
10	King George III	UK	1760–1820	22	59#

* Paramount chief until 1967, when Great Britain recognized him as king with the granting of internal self-government

Precise differences between reign days distinguish between those of identical duration in years

King Harald I of Norway is said to have ruled for 70 years from 870–940, and the even longer reigns of 95 and 94 years are credited respectively to King Mihti of Arakan (Myanmar) around 1279–1374, and Pharaoh Phiops (Pepi) II of Egypt (Neferkare) around 2269–2175 BC, but there is inadequate historical evidence to substantiate any of these claims.

➜ **Long reigns**
Clockwise, from top left: Christian IV, Hirohito, Franz-Josef, and Queen Victoria. Acceding to a throne in their youth, a long life, and the avoidance of the risks that traditionally threaten monarchs, allowed each of these to reign for 60 or more years. Queen Victoria survived no fewer than eight attempts on her life: had the first, by Edward Oxford on 10 June 1840, succeeded, her reign would have lasted less than three years.

The First To...

the 10 FIRST PEOPLE TO **CROSS NIAGARA FALLS** BY TIGHTROPE

TIGHTROPE WALKER	DATE
1 Blondin (Jean François Gravelet)	30 June 1859
2 Signor Guillermo Antonio Farini (William Leonard Hunt)	15 Aug 1860
3 Harry Leslie	15 June 1865
4 J.F. "Professor" Jenkins	25 Aug 1869
5 Signor Henri Belleni	25 Aug 1873
6 Stephen Peer	10 Sept 1873
7 Maria Spelterini	8 July 1876
8 Samuel Dixon	6 Sept 1890
9 Clifford Caverley	12 Oct 1892
10 James Hardy	1 July 1896

Several of these funambulists were members of the making-things-as-difficult-as-possible school: on one of his crossings Blondin pushed a wheelbarrow, Farini strapped a washing machine on to his back, and Professor Jenkins rode a bicycle, while Maria Spelterini had her ankles and wrists manacled and wore peach baskets on her feet. Most walkers made more than one crossing.

the 10 FIRST MOUNTAINEERS TO **CLIMB EVEREST**

MOUNTAINEER / NATIONALITY	DATE
1 Edmund Hillary, New Zealander	29 May 1953
2 Tenzing Norgay, Nepalese	29 May 1953
3 Jürg Marmet, Swiss	23 May 1956
4 Ernst Schmied, Swiss	23 May 1956
5 Hans-Rudolf von Gunten, Swiss	24 May 1956
6 Adolf Reist, Swiss	24 May 1956
7 Wang Fu-chou, Chinese	25 May 1960
8 Chu Ying-hua, Chinese	25 May 1960
9 Konbu, Tibetan	25 May 1960
10 = Nawang Gombu, Indian	1 May 1963
= James Whittaker, American	1 May 1963

Some 15 reconnaissance expeditions and attempts on Everest – several resulting in the deaths of the mountaineers – preceded the first successful conquest of the world's tallest peak. Nawang Gombu and James Whittaker are 10th equal because, neither wishing to deny the other the privilege of being first, they ascended the last steps to the summit side by side.

🔼 **Rope trick**
French tightrope walker Blondin is dwarfed by Niagara Falls as he makes the first of his 21 crossings on 30 June 1859.

the 10 FIRST EXPEDITIONS TO **REACH THE NORTH POLE OVERLAND**

EXPEDITION LEADER OR CO-LEADER / NATIONALITY / DATE

1 **Ralph S. Plaisted**, American, 19 Apr 1968 **2** **Wally W. Herbert**, British, 5 Apr 1969 **3** **Naomi Uemura**, Japanese, 1 May 1978

4 **Dmitri Shparo**, Soviet, 31 May 1979 **5** **Sir Ranulph Fiennes/Charles Burton**, British, 11 Apr 1982

6 **Will Steger/Paul Schurke**, American, 1 May 1986 **7** **Jean-Louis Etienne**, French 11 May 1986

8 **Fukashi Kazami**, Japanese, 20 Apr 1987 **9** **Helen Thayer**, American*, 20 Apr 1988 **10** **Robert Swan**, British, 14 May 1989

* New Zealand-born

the 10 FIRST PEOPLE TO **REACH THE SOUTH POLE**

Just 33 days separated the first two expeditions to reach the South Pole. Scott's British Antarctic Expedition was organized with its avowed goal "to reach the South Pole and to secure for the British Empire the honour of this achievement". Meanwhile, Norwegian explorer Roald Amundsen also set out on an expedition to the Pole. When Scott eventually reached his goal, he discovered that the Norwegians had beaten them. Demoralized, Scott's team began the arduous return journey, but, plagued by illness, hunger, bad weather, and exhaustion, the entire expedition died just as Amundsen's triumph was being reported to the world.

➲ Pole position
Roald Amundsen records his conquest of the South Pole a month ahead of Captain Scott's expedition, which ended in disaster.

14 December 1911

EXPLORER / NATIONALITY

1
= **Roald Amundsen***, Norwegian
= **Olav Olavsen Bjaaland**, Norwegian
= **Helmer Julius Hanssen**, Norwegian
= **Helge Sverre Hassel**, Norwegian
= **Oscar Wisting**, Norwegian
* Expedition leader

SOUTH POLE

17 January 1912

EXPLORER / NATIONALITY

6
= **Robert Falcon Scott***, British
= **Henry Robertson Bowers**, British
= **Edgar Evans**, British
= **Lawrence Edward Grace Oates**, British
= **Edward Adrian Wilson**, British
* Expedition leader

SCOTT'S ROUTE ———

AMUNDSEN'S ROUTE ———

Crime & Punishment

the 10 COUNTRIES WITH THE **HIGHEST MURDER** RATES

COUNTRY	REPORTED MURDERS PER 100,000 POPULATION, 2002*
1 Honduras	154.02
2 South Africa	114.84
3 Colombia	69.98
4 Lesotho	50.41
5 Rwanda	45.08
6 Jamaica	43.71
7 El Salvador	34.33
8 Venezuela	33.20
9 Bolivia	31.98
10 Namibia	26.32
England and Wales	*2.01*

* Or latest year for which data available

Source: Interpol

the 10 MOST COMMON MURDER **WEAPONS AND METHODS** IN ENGLAND AND WALES

	WEAPON OR METHOD	VICTIMS, 2003–04
1	Sharp instrument	237
2	Hitting and kicking	139
3	Not known	105
4	Shooting	73
5	Blunt instrument	67
6	Strangulation (including asphyxiation)	65
7	Burning	27
8	= Drowning	25*
	= Motor vehicle	25#
10	Poison or drugs	23

* Includes 20 cockle pickers drowned in Morecambe Bay

\# Excludes death by careless/dangerous driving and aggravated vehicle taking

Source: Home Office, *Crime in England and Wales 2003/2004: Supplementary Volume*

the 10 COUNTRIES WITH THE **HIGHEST REPORTED CRIME** RATES

COUNTRY	CRIMES PER 100,000, 2002*
1 Finland	14,525.74
2 Sweden	13,350.27
3 Guyana	12,933.18
4 New Zealand	12,586.64
5 England and Wales	11,326.60
6 Grenada	10,177.89
7 Norway	9,822.91
8 Denmark	9,005.77
9 Belgium	8,597.66
10 Canada	8,572.50
Scotland	*8,225.76*
Northern Ireland	*2,389.16*

* Or latest year for which data available

Source: Interpol

An appearance in this list does not necessarily confirm these as the most crime-ridden countries, since the rate of reporting relates closely to such factors as confidence in local law enforcement authorities. However, a rate of approximately 1,000 per 100,000 may be considered average, so those in the Top 10 are well above it.

the 10 COUNTRIES WITH THE **HIGHEST PRISON POPULATION** RATE

COUNTRY	PRISONERS PER 100,000*
1 USA	701
2 Russia	606
3 Kazakhstan	522
4 Turkmenistan	489
5 = Belarus	459
= Belize	459
7 Surinam	437
8 Dominica	420
9 Ukraine	415
10 Maldives	414
England and Wales	*141*
Scotland	*129*

* Most figures relate to the period 1999–2003

Source: British Home Office, *World Prison Population List*, 5th edition

the 10 COUNTRIES WITH THE **MOST EXECUTIONS**

COUNTRY	EXECUTIONS*, 2003
1 China	726
2 Iran	108
3 USA	65
4 Vietnam	64
5 Saudi Arabia	53
6 Chad	9
7 Singapore	8
8 Jordan	7
9 = Botswana	4
= Thailand	4
= Zimbabwe	4

* Verifiable reported executions

Some 118 countries have abolished the death penalty in law or practice, while 78 retain it. According to Amnesty International, in 2003 a total of at least 1,146 people were executed in 28 countries.

the 10 WORST GUN MASSACRES*

PERPETRATOR / LOCATION / DATE / CIRCUMSTANCES

KILLED 57

1

Woo Bum Kong
Sang-Namdo, South Korea
28 April 1982

Off-duty policeman Woo Bum Kong (or Wou Bom-Kon), 27, went on a drunken rampage with rifles and hand grenades, killing 57 and injuring 38 before blowing himself up with a grenade.

KILLED 35

2

Martin Bryant
Port Arthur, Tasmania, Australia
28 April 1996

Bryant, a 28-year-old Hobart resident, used a rifle in a horrific spree that began in a restaurant and ended with a siege in a guesthouse in which he held hostages and set it on fire before being captured by police.

3

KILLED 29

Baruch Goldstein
Hebron, occupied West Bank, Israel
25 February 1994

Goldstein, a 42-year-old US immigrant doctor, carried out a gun massacre of Palestinians at prayer at the Tomb of the Patriarchs before being beaten to death by the crowd.

4

KILLED 28

Campo Elias Delgado
Bogota, Colombia
4 December 1986

Delgado, a Vietnamese war veteran and electronics engineer, stabbed two and shot a further 26 people before being killed by police.

KILLED 22

5=

= George Jo Hennard
Killeen, Texas, USA
16 October 1991

Hennard drove his pick-up truck through the window of Luby's Cafeteria and, in 11 minutes, killed 22 with semi-automatic pistols before shooting himself.

KILLED 22

= James Oliver Huberty
San Ysidro, California, USA
18 July 1984

Huberty, aged 41, opened fire in a McDonald's restaurant, killing 21 before being shot dead by a SWAT marksman. A further 19 were wounded, including a victim who died the following day.

7=

KILLED 17

= Thomas Hamilton
Dunblane, Stirling, UK
13 March 1996

Hamilton, 43, shot 16 children and a teacher in Dunblane Primary School before killing himself in the UK's worst-ever shooting incident.

= Robert Steinhäuser
Erfurt, Germany
26 April 2002

KILLED 17

Former student Steinhäuser returned to Johann Gutenberg Secondary School and killed 14 teachers, two students, and a police officer with a handgun before shooting himself.

KILLED 16

= Michael Ryan
Hungerford, Berkshire, UK
19 August 1987

Ryan, 26, shot 14 dead and wounded 16 others (two of whom died later) before shooting himself.

9=

= Ronald Gene Simmons
Russellville, Arkansas, USA
28 December 1987

Simmons, 47, killed 16, including 14 members of his own family, by shooting or strangling. He was caught and on 10 February 1989 sentenced to death.

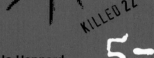

KILLED 16

= Charles Joseph Whitman
Austin, Texas, USA
31 July–1 August 1966

Ex-Marine marksman Whitman, 25, killed his mother and wife and the following day took the lift to the 27th floor of the campus tower and ascended to the observation deck at the University of Texas at Austin, from where he shot 14 and wounded 34 before being shot dead by police officer Romero Martinez.

* By individuals, excluding terrorist and military actions; totals exclude perpetrator.

World War II

the 10 WORST MILITARY SHIP LOSSES OF WORLD WAR II

SHIP*	COUNTRY	DATE	APPROX. NO. KILLED
1 Wilhelm Gustloff	Germany	30 Jan 1945	7,800
2 Goya	Germany	16 Apr 1945	6,202
3 Cap Arcona	Germany	26 Apr 1945	6,000
4 Junyo Maru	Japan	18 Sept 1944	5,620
5 Toyama Maru	Japan	29 June 1944	5,400
6 Arcona	Germany	3 May 1945	5,000
7 Lancastria	UK	17 June 1940	3,050
8 Steuben	Germany	9 Feb 1945	3,000
9 Thielbeck	Germany	3 May 1945	2,750
10 Yamato	Japan	7 Apr 1945	2,498

* Includes warships and passenger vessels used for troop and refugee transport

The German liner *Wilhelm Gustloff*, laden with civilian refugees and wounded German soldiers and sailors, was torpedoed off the coast of Poland by a Soviet submarine, *S-13*. Although imprecise, some sources even suggest a figure as high as 9,400, the probable death toll is some five times as great as that of the *Titanic*.

⬇ Scramble!
Fighter pilots race for their planes during the Battle of Britain. The UK's aircraft losses were less than one-third those of Germany or the USSR.

the 10 COUNTRIES SUFFERING THE GREATEST AIRCRAFT LOSSES IN WORLD WAR II

COUNTRY	AIRCRAFT LOST
1 Germany	116,584
2 USSR	106,652
3 USA	59,296
4 Japan	49,485
5 UK	33,090
6 Australia	7,160
7 Italy	5,272
8 Canada	2,389
9 France	2,100
10 New Zealand	684

Reports of aircraft losses vary considerably from country to country, some of them including aircraft damaged, lost due to accidents, or scrapped, as well as those destroyed during combat. The Japanese figure for combat-only losses, for example, is sometimes reported as 38,105. The huge Soviet losses, which were undisclosed at the time, are believed to include aircraft withdrawn from frontlines as well as those destroyed. Very precise combat loss figures exist for the Battle of Britain – during the period 10 July to 31 October 1940, 1,065 RAF aircraft were destroyed, compared with 1,922 Luftwaffe fighters, bombers, and other aircraft.

the 10 COUNTRIES SUFFERING THE **GREATEST MILITARY LOSSES** IN WORLD WAR II

COUNTRY / APPROX. NO. KILLED

1 **USSR** 13,600,000*
2 **Germany** 3,300,000
3 **China** 1,324,516
4 **Japan** 1,140,429
5 **British Empire**# 357,116
   (UK 264,000)
6 **Romania** 350,000
7 **Poland** 320,000
8 **Yugoslavia** 305,000
9 **USA** 292,131
10 **Italy** 279,800
   Total 21,268,992

* Total, of which 7.8 million battlefield deaths

Including Australia, Canada, India, New Zealand, etc.

the 10 COUNTRIES SUFFERING THE **GREATEST CIVILIAN LOSSES** IN WORLD WAR II

COUNTRY / APPROX. NO. KILLED*

1 **China** 8,000,000
2 **USSR** 6,500,000
3 **Poland** 5,300,000
4 **Germany** 2,350,000
5 **Yugoslavia** 1,500,000
6 **France** 470,000
7 **Greece** 415,000
8 **Japan** 393,400
9 **Romania** 340,000
10 **Hungary** 300,000

* During World War II, many deaths among civilians – especially in China and the USSR – resulted from famine and internal purges. For political and propaganda reasons, totals are less well-documented than military losses.

the 10 **NAZI WAR CRIMINALS** HANGED AT NUREMBERG

NAME / AGE / DETAILS

1 **Joachim Von Ribbentrop**, 53, former Ambassador to Great Britain and Hitler's last Foreign Minister (the first to be hanged, at 1.02 am on 16 Oct 1946)
2 **Field Marshal Wilhelm Von Keitel**, 64, who had ordered the killing of 50 Allied air force officers after the Great Escape
3 **General Ernst Kaltenbrunner**, 44, SS and Gestapo leader
4 **Reichminister Alfred Rosenberg**, 53, ex-Minister for Occupied Eastern territories
5 **Reichminister Hans Frank**, 46, ex-Governor of Poland
6 **Reichminister Wilhelm Frick**, 69, former Minister of the Interior
7 **Gauleiter Julius Streicher**, 61, editor of anti-Semitic magazine *Die Stürmer*
8 **Reichminister Fritz Sauckel**, 52, ex-General Plenipotentiary for the Utilization of Labour (the slave-labour programme)
9 **Colonel-General Alfred Jodl**, 56, former Chief of the General Staff
10 **Gauleiter Artur Von Seyss-Inquart**, 53, Governor of Austria and later Commissioner for Occupied Holland

The actual numbers killed in World War II have been the subject of intense argument. The immense military casualty rate of the USSR in particular is hard to comprehend. Most authorities now reckon that of the 30 million Soviets who bore arms, there were 13.6 million military deaths, but it should also be borne in mind that these were military losses – to these should be added many millions of civilian war deaths, while recent estimates have suggested an additional figure of up to 25 million civilian deaths as a result of Stalinist purges which began just before the war.

During the International Military Tribunal trials from 20 November 1945 to 31 August 1946, 24 Nazi war criminals stood trial. Of them, 12 were found guilty and sentenced to death (including Martin Bormann, who had escaped, and was tried *in absentia*, and Herman Goering, who cheated the gallows by committing suicide with a capsule of cyanide at 10.50 pm the previous day. The remaining 10 were hanged on 16 October 1946.

⊕ **War graves**
A US military cemetery in France shows the scale of the losses sustained by one country in a single campaign.

Military Might

⊕ **Balance of power** China and the US represent the greatest military strengths today in a world facing the threats of global terrorism and rogue states.

top 10 **LARGEST** ARMED FORCES

	COUNTRY	ESTIMATED TOTAL ACTIVE FORCES			
		(ARMY	NAVY	AIR)	TOTAL
1	**China**	1,600,000	255,000	400,000	2,255,000
2	**USA**	502,000	400,000	379,500	1,456,850*
3	**India**	1,100,000	55,000	170,000	1,325,000
4	**North Korea**	1,106,000	46,000	110,000	1,262,000
5	**Russia**	360,000	155,000	184,600	1,058,700#
6	**South Korea**	560,000	63,000	64,700	687,700
7	**Pakistan**	550,000	25,000	45,000	620,000
8	**Iran**	350,000	18,000	52,000	540,000†
9	**Turkey**	402,000	52,750	60,100	514,850
10	**Vietnam**	412,000	42,000	30,000	484,000
	UK	*116,760*	*40,630*	*48,500*	*205,890*

* Includes 175,350 Marine Corps

\# Includes Strategic Deterrent Forces, Paramilitary, National Guard, etc.

† Includes 120,000 Revolutionary Guards

In addition to the active forces listed here, many of the world's foremost countries have substantial reserves on standby; South Korea's has been estimated at some 4.5 million, Vietnam's at three to four million, and China's 800,000. China is also notable for having a massive arsenal of military equipment at its disposal, including some 7,850 tanks and 3,000 combat aircraft. North Korea has the world's highest military/civilian ratio: 558 out of every 10,000 of the population serve in its forces, compared with South Korea's 144 per 10,000. The UK ratio is 35 per 10,000.

top 10 **SMALLEST** ARMED FORCES*

	COUNTRY	ESTIMATED TOTAL ACTIVE FORCES
1	**Antigua and Barbuda**	170
2	**Seychelles**	450
3	**Barbados**	610
4	**Gambia**	800
5	**Bahamas**	860
6	**Luxembourg**	900
7	**Belize**	1,050
8	**Cape Verde**	1,200
9	**Equatorial Guinea**	1,320
10	**Guyana**	1,600

* Includes only those countries that declare a defence budget

A number of small countries maintain military forces for ceremonial purposes, national prestige, or reasons other than national defence, and would clearly be inadequate to resist an invasion by their much larger neighbours. Luxembourg's army, however, took an active part in peacekeeping duties in former Yugoslavia.

🔿 **Soaring costs** The US and India, both notable for their multi-billon dollar and ever-increasing defence budgets, join forces in an aerial military exercise.

top 10 COUNTRIES WITH THE LARGEST DEFENCE BUDGETS

	COUNTRY	BUDGET ($)
1	USA	404,920,000,000
2	Russia	62,200,000,000
3	China	55,948,000,000
4	France	45,695,000,000
5	Japan	42,835,000,000
6	UK	42,782,000,000
7	Germany	35,145,000,000
8	Italy	27,751,000,000
9	Saudi Arabia	18,747,000,000
10	India	15,508,000,000

The so-called "peace dividend" – the reduction in defence expenditure since the end of the Cold War between the West and the former Soviet Union – was short-lived. In response to the threats of international terrorism and "rogue states", such as Iraq, the budgets of the USA (which stood at $305,500,000 in 2001) and her allies have increased to record levels. Globally, the total defence expenditure is now almost $1 trillion, of which over $600 billion is by NATO countries. The budget of North Korea, an impoverished country with a population of just 22 million, is a remarkable $5.5 billion.

top 10 COUNTRIES WITH THE SMALLEST DEFENCE BUDGETS

	COUNTRY*	BUDGET ($)
1	Gambia	2,000,000
2	Antigua and Barbuda	4,000,000
3 =	Cape Verde	5,000,000
=	Guyana	5,000,000
5	Equatorial Guinea	6,000,000
6	Surinam	8,000,000
7	Guinea-Bissau	9,000,000
8	Malawi	11,000,000
9	Seychelles	12,000,000
10 =	Barbados	13,000,000
=	Mauritius	13,000,000

* Includes only those countries that declare defence budgets

Compared with the multi-billion dollar defence budgets of the world's biggest military spenders, those of these countries are minute. However, if expressed as a proportion of their gross domestic product, with expenditure amounting to more than one per cent, several of these countries are actually on a par with many larger and wealthier nations. Gambia's minuscule $2 million budget supports an army of 800 and a marine unit of 70, plus a tiny UN peacekeeping force.

Religions

top 10 LARGEST CHRISTIAN POPULATIONS

	COUNTRY	CHRISTIAN POPULATION (2004)
1	USA	246,543,000
2	Brazil	164,122,000
3	China	106,902,000
4	Mexico	101,541,000
5	Russia	85,234,000
6	Philippines	73,862,000
7	India	68,125,000
8	Germany	62,557,000
9	Nigeria	59,148,000
10	Dem. Rep. of Congo	55,340,000

Source: World Christian Database

The Christian populations of these 10 countries make up almost 50 per cent of the world total. Although Christian communities are found in virtually every country in the world, it is difficult to put a precise figure on nominal membership (a declared religious persuasion) rather than active participation (regular attendance at a place of worship).

⬇ Muslim population

Interdum volgus rectum videt, est ubi peccat. Si veteres ita miratur laudatque poetas, ut nihil anteferat, nihil illis comparet, errat. Si quaedam nimis antique, si peraque dure dicere credit.

top 10 LARGEST JEWISH POPULATIONS

	COUNTRY	JEWISH POPULATION (2004)
1	USA	5,795,000
2	Israel	5,096,000
3	France	599,000
4	Argentina	490,000
5	Canada	420,000
6	Palestine	400,000
7	Brazil	379,000
8	UK	312,000
9	Germany	225,000
10	Russia	210,000

Source: *World Christian Encyclopedia*

The Diaspora, or scattering of Jewish people, has been in progress for nearly 2,000 years, and as a result Jewish communities are found in virtually every country in the world. In 1939 it was estimated that the total world Jewish population was 17 million. Some 6 million fell victim to Nazi persecution, reducing the figure to about 11 million, but it is now estimated to have grown to exceed 13 million.

top 10 LARGEST MUSLIM POPULATIONS

	COUNTRY	MUSLIM POPULATION (2004 EST.)
1	Pakistan	150,850,000
2	India	132,480,000
3	Bangladesh	128,700,000
4	Indonesia	120,670,000*
5	Turkey	70,250,000
6	Iran	66,890,000
7	Egypt	61,900,000
8	Nigeria	53,500,000
9	Algeria	31,300,000
10	Morocco	30,560,000

* An additional 46 million people are considered Muslims by the Indonesian government but are more properly categorized as New Religionists (islamized syncretistic religions)

Source: World Christian Database, www.worldchristiandatabase.org, October 2003

top 10 LARGEST HINDU POPULATIONS

	COUNTRY	HINDU POPULATION (2004 EST.)
1	India	801,360,000
2	Nepal	19,030,000
3	Bangladesh	18,500,000
4	Indonesia	7,550,000
5	Sri Lanka	2,170,000
6	Pakistan	2,050,000
7	Malaysia	1,830,000
8	USA	1,130,000
9	South Africa	1,080,000
10	Myanmar	1,000,000

Source: World Christian Database, www.worldchristiandatabase.org, October 2003

Hindus constitute some 75 per cent of the population of India and 70 per cent of that of Nepal, but only 13 per cent of that of Bangladesh and as little as three per cent of Indonesia's.

→ Cross road
Christianity is predicted to maintain its status as the world's foremost religion, with some estimates forecasting a total global population of around 3 billion Christians by 2025.

top 10 **RELIGIOUS BELIEFS** IN THE **UK**

RELIGION	FOLLOWERS, 2006 EST.
1 Christianity	48,631,000
2 Agnosticism	7,380,000
3 Islam	1,369,000
4 Atheism	858,000
5 Hinduism	494,000
6 Judaism	308,000
7 Sikhism	238,000
8 Buddhism	172,000
9 Zoroastrianism	90,100
10 Spiritualism	70,700

Source: Center for the Study of Global Christianity, Gordon-Conwell Theological Seminary

Reliable statistical data on religions is notoriously difficult to assemble: many individuals consider questions about their religion intrusive and decline to answer, while there is inevitably a distinction between those who profess and those who actively practise a particular religion. The Center for the Study of Global Christianity at the Gordon-Conwell Theological Seminary is considered the most authoritative source. It gathers statistics on all Christian denominations and world religions, and provides the most reliable available overview of the current numbers of people claiming affiliation to each religious group – including agnosticism (the belief that knowledge of a god or gods can not be known with certainty) and atheism (the denial of the existence of a god).

top 10 **RELIGIOUS BELIEFS**

RELIGION	FOLLOWERS, 2006 EST.
1 Christianity	2,159,841,000
2 Islam	1,342,394,000
3 Hinduism	877,126,000
4 Agnosticism	772,177,000
5 Chinese folk-religions	406,889,000
6 Buddhism	382,155,000
7 Ethnic religions	257,888,000
8 Atheism	152,152,000
9 New religions	108,939,000
10 Sikhism	25,731,000

Source: Center for the Study of Global Christianity, Gordon-Conwell Theological Seminary

These authoritative estimates imply that almost one-third of the world's population are nominally (self-declared), if not practising, Christians, and one-fifth followers of Islam. Alongside the growth of some religious groups, mainstream religions have seen a decline in formal attendance as increasing numbers of people describe themselves as "spiritual" rather than "religious", while it is reckoned that at least 15 per cent of the world population profess no religious beliefs of any kind.

top 10 countries with the longest coastlines: page 82

Chapter
4

top 10 tallest habitable buildings: page 90

top 10 most populated countries: page 84

top 10 countries with most neighbours: page 83

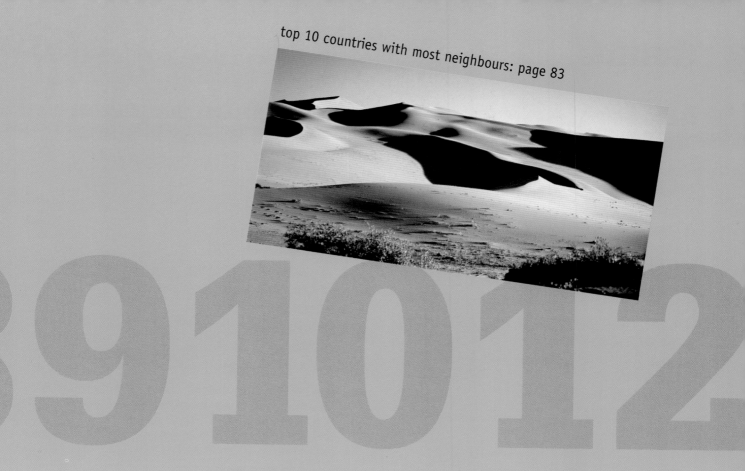

Town & Country

top 10 largest US states: page 88

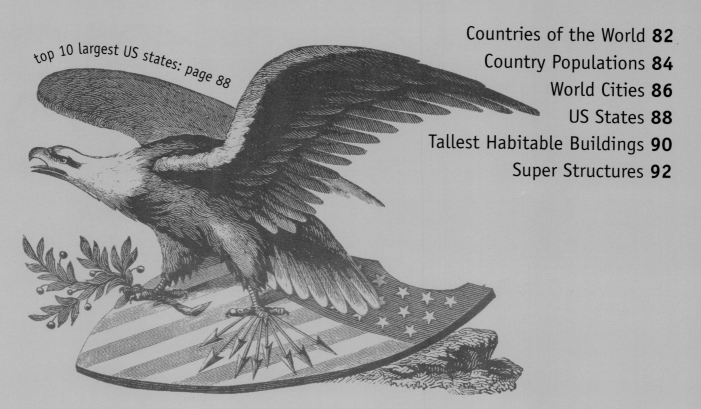

Countries of the World

top 10 LARGEST COUNTRIES

COUNTRY	(SQ KM)	AREA (SQ MILES)	PERCENTAGE OF WORLD TOTAL
1 Russia	17,075,400	6,592,850	13.0
2 Canada	9,984,670	3,855,103	7.6
3 China	9,326,411	3,600,948	7.1
4 USA	9,166,601	3,539,245	6.9
5 Brazil	8,456,511	3,265,077	6.4
6 Australia	7,617,931	2,941,300	5.8
7 India	2,973,190	1,148,148	2.2
8 Argentina	2,736,690	1,056,642	2.1
9 Kazakhstan	2,717,300	1,049,155	2.0
10 Algeria	2,381,741	919,595	1.8
UK	*241,590*	*93,278*	*0.2*
World total	*131,003,055*	*50,580,568*	*100.0*

Source: US Census Bureau, International Data Base/Statistics Canada

top 10 SMALLEST COUNTRIES

COUNTRY	AREA (SQ KM)	(SQ MILES)
1 Vatican City	0.44	0.2
2 Monaco	2	0.7
3 Nauru	21	8
4 Tuvalu	26	10
5 San Marino	60	23
6 Liechtenstein	161	62
7 Marshall Islands	181	70
8 Maldives	300	115
9 Malta	321	124
10 Grenada	339	130

Source: US Census Bureau, International Database

The "country" status of the Vatican is questionable, since its government and other features are intricately linked with those of Italy. The Vatican did become part of unified Italy in the 19th century, but its identity as an independent state was recognized by a treaty on 11 February 1929.

top 10 COUNTRIES WITH THE LONGEST COASTLINES

COUNTRY / TOTAL COASTLINE LENGTH (KM / MILES)

1 Canada 202,080 km / 125,566 miles

2 Indonesia 54,716 km / 33,999 miles   **3 Russia** 37,653 km / 23,396 miles   **4 Philippines** 36,289 km / 22,559 miles

5 Japan 29,751 km / 18,486 miles   **6 Australia** 25,760 km / 16,007 miles   **7 Norway** 21,925 km / 13,624 miles

8 USA 19,924 km / 12,380 miles   **9 New Zealand** 15,134 km / 9,404 miles   **10 China** 14,500 km / 9,010 miles

Including all its islands, the coastline of Canada is more than six times as long as the distance around the Earth at the Equator (40,076 km/24,902 miles). The coastline of the UK (12,429 km/ 7,723 miles) is longer than the distance from London to Honolulu, which puts it in 13th place after Greece's 13,676-km (8,498-mile) coastline. Greenland (44,087 km/27,394 miles) is a self-governed Danish territory. If it were a country in its own right, it would rank in 3rd place in this list.

⬆ **From one extreme to the other** China has frontiers with 14 other countries, its neighbours representing landscapes as diverse as Nepal's Himalayas and Mongolia's Gobi Desert.

top 10 COUNTRIES WITH **MOST** NEIGHBOURS

COUNTRY / NEIGHBOURS	NO. OF NEIGHBOURS
1 = China	14
Afghanistan, Bhutan, India, Kazakhstan, Kyrgyzstan, Laos, Mongolia, Myanmar, Nepal, North Korea, Pakistan, Russia, Tajikistan, Vietnam	
= Russia	14
Azerbaijan, Belarus, China, Estonia, Finland, Georgia, Kazakhstan, Latvia, Lithuania, Mongolia, North Korea, Norway, Poland, Ukraine	
3 Brazil	10
Argentina, Bolivia, Colombia, French Guiana, Guyana, Paraguay, Peru, Suriname, Uruguay, Venezuela	
4 = Dem. Rep. of Congo	9
Angola, Burundi, Central African Republic, Congo, Rwanda, Sudan, Tanzania, Uganda, Zambia	
= Germany	9
Austria, Belgium, Czech Republic, Denmark, France, Luxembourg, Netherlands, Poland, Switzerland	
= Sudan	9
Central African Republic, Chad, Dem. Rep. of Congo, Egypt, Eritrea, Ethiopia, Kenya, Libya, Uganda	
7 = Austria	8
Czech Republic, Germany, Hungary, Italy, Liechtenstein, Slovakia, Slovenia, Switzerland	

COUNTRY / NEIGHBOURS	NO. OF NEIGHBOURS
= France	8
Andorra, Belgium, Germany, Italy, Luxembourg, Monaco, Spain, Switzerland	
= Turkey	8
Armenia, Azerbaijan, Bulgaria, Georgia, Greece, Iran, Iraq, Syria	
10 = Mali	7
Algeria, Burkina Faso, Côte d'Ivoire, Guinea, Mauritania, Niger, Senegal	
= Niger	7
Algeria, Benin, Burkina Faso, Chad, Libya, Mali, Nigeria	
= Saudi Arabia	7
Iraq, Jordan, Kuwait, Oman, Qatar, United Arab Emirates, Yemen	
= Tanzania	7
Burundi, Kenya, Malawi, Mozambique, Rwanda, Uganda, Zambia	
= Ukraine	7
Belarus, Hungary, Moldova, Poland, Romania, Russia, Slovakia	
= Zambia	7
Angola, Dem. Rep. of Congo, Malawi, Mozambique, Namibia, Tanzania, Zimbabwe	

It should be noted that some countries have more than one discontinuous border with the same country; this has been counted only once.

Country Populations

top 10 MOST POPULATED COUNTRIES

COUNTRY	POPULATION, EST. 2006
1 China	1,313,973,713
2 India	1,095,351,995
3 USA	298,444,215
4 Indonesia	245,452,739
5 Brazil	188,078,227
6 Pakistan	165,803,560
7 Bangladesh	147,365,352
8 Russia	142,893,540
9 Nigeria	131,866,254
10 Japan	127,463,611
World	*6,529,645,083*
UK	*60,609,153*

Source: US Census Bureau, International Data Base

top 10 MOST POPULATED COUNTRIES IN 2050

COUNTRY	POPULATION, EST. 2050
1 India	1,601,004,572
2 China	1,424,161,948
3 USA	420,080,587
4 Nigeria	356,544,098
5 Indonesia	336,247,428
6 Pakistan	294,995,104
7 Bangladesh	279,955,405
8 Brazil	228,426,737
9 Dem Rep. of Congo	181,260,098
10 Mexico	147,907,650
World	*9,190,252,532*
UK	*63,977,435*

Source: US Census Bureau, International Data Base

➲ Most populated

China has been the world's most populated country since ancient times: even 2,000 years ago it contained a quarter of the world's inhabitants, a picture that is scheduled to be eclipsed by India.

top 10 COUNTRIES WITH THE **HIGHEST PROPORTION** OF IMMIGRANTS

COUNTRY / EST. NET NO. OF IMMIGRANTS
PER 1,000 POPULATION, 2006

1 **Kuwait** 15.7

2 **Qatar** 14.1

3 **San Marino** 10.7

4 **Singapore** 9.1

5 **Luxembourg** 8.8

6 **Monaco** 7.7

7 **Andorra** 6.5

8 **Jordan** 6.3

9 **Botswana** 6.1

10 **Canada** 5.8

UK 2.2

Source: US Census Bureau, International Data Base

A number of island territories would figure strongly in this list if they had country status: Cayman Islands with an estimated net migration of 17.8 per 1,000 in 2006, Turks and Caicos with 10.5, and British Virgin Islands with 9.2.

top 10 COUNTRIES WITH THE **HIGHEST PROPORTION** OF EMIGRANTS

COUNTRY / EST. NET NO. OF EMIGRANTS
PER 1,000 POPULATION, 2006

1 **Micronesia** 21.0

2 **Grenada** 12.6

3 **Cape Verde** 11.9

4 **Samoa** 11.8

5 **Trinidad and Tobago** 10.9

6 **Dominica** 9.3

7 **Surinam** 8.8

8 **St. Vincent and the Grenadines** 7.6

9 **Guyana** 7.5

10 **Antigua and Barbuda** 6.1

Source: US Census Bureau, International Data Base

Economic migration from small island communities is especially prevalent: few have industries other than tourism and many inhabitants opt to leave in search of the attractions of work and life offered by neighbouring mainlands.

top 10 **COUNTRIES OF ORIGIN** OF UK IMMIGRANTS

COUNTRY / TOTAL NO. OF IMMIGRANTS, 2003

1 **Pakistan** 13,040 2 **India** 11,460 3 **South Africa** 8,930 4 **Nigeria** 7,690

5 **Somalia** 6,075 6 **USA** 5,695 7 **Bangladesh** 5,610 8 **Jamaica** 4,500

9 **Turkey** 4,325 10 **Australia** 4,160

Source: UK Home Office

These are the leading countries of origin of immigrants to the UK based on Home Office Grants of Settlement, of which a total of 143,845 were issued in 2003. The largest region of origin is Asia, with 55,040 immigrants, followed by Africa with 44,815, Europe with 18,920, and the Americas with 16,735.

World Cities

top 10 LARGEST CAPITAL CITIES

CITY / COUNTRY	ESTIMATED POPULATION*
1 Tokyo (including Yokohama and Kawasaki), Japan	34,000,000
2 Mexico City (including Nezahualcóyotl, Ecatepec, and Naucalpan), Mexico	22,350,000
3 Seoul (including Bucheon, Goyang, Incheon, Seongnam, and Suweon), South Korea	22,050,000
4 Delhi (including Faridabad and Ghaziabad), India	19,000,000
5 Jakarta (including Bekasi, Bogor, Depok, and Tangerang), Indonesia	16,850,000
6 Cairo (including Al-Jizah and Shubra al-Khaymah), Egypt	15,250,000
7 Manila (including Kalookan and Quezon City), Philippines	14,550,000
8 Moscow, Russia	13,650,000
9 Buenos Aires (including San Justo and La Plata), Argentina	13,350,000
10 Dhaka, Bangladesh	12,750,000

* As at 30 Jan 2005

Source: Th. Brinkhoff: *The Principal Agglomerations of the World*, http://www.citypopulation.de

These populations are of the "urban agglomerations" – city centres and their densely populated outlying suburbs, with the strict definition taking account of population density in determining the boundaries of the agglomeration. They often encompass other neighbouring cities and their suburbs, the resulting totals inevitably exceeding those of the city proper.

top 10 LARGEST NON-CAPITAL CITIES

CITY / COUNTRY	ESTIMATED POPULATION*
1 New York (including Newark and Paterson), USA	21,800,000
2 São Paulo (including Guarulhos), Brazil	20,000,000
3 Mumbai (including Kalyan, Thane, and Ulhasnagar), India	19,400,000
4 Los Angeles (including Riverside and Anaheim), USA	17,750,000
5 Osaka (including Kobe and Kyoto), Japan	16,750,000
6 Calcutta[#] (including Haora), India	15,350,000
7 Karachi[#], Pakistan	13,800,000
8 Shanghai, China	13,400,000
9 Rio de Janeiro[#] (including Nova Iguaçu and São Gonçalo), Brazil	12,000,000
10 Istanbul[#], Turkey	11,250,000

* As at 30 Jan 2005

[#] Former capital

Source: Th. Brinkhoff: *The Principal Agglomerations of the World*, http://www.citypopulation.de

top 10 FASTEST-GROWING CITIES

CITY / COUNTRY	AVERAGE ANNUAL POPULATION GROWTH RATE* (PERCENTAGE), 2000–05
1 **Ansan**, South Korea	9.15
2 **Toluca**, Mexico	6.15
3 **Sana'a**, Yemen	5.83
4 **Niamey**, Niger	5.70
5 **Songnam**, South Korea	5.47
6 **P'ohang**, South Korea	5.43
7 **Rajshahi**, Bangladesh	5.29
8 **Kabul**, Afghanistan	5.10
9 = **Antananarivo**, Madagascar	5.05
= **Campo Grande**, Brazil	5.05
Tyneside (Newcastle), UK	*0.60*

* Of urban agglomerations with 750,000 inhabitants or more

Source: United Nations Population Division, *World Urbanization Report: The 2001 Revision*

These cities, which include several capitals (Sana'a, Naimey, Kabul, and Antananarivo) have experienced recent population increases for a variety of reasons: in the case of Naimey, for example, as a result of droughts elsewhere in the country.

top 10 CITIES THAT ARE HOME TO THE LARGEST PROPORTIONS OF THEIR COUNTRIES' POPULATIONS

CITY / COUNTRY	POPULATION, 2003 (TOTAL)	(PERCENTAGE OF COUNTRY)
1 = **Hong Kong**, China	7,000,000	100.0
= **Singapore**, Singapore	4,300,000	100.0
3 **San Juan**, Puerto Rico	2,300,000	60.1
4 **Beirut**, Lebanon	1,800,000	49.1
5 **Kuwait City**, Kuwait	1,200,000	48.5
6 **Tel Aviv**, Israel	2,900,000	45.3
7 **Montevideo**, Uruguay	1,300,000	39.3
8 **Tripoli**, Libya	2,000,000	36.1
9 **Yerevan**, Armenia	1,100,000	35.3
10 **Santiago**, Chile	5,500,000	34.7
London, UK	*7,600,000*	*12.9*

Source: United Nations Population Division, *Urban Agglomerations 2003*

⊕ City of angels

In 1900 the population of the city of Los Angeles was just 102,479. By the 2000 Census the city centre population had reached 3,694,820, while the expanding conurbation is home to five times that number.

US States

top 10 LARGEST US STATES

STATE	LAND AREA* (SQ KM)	(SQ MILES)
1 Alaska	1,481,347	571,951
2 Texas	678,051	261,797
3 California	403,933	155,959
4 Montana	376,979	145,552
5 New Mexico	314,309	121,356
6 Arizona	294,312	113,635
7 Nevada	284,448	109,826
8 Colorado	268,627	103,718
9 Wyoming	251,489	97,100
10 Oregon	248,631	95,997

* Excluding water

The total land area of the USA has grown progressively – in 1800 it was 2,248,058 sq km (867,980 sq miles), and by 1900 it had grown to 7,703,036 sq km (2,974,159 sq miles). The admission of Alaska into the Union on 3 January and Hawaii on 20 August 1959 increased the land area by almost 20 per cent, bringing the total to its present 9,171,146 sq km (3,540,999 sq miles).

top 10 SMALLEST US STATES

STATE	LAND AREA* (SQ KM)	(SQ MILES)
1 Rhode Island	2,706	1,045
2 Delaware	5,063	1,955
3 Connecticut	12,548	4,845
4 Hawaii	16,635	6,423
5 New Jersey	19,215	7,419
6 Massachusetts	20,300	7,838
7 New Hampshire	23,229	8,969
8 Vermont	23,955	9,249
9 Maryland	25,317	9,775
10 West Virginia	62,385	24,087

* Excluding water

The smallest state, Rhode Island, has the longest official name – "State of Rhode Island and Providence Plantations". A total of 546 Rhode Islands – which also includes some 1,295 sq km (500 sq miles) of inland water – could fit into the land area of the largest state, Alaska.

top 10 US STATES WITH THE HIGHEST ELEVATIONS

STATE	PEAK	HIGHEST ELEVATION* (M)	(FT)
1 Alaska	Mount McKinley	6,194	20,320
2 California	Mount Whitney	4,418	14,494
3 Colorado	Mount Elbert	4,399	14,433
4 Washington	Mount Rainier	4,392	14,410
5 Wyoming	Gannett Peak	4,207	13,804
6 Hawaii	Mauna Kea	4,205	13,796
7 Utah	Kings Peak	4,123	13,528
8 New Mexico	Wheeler Peak	4,011	13,161
9 Nevada	Boundary Peak	4,005	13,140
10 Montana	Granite Peak	3,901	12,799

* Only the highest elevation in each state is included; many states have further peaks of lesser height

Alaska not only has the USA's tallest mountain, but a further 12 that are taller than the next highest, California's Mount Whitney. All of them are in Denali National Park with Mount McKinley, or in Wrangel-St. Elias National Park, with the single exception of Fairweather, which is in Glacier Bay National Park.

← American high

Mount McKinley (also known as Denali) – the tallest US peak – was first climbed on 7 June 1912 by a party led by Hudson Stuck, the British-born Archdeacon of the Yukon.

top 10 LEAST POPULATED US STATES

STATE	POPULATION 2004
1 Wyoming	506,529
2 Vermont	621,394
3 North Dakota	634,366
4 Alaska	655,435
5 South Dakota	770,883
6 Delaware	830,364
7 Montana	926,865
8 Rhode Island	1,080,632
9 Hawaii	1,262,840
10 New Hampshire	1,299,500

Source: US Census Bureau

With a high proportion of its area devoted to agriculture and almost half the land area of Wyoming federally owned, the low population density of the state is likely to maintained.

top 10 MOST DENSELY POPULATED US STATES

STATE	POPULATION* PER (SQ KM)	(SQ MILE)
1 New Jersey	452.7	1,172.7
2 Rhode Island	415.1	1,075.3
3 Massachusetts	315.9	818.4
4 Connecticut	279.1	723.1
5 Maryland	219.5	568.6
6 Delaware	164.0	425.0
7 New York	157.2	407.2
8 Florida	124.5	322.6
9 Ohio	108.0	279.8
10 Pennsylvania	106.8	276.8

* Of land area as at 2004

Source: US Census Bureau

The population densities of the states have increased dramatically over the past 200 years: that of New Jersey, for example, was 96.8 per sq km (250.7 per sq mile) in 1900, and just 10.8 per sq km (28.1 per sq mile) in 1800.

top 10 US STATES WITH THE LONGEST SHORELINES

STATE	SHORELINE (KM)	(MILES)
1 Alaska	54,563	33,904
2 Florida	13,560	8,426
3 Louisiana	12,426	7,721
4 Maine	5,597	3,478
5 California	5,515	3,427
6 North Carolina	5,432	3,375
7 Texas	5,406	3,359
8 Virginia	5,335	3,315
9 Maryland	5,134	3,190
10 Washington	4,870	3,026

Pennsylvania's 143-km (89-mile) shoreline is the shortest among states that have one – 26 states, plus Washington, DC, have no shoreline at all.

◗ Soaring symbol
The bald eagle has been a symbol of the USA since 1782, when the design of the Great Seal depicted it clutching an olive branch and 13 arrows in its talons, representing peace and war.

top 10 **TALLEST** HABITABLE BUILDINGS

BUILDING / LOCATION / YEAR COMPLETED	STOREYS	HEIGHT (M)	(FT)
1 Taipei 101, Taipei, Taiwan, 2004	101	509	1,669
2 Petronas Towers, Kuala Lumpur, Malaysia, 1998	88	452	1,482
3 Sears Tower, Chicago, USA, 1974	108	442	1,450
4 Jin Mao Building, Shanghai, China, 1998	88	421	1,381
5 Two International Finance Centre, Hong Kong, China, 2003	90	415	1,361
6 CITIC Plaza, Guangzhou, China, 1997	80	391	1,282
7 Shun Hing Square, Shenzen, China, 1996	69	384	1,259
8 Empire State Building, New York, USA, 1931	102	381	1,250
9 Central Plaza, Hong Kong, China, 1992	78	374	1,227
10 Bank of China Tower, Hong Kong, China, 1990	72	367	1,204

According to rules established by the Council on Tall Buildings and Urban Habitat, the height of a building is taken from street level to the structural top of the building. This includes spires, but not subterranean floors or non-structural additions such as masts, antennae, or flagpoles.

⬅ **Taipei 101**

So named because it has 101 storeys above ground level, Taipei 101 is the world's tallest building (according to the definition that allows certain architectural structures). Taipei 101 has a spire which contributes to its total height.

➡ **Petronas Towers**

Once the record-holder and still the tallest twin towers, the Petronas Towers are connected by a sky bridge between the 41st and 42nd floors. The building was featured in the Sean Connery/ Catherine Zeta-Jones film *Entrapment* (1999).

Super Structures

top 10 LONGEST BRIDGES

BRIDGE* / LOCATION / YEAR COMPLETED / LENGTH OF MAIN SPAN (M / FT)

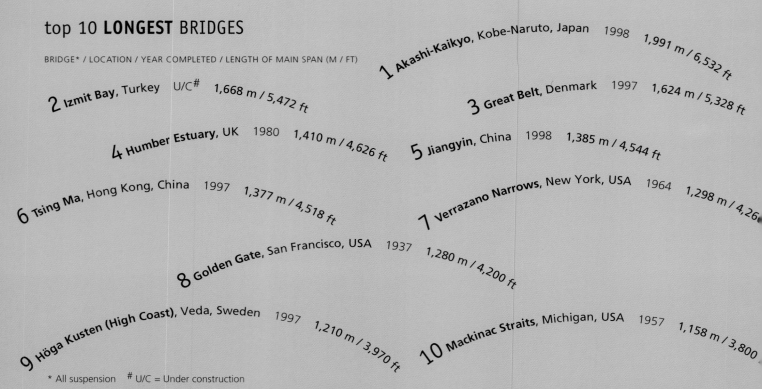

1 Akashi-Kaikyo, Kobe-Naruto, Japan   1998   1,991 m / 6,532 ft

2 Izmit Bay, Turkey   U/C#   1,668 m / 5,472 ft

3 Great Belt, Denmark   1997   1,624 m / 5,328 ft

4 Humber Estuary, UK   1980   1,410 m / 4,626 ft

5 Jiangyin, China   1998   1,385 m / 4,544 ft

6 Tsing Ma, Hong Kong, China   1997   1,377 m / 4,518 ft

7 Verrazano Narrows, New York, USA   1964   1,298 m / 4,26

8 Golden Gate, San Francisco, USA   1937   1,280 m / 4,200 ft

9 Höga Kusten (High Coast), Veda, Sweden   1997   1,210 m / 3,970 ft

10 Mackinac Straits, Michigan, USA   1957   1,158 m / 3,800

* All suspension   # U/C = Under construction

The Messina Strait Bridge between Sicily and Calabria, Italy, received the go-ahead in June 2002, with work to begin in 2005; it will take six years and cost €4.6/£3.1 billion. Designed to carry road and rail traffic on a 60-m (197-ft) deck, it will have by far the longest centre span of any bridge at 3,300 m (10,827 ft), although at 3,910 m (12,828 ft,) Japan's Akashi-Kaikyo bridge, is the world's longest overall.

top 10 LONGEST TUNNELS*

TUNNEL# / COUNTRY / YEAR COMPLETED / LENGTH (KM / MILES)

Several of the tunnels listed presented the additional challenge of being bored beneath the sea: the Channel Tunnel, one of the most ambitious tunnelling projects of all time, defeated engineers for almost 200 years before finally being realized.

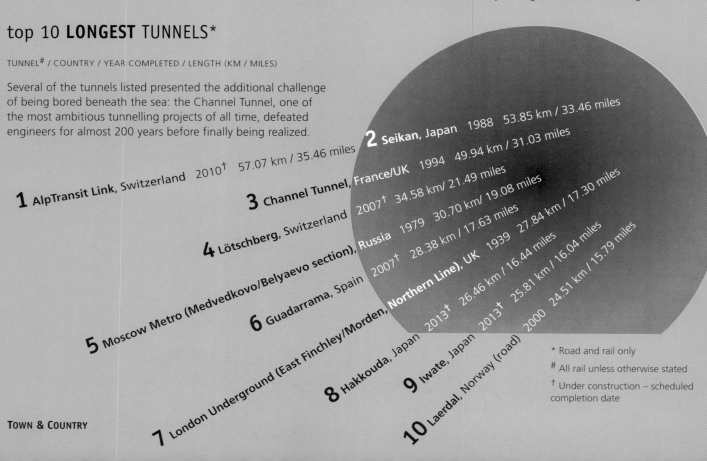

1 AlpTransit Link, Switzerland   2010†   57.07 km / 35.46 miles

2 Seikan, Japan   1988   53.85 km / 33.46 miles

3 Channel Tunnel, France/UK   1994   49.94 km / 31.03 miles

4 Lötschberg, Switzerland   2007†   34.58 km/ 21.49 miles

5 Moscow Metro (Medvedkovo/Belyaevo section), Russia   1979   30.70 km/ 19.08 miles

6 Guadarrama, Spain   2007†   28.38 km / 17.63 miles

7 London Underground (East Finchley/Morden, Northern Line), UK   1939   27.84 km / 17.30 miles

8 Hakkouda, Japan   2013†   26.46 km / 16.44 miles

9 Iwate, Japan   2013†   25.81 km / 16.04 miles

10 Laerdal, Norway (road)   2000   24.51 km / 15.79 miles

* Road and rail only

All rail unless otherwise stated

† Under construction – scheduled completion date

top 10 **TALLEST** TELECOMMUNICATIONS TOWERS

	TOWER / LOCATION	COMPLETED	HEIGHT (M)	(FT)
1	**CN Tower**, Toronto, Canada	1975	555	1,821
2	**Ostankino Tower***, Moscow, Russia	1967	537	1,762
3	**Oriental Pearl Broadcasting Tower**, Shanghai, China	1995	468	1,535
4	**Borj-e Milad Telecommunications Tower**, Tehran, Iran	2003	435	1,426
5	**Menara Telecom Tower**, Kuala Lumpur, Malaysia	1996	421	1,381
6	**Tianjin TV and Radio Tower**, Tianjin, China	1991	415	1,362
7	**Central Radio and TV Tower**, Beijing, China	1994	405	1,328
8	**Kiev TV Tower**, Kiev, Ukraine	1973	385	1,263
9	**TV Tower**, Tashkent, Uzbekistan	1983	375	1,230
10	**Liberation Tower**, Kuwait City, Kuwait	1998	372	1,220

* Severely damaged by fire, Aug 2000

All the towers listed are self-supporting, rather than masts braced with guy wires, and all have observation facilities, the highest being that in the CN Tower, Toronto (the world's tallest self-supporting structure of any kind) at 447 m (1,467 ft). The proposed Jakarta TV Tower, scheduled for completion in 2009, will top this list at 558 m (1,831 ft).

First Fact

Proposed for construction at Buronga, New South Wales, Australia, the EnviroMission Solar Tower will be a revolutionary and environmentally-friendly power station – the first of five planned for Australia. The original concept proposed by German civil engineer Jörg Schlaich uses solar energy to heat air under a vast greenhouse surface. The heated air is then drawn through turbines around the base of a 1-km (3,280-ft) high hollow tower – which will be the world's tallest structure. The constant movement of air will power the turbines to generate more than 200 MW of electricity, enough for more than 200,000 households.

top 10 **LARGEST VOLUME** DAMS*

	DAM	LOCATION	COMPLETED	VOLUME (CU M)	VOLUME (CU YD)
1	**Syncrude Tailings**	Alberta, Canada	1992	540,000,000	706,293,000
2	**Chapetón**	Paraná, Argentina	U/C#	296,200,000	387,415,000
3	**Pati**	Paraná, Argentina	1990	230,180,000	301,064,000
4	**New Cornelia Tailings**	Arizona, USA	1973	209,500,000	274,016,000
5	**Tarbela**	Indus, Pakistan	1976	121,720,000	159,210,000
6	**Kambaratinsk**	Naryn, Kyrgyzstan	U/C#	112,200,000	146,752,000
7	**Fort Peck**	Missouri/Montana, USA	1937	96,050,000	125,629,000
8	**Lower Usuma**	Usuma, Nigeria	1990	93,049,000	121,703,000
9	**Cipasang**	Cimanuk, Indonesia	U/C#	90,000,000	117,716,000
10	**Atatürk**	Euphrates, Turkey	1990	84,500,000	110,522,000

* Volume of material used in construction (earth, rocks, concrete, etc.)
# U/C = Under construction

➲ EnviroMission Solar Tower
The progressive increase in height of the world's tallest structure, from the Great Pyramid to the EnviroMission Solar Tower, is graphically depicted in this artist's impression.

RMIT University, Melbourne Australia and EnviroMission Limited.

Chapter

45678

No. 27

64
PAGES
OF
ACTION!

MAY, 1939

Detective COMICS

10¢

STARTING THIS ISSUE:
THE AMAZING AND
UNIQUE ADVENTURES OF
THE BATMAN!

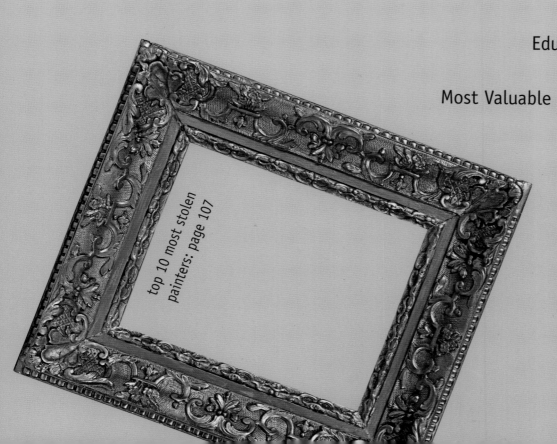

top 10 largest libraries: page 99

top 10 countries with the most English language speakers: page 96

top 10 most stolen painters: page 107

Culture & Learning

World Wide Words

top 10 COUNTRIES WITH THE **MOST ENGLISH LANGUAGE** SPEAKERS

	COUNTRY	APPROXIMATE NO. OF SPEAKERS*
1	USA	215,423,557
2	UK	58,190,000
3	Canada	20,000,000
4	Australia	14,987,000
5	Ireland	3,750,000
6	=New Zealand	3,700,000
	=South Africa	3,700,000
8	Jamaica#	2,600,000
9	Trinidad and Tobago#	1,145,000
10	Guyana#	650,000

* People for whom English is their mother-tongue

Includes English Creole

The Top 10 represents the countries with the greatest numbers of inhabitants who speak English as their mother-tongue. After the 10th entry, the figures dive to 260,000 or fewer in the case of the Bahamas, Barbados, and Zimbabwe. These and other countries comprise a world total of over 500 million, with perhaps one billion speaking English as a second language: a large proportion of the population of the Philippines, for example, speaks English, and there are many countries where English is either an official language or is widely understood and used in conducting legal affairs, in government, and business.

⊕ **Strong character**
While Chinese remains the world's most spoken language, English is increasingly considered the *lingua franca* of the world's youth.

top 10 **EUROPEAN COUNTRIES** SPEAKING ENGLISH AS A FOREIGN LANGUAGE

	COUNTRY*	PERCENTAGE SPEAKING ENGLISH AS A FOREIGN LANGUAGE
1	Malta	84
2	Denmark	79
3	Sweden	76
4	Netherlands	75
5	Cyprus	67
6	Austria	55
7	Finland	50
8	=Luxembourg	46
	=Slovenia	46
10	Germany	44

* EU member states

While Maltese is the first language of most of Malta's inhabitants, English is a second official language spoken by the majority of the population. Malta was liberated by the British from occupation by Napoleon and was a British colony for 150 years from 1814, becoming an important naval base with long-standing links with the UK. Its role during World War II resulted in the entire island's uniquely receiving the George Cross, Britain's highest award for bravery.

top 10 LANGUAGES THAT WILL BE **SPOKEN BY THE YOUTH** OF 2050

	LANGUAGE	ESTIMATED NO. OF 15–24-YEAR-OLD SPEAKERS (1995)	(2050)
1	Chinese	201,600,000	166,000,000
2	Hindu/Urdu	59,800,000	73,700,000
3	Arabic	39,500,000	72,200,000
4	English	51,700,000	65,000,000
5	Spanish	58,000,000	62,800,000
6	Portuguese	32,200,000	32,500,000
7	Bengali	25,200,000	31,600,000
8	Russian	14,800,000	22,500,000
9	Japanese	11,300,000	18,200,000
10	Malay	9,500,000	10,500,000

Source: David Graddol, *The Future of English?*, British Council

By 2050, it is estimated that German and French, which ranked 10 and 11 in the 1995 Top 10, will be pushed further down the scale by the rise in young people speaking Malay.

top 10 MOST COMMONLY **MISSPELLED** WORDS IN ENGLISH

MISSPELLING	CORRECT SPELLING
1 suppose to	supposed to
2 caffiene	caffeine
3 recieve	receive
4 seperate	separate
5 adress	address
6 occured	occurred
7 definately	definitely
8 therefor	therefore
9 usefull	useful
10 transfered	transferred

Source: *Bloomsbury English Dictionary*, 2nd edition, 2004

top 10 MOST SPOKEN LANGUAGES

LANGUAGE	APPROXIMATE NO. OF SPEAKERS
1 Chinese (Mandarin)	1,120,000,000
2 English	480,000,000
3 Spanish	320,000,000
4 Russian	285,000,000
5 French	265,000,000
6 Hindustani*	250,000,000
7 Arabic#	221,000,000
8 Portuguese	188,000,000
9 Bengali	185,000,000
10 Japanese	133,000,000

* Hindi and Urdu are essentially the same language, Hindustani. As the official language of Pakistan it is written in modified Arabic script and called Urdu. As the official language of India it is written in the Devanagari script and called Hindi.

Includes 16 variants of the Arabic language

There are 11 further languages that are spoken by between 60 and 100 million people, including Korean, French, Chinese, Javanese, Chinese (Yue), Telugu, Marathi, Vietnamese, Tamil, Italian, and Turkish.

⊕ Sign of the times
Although understood only by some 25 million inhabitants of Thailand, the Thai script is almost redundant, such is the graphic and universal impact of a stop sign.

top 10 **ONLINE** LANGUAGES

LANGUAGE	INTERNET USERS*
1 English	286,642,757
2 Chinese	105,736,236
3 Japanese	66,763,838
4 Spanish	55,887,063
5 German	54,234,545
6 French	36,412,050
7 Korean	30,670,000
8 Italian	28,610,000
9 Portuguese	23,058,254
10 Dutch	13,657,170
World total	*814,931,592*

* Latest figures at 3 Dec 2004

Source: Nielsen//NetRatings/International Telecommunications Union/Internet World Stats

⊕ Multi-lingual
Mandarin and Arabic co-exist on a shop sign in the Chinese city of Urumqi, Xinjiang Province.

Education & Learning

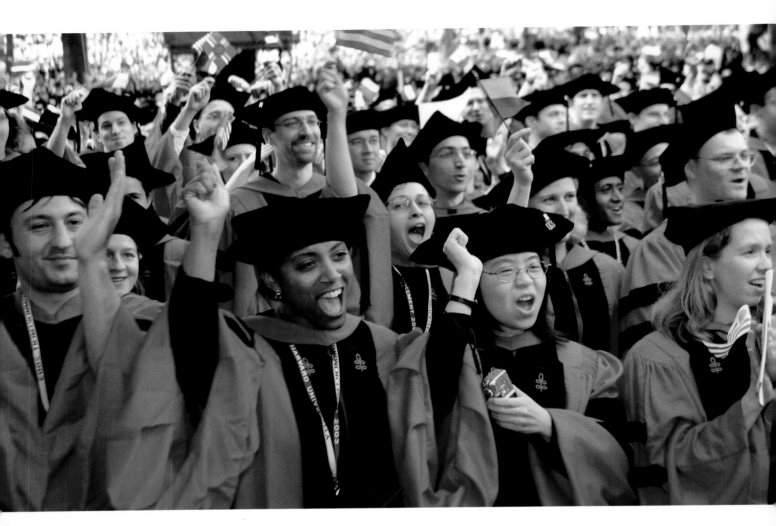

top 10 **UNIVERSITIES**

	UNIVERSITY / LOCATION	POINTS*
1	**Harvard University**, Massachusetts, USA	1,000
2	**University of California, Berkeley**, USA	880.2
3	**Massachusetts Institute of Technology**, USA	788.9
4	**California Institute of Technology**, USA	738.9
5	= **Cambridge University**, UK	731.8
	= **Oxford University**, UK	731.8
7	**Stanford University**, California, USA	688.0
8	**Yale University**, Connecticut, USA	582.8
9	**Princeton University**, New Jersey, USA	557.5
10	**ETH Zurich**, Switzerland	553.7

* Scaled by awarding the top university 1,000 points and ranking all others proportionately

Source: Times University Guides, *Times Higher Education Supplement* (*THES*)

⬆ Reason to cheer at Harvard
Graduates of Harvard – ranked as the world's leading university – celebrate the completion of their degree courses.

This Top 10 has been taken from a table of 50 universities ranked in accordance with the findings of a survey undertaken by the *THES*, in which 1,300 academics across 88 countries were asked which universities they thought were the best in their fields of expertise. Also taken into account in the ranking were data on cited research of faculty members; ratios of faculty/student numbers; and success in attracting foreign students and internationally renowned academics.

Harvard, which came out top of this survey, was founded in 1636 as the "New College", but was renamed three years later in honour of British-born clergyman John Harvard (1607–38), who endowed the college with half of his estate and his collection of 400 books. Five US Presidents attended Harvard, along with innumerable celebrities, from billionaire Bill Gates (who did not graduate) to actress Natalie Portman.

top 10 LARGEST LIBRARIES

LIBRARY / LOCATION	YEAR FOUNDED	NO. OF VOLUMES
1 **Russian State Library***, Moscow, Russia	1862	43,000,000
2 **National Library of Russia**, St. Petersburg, Russia	1795	32,064,000
3 **Library of Congress**, Washington DC, USA	1800	29,000,000
4 **National Library of China**, Beijing, China	1909	22,000,000
5 **Library of the Russian Academy of Sciences**, St. Petersburg, Russia	1714	20,000,000
6 **National Library of Canada**, Ottawa, Canada	1953	19,500,000
5 **Deutsche Bibliothek**#, Frankfurt, Germany	1990	19,133,986
6 **British Library**†, London, UK	1753	16,000,000
7 **Vernadsky National Scientific Library of Ukraine**, Kiev, Ukraine	1919	14,000,000
8 **Institute for Scientific Information on Social Sciences of the Russian Academy of Sciences**, Moscow, Russia	1969	13,500,000
9 **Harvard University Library**, Massachusetts, USA	1638	13,143,330
10 **Library for Natural Sciences of the Russian the Russian Academy of Sciences**, Moscow, Russia	1973	12,549,000

* Founded 1862 as Rumyantsev Library, formerly State V.I. Lenin Library

Formed in 1990 through the unification of the Deutsche Bibliothek, Frankfurt (founded 1947) and the Deutsche Bucherei, Leipzig

† Founded as part of the British Museum, 1753; became an independent body in 1973

top 10 OLDEST UNIVERSITIES IN THE UK

UNIVERSITY	YEAR FOUNDED
1 **Oxford**	1160
2 **Cambridge**	1209
3 **St. Andrews**	1411
4 **Glasgow**	1451
5 **Aberdeen**	1495
6 **Edinburgh**	1583
7 **Durham***	1832
8 **London**#	1836
9 **Manchester**	1851
10 **University of Wales**†	1893

* A short-lived Cromwellian establishment was set up in 1657

Constituent colleges founded earlier: University College 1826, King's College 1828

† Constituent colleges founded earlier: Lampeter 1822, Aberystwyth 1872, Cardiff 1883, Bangor 1884, Swansea 1920

top 10 COUNTRIES WITH THE FEWEST PRIMARY SCHOOL PUPILS PER TEACHER

COUNTRY	PUPIL / TEACHER RATIO IN PRIMARY SCHOOLS, 2001–02*
1 **San Marino**	5
2 **Libya**	8
3 = **Denmark**	10
= **Hungary**	10
= **Netherlands**	10
6 = **Iceland**	11
= **Italy**	11
= **Sweden**	11
9 = **Belgium**	12
= **Israel**	12
= **Luxembourg**	12
= **Qatar**	12
= **Saudi Arabia**	12
UK	*18*

* Or latest year for which data available

Source: UNESCO

top 10 COUNTRIES SPENDING THE MOST ON EDUCATION

COUNTRY	PUBLIC EXPENDITURE AS PERCENTAGE OF GNP*, 2001–02#
1 **Lesotho**	13.0
2 **Zimbabwe**	11.1
3 **Yemen**	10.6
4 **St. Vincent and the Grenadines**	8.9
5 **Cuba**	8.7
6 = **Palau**	8.6
= **Vanuatu**	8.6
8 **Malaysia**	8.5
9 **Denmark**	8.4
10 **Saudi Arabia**	8.3
UK	*4.7*

* GNP = Gross National Product

Or latest year available; in those countries for which data available

Source: UNESCO

If the Marshall Islands were a country, it would top this list, with the 2001–02 public expenditure on education at 16.4 per cent of this US territory's gross national income.

Books

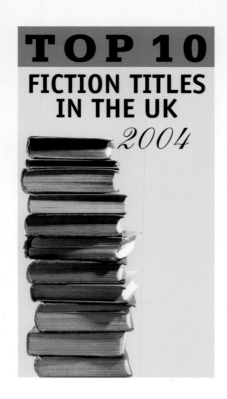

TOP 10 FICTION TITLES IN THE UK *2004*

TITLE	AUTHOR	SALES
1 The Da Vinci Code	Dan Brown	1,639,580
2 The Curious Incident of the Dog in the Night-time (adult edition)	Mark Haddon	990,972
3 The Lovely Bones	Alice Sebold	664,629
4 Angels and Demons	Dan Brown	611,603
5 The Star of the Sea	Joseph O'Connor	523,028
6 Brick Lane	Monica Ali	507,503
7 Digital Fortress	Dan Brown	502,495
8 The No. 1 Ladies' Detective Agency	Alexander McCall Smith	478,850
9 Deception Point	Dan Brown	458,705
10 PS, I Love You	Cecelia Ahern	389,798

Source: Nielsen BookScan

Dan Brown's *The Da Vinci Code* was the international hit of 2004 and carried on topping the UK chart in 2005, when its overall sales topped two million. Its huge popularity and the publicity attaching to its controversial subject enabled its predecessor, *Angels and Demons*, and two successors, *Digital Fortress* and *Deception Point*, to board the Brown bandwagon. The *Code*'s closest rival, Whitbread Prize-winner *The Curious Incident of the Dog in the Night-time*, benefited from appealing to both adults and children.

the 10 LATEST WINNERS OF THE WHITBREAD "BOOK OF THE YEAR" AWARD

	TITLE	AUTHOR
2004	Small Island	Andrea Levy
2003	The Curious Incident of the Dog in the Night-time	Mark Haddon
2002	Samuel Pepys: The Unequalled Self	Claire Tomalin
2001	The Amber Spyglass	Philip Pullman
2000	English Passengers	Matthew Kneale
1999	Beowulf	Seamus Heaney
1998	Birthday Letters	Ted Hughes
1997	Tales from Ovid	Ted Hughes
1996	The Spirit Level	Seamus Heaney
1995	Behind the Scenes at the Museum	Kate Atkinson

top 10 NON-FICTION TITLES IN THE UK, 2004

TITLE / AUTHOR	SALES
1 A Short History of Nearly Everything, Bill Bryson	790,419
2 You Are What You Eat: The Plan That Will Change Your Life, Gillian McKeith	743,664
3 Eats, Shoots & Leaves: The Zero Tolerance Approach to Punctuation, Lynne Truss	564,565
4 Himalaya, Michael Palin	517,925
5 Jamie's Dinners, Jamie Oliver	410,531
6 The Two of Us: My Life with John Thaw, Sheila Hancock	386,363
7 Guinness World Records 2005	361,287
8 Feel: Robbie Williams, Chris Heath	324,936
9 Being Jordan, Katie Price	315,522
10 The Bookseller of Kabul, Asne Seierstad	303,086

Source: Nielsen BookScan

top 10
BESTSELLING
BOOKS OF ALL TIME

	TITLE / AUTHOR / FIRST PUBLISHED	APPROXIMATE SALES*
1	**The Bible**, c.1451–55	more than 6,000,000,000
2	**Quotations from the Works of Mao Tse-tung**, 1966	900,000,000
3	**The Lord of the Rings**, J.R.R. Tolkien, 1954–55	over 100,000,000
4	**American Spelling Book**, Noah Webster, 1783	up to 100,000,000
5	**The Guinness Book of Records** (now Guinness World Records), 1955	more than 95,000,000#
6	**World Almanac**, 1868	more than 80,000,000#
7	**The McGuffey Readers**, William Holmes McGuffey, 1836	60,000,000
8	**The Common Sense Book of Baby and Child Care**, Benjamin Spock, 1946	more than 50,000,000
9	**A Message to Garcia**, Elbert Hubbard, 1899	more than 40,000,000
10 =	**In His Steps: "What Would Jesus Do?"**, Rev. Charles Monroe Sheldon, 1896	more than 30,000,000
=	**Valley of the Dolls**, Jacqueline Susann, 1966	more than 30,000,000

* Including translations

Aggregate sales of annual publication

The publication of multiple editions, translations, and pirated copies – and often exaggerated sales claims – make it notoriously problematic to establish precise sales of many recently published books. It is even more difficult with books published before sales figures were recorded. Globally, the Bible tops this list (the Koran may rival it, but sales estimates are speculative). Chairman Mao's "Little Red Book" could hardly fail to become a bestseller, since in the years 1966–71 it was compulsory for every Chinese adult to own a copy. The *American Spelling Book* and *The McGuffey Readers* were long-standing school textbooks, while *A Message to Garcia* was bought in bulk and distributed to employees in vast numbers. Many standard works, from *Roget's Thesaurus* and translations of books by Karl Marx to the *Complete Works of Shakespeare* and Conan Doyle's *Sherlock Holmes* stories have been sold in countless editions of unknown magnitude. There may be other single novels with a valid claim to a place in the Top 10, including Margaret Mitchell's *Gone With the Wind* (1936) and Harper Lee's *To Kill a Mockingbird* (1960), which may each have sold over 30 million copies. In the realm of non-fiction, Boy Scout founder Robert Baden-Powell's manual *Scouting for Boys* (1908) could be one of the 20th-century's bestselling books, since almost every boy in the world who became a Scout once owned a copy.

top 10 MOST VALUABLE
AMERICAN COMICS

COMIC	VALUE ($)*
1 **Action Comics No. 1** Published in June 1938, the first issue of *Action Comics* marked the original appearance of Superman.	440,000
2 **Detective Comics No. 27** Issued in May 1939, it is prized as the first comic book to feature Batman.	375,000
3 **Marvel Comics No. 1** The Human Torch and other heroes were first introduced in the issue dated October 1939.	330,000
4 **Superman No. 1** The first comic book devoted to Superman, reprinting the original *Action Comics* story, was published in summer 1939.	270,000
5 **All American Comics No. 16** The Green Lantern made his debut in the issue dated July 1940.	160,000
6= **Batman No. 1** Published in spring 1940, this was the first comic book devoted to Batman.	125,000
Captain America Comics No. 1 Published in March 1941, this was the original comic book in which Captain America appeared.	125,000
8 **Flash Comics No. 1** Dated January 1940, and featuring The Flash, it is rare because it was produced in small numbers for promotional purposes, and was unique as issue #2 was retitled *Whiz Comics*.	97,000
9= **More Fun Comics No. 52** The Spectre made his debut in the issue dated February 1940.	84,000
Whiz Comics No. 1 Published in February 1940 – and confusingly numbered "2" – it was the first comic book to feature Captain Marvel.	84,000

* For example in "Near Mint" condition

➔ **Caped crusader**
Following the success of Superman, artist Bob Kane created Batman, whose debut appearance is among the most prized comics of the "Golden Age".

↑ **All-American hero**
First published at the height of World War II, Captain America appealed to the anti-Nazi sentiments of the period.

THE ⚬~⚬ PRESS

Top 10 English-Language Daily Newspapers

Newspaper / Country	Average daily circulation, 2004
1 **The Sun**, UK	3,332,831
2 **USA Today**, USA	2,617,000
3 **The Daily Mail**, UK	2,412,261
4 **The Wall Street Journal**, USA	2,091,000
5 **The Mirror**, UK	1,828,938
6 **The New York Times**, USA	1,677,000
7 **Los Angeles Times**, USA	1,379,000
8 **The Times of India**, India	1,284,000
9 **The Washington Post**, USA	1,030,000
10 **Chicago Tribune**, USA	1,002,000

Source: World Association of Newspapers, *World Press Trends* 2004, www.wan-press.org/Audit Bureau of Circulations Ltd.

The world's bestselling English language dailies represent both long-established publications and relative newcomers: the *Daily Herald*, the first paper to ever sell two million copies, was launched in 1911, became *The Sun* in 1964, and was re-launched as a tabloid in 1969. *The Daily Mail* started in 1896, absorbing the *News Chronicle* in 1960 and *Daily Sketch* in 1971. *USA Today*, launched in 1982, was one of the first newspapers to use computers and to transmit editions for simultaneous publication around the world. *The Times of India* began in 1838 as *The Bombay Times and Journal of Commerce*, changing to its present name in 1861.

⊙ Press ahead
Despite the inexorable growth of other sources of news, from television to the Internet, daily newspapers have maintained their role as the medium of choice for a high proportion of the English-speaking public.

Top 10 Daily Newspapers

Newspaper / Country	Average daily circulation, 2004
1 **Yomiuri Shimbun**, Japan	14,081,000
2 **The Asahi Shimbun**, Japan	12,235,000
3 **Nihon Keizai Shimbun**, Japan	4,643,000
4 **Chunichi Shimbun**, Japan	4,542,000
5 **Bild**, Germany	3,989,000
6 **Mainichi Shimbun**, Japan	3,957,000
7 **The Sun**, UK	3,332,831
8 **Sankei Shimbun**, Japan	2,723,000
9 **Canako Xiaoxi (Beijing)**, China	2,670,000
10 **USA Today**, USA	2,617,000

Source: World Association of Newspapers, *World Press Trends 2004*, www.wan-press.org

Top 10 Daily Newspapers in the UK

Newspaper	Average daily circulation, 2004
1 **The Sun**	3,332,831
2 **The Daily Mail**	2,412,261
3 **The Mirror**	1,828,938
4 **Daily Express**	939,134
5 **The Daily Telegraph**	910,470
6 **Daily Star**	890,244
7 **The Times**	657,716
8 **Daily Record**	487,564
9 **Financial Times**	431,636
10 **The Guardian**	376,301

Source: Audit Bureau of Circulations Ltd.

Top 10 Newspaper-reading Countries

Country	Daily copies per 1,000 people, 2004
1 **Iceland**	705.9
2 **Norway**	684.0
3 **Japan**	646.9
4 **Sweden**	590.0
5 **Finland**	524.2
6 **Bulgaria**	472.7
7 **Macau**	448.9
8 **Denmark**	436.6
9 **Switzerland**	419.6
10 **UK**	393.4

Source: World Association of Newspapers, *World Press Trends 2004*, www.wan-press.org

In January 2002 *Yomiuri Shimbun*, Japan's and the world's bestselling daily newspaper, achieved a record sale average of 14,323,781 copies a day.

Founded in 1874, "Yomiuri" ("selling by reading"), refers to the Japanese practice of vendors reading aloud from newssheets in the era before moveable type.

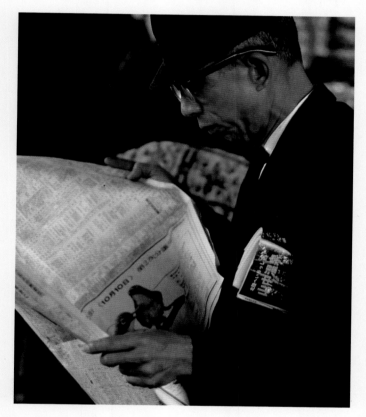

Top 10 Consumer Magazines in the UK

Magazine	Average UK circulation per issue*
1 **What's On TV**	1,587,251
2 **Take a Break**	1,211,016
3 **TV Choice**	1,102,989
4 **Radio Times**	1,088,098
5 **Reader's Digest**	725,998
6 **Chat**	623,567
7 **Now**	597,733
8 **That's Life**	597,016
9 **Saga Magazine**	594,286
10 **Glamour**	579,761

* Actively purchased circulation in six-month period to 31 Dec 2004

Source: Audit Bureau of Circulations Ltd.

↑ Avid readers
With a large, loyal, and highly literate readership among its population of 127 million, six of the world's Top 10 bestselling daily newspapers are Japanese.

Art

top 10 BEST-ATTENDED ART EXHIBITIONS, 2004

EXHIBITION / VENUE / CITY / DATES	TOTAL ATTENDANCE / DAILY ATTENDANCE*
1 **MoMA Museum of Modern Art**, Neue Nationalgalerie, Berlin, 20 Feb–19 Sept	**1,200,000** / 6,568
2 **Pre-Raphaelites in Florence**, Galleria degli Uffizi, Florence, 6 Apr–31 Aug	**693,847** / 5,507
3 **Art in the Age of Dante**, Gallerie dell'Accademia, Florence, 1 June–26 Sept	**512,498** / 4,343
4 **James Rosenquist: A Retrospective**, Guggenheim Museum, Bilbao, 13 May–17 Oct	**487,582** / 3,596
5 **Joan Miró 1917–34: the Birth of the World**, Centre Georges Pompidou, Paris, 3 Mar–28 June	**475,601** / 4,742
6 **Mark Rothko: Walls of Light**, Guggenheim Museum, Bilbao, 8 June–24 Oct	**451,275** / 3,783
7 **Henri Matisse: Process/Variation**, National Museum of Western Art, Tokyo, 10 Sept–12 Dec	**451,105** / 5,389
8 **Edward Hopper**, Tate Modern, London, 27 May–5 Sept	**429,909** / 4,215
9 **Fashion and Furniture in the 18th Century**, Metropolitan Museum of Art, New York, 29 Apr–6 Sept	**420,234** / 3,738
10 **Edouard Manet: Impressions of the Sea**, Van Gogh Museum, Amsterdam, 18 June–26 Sept	**400,000** / 3,960

* Approximate totals provided by museums; excludes exhibitions that began in 2003   Source: *The Art Newspaper*

top 10 MOST EXPENSIVE PAINTINGS

PAINTING / ARTIST / SALE / DATE	PRICE
1 **Garçon à la Pipe**, Pablo Picasso (Spanish; 1881–1973), Sotheby's, New York, 5 May 2004	£51,955,308 ($93,000,000)
2 **Massacre of the Innocents**, Sir Peter Paul Rubens (Flemish; 1577–1640), Sotheby's, London, 10 July 2002	£45,000,000
3 **Portrait du Dr. Gachet**, Vincent van Gogh (Dutch; 1853–90), Christie's, New York, 15 May 1990	£44,378,696 ($75,000,000)
4 **Au Moulin de la Galette**, Pierre-Auguste Renoir (French; 1841–1919), Sotheby's, New York, 17 May 1990	£42,011,832 ($71,000,000)
5 **Portrait de l'Artiste Sans Barbe**, Vincent van Gogh Christie's, New York, 19 Nov 1998	£39,393,940 ($65,000,000)
6 **Femme aux Bras Croises**, Pablo Picasso Christie's Rockefeller, New York, 8 Nov 2000	£34,965,036 ($50,000,000)
7 **Rideau, Cruchon et Compôtier**, Paul Cézanne (French; 1839–1906), Sotheby's, New York, 10 May 1999	£33,950,616 ($55,000,000)
8 **Les Noces de Pierrette**, **1905**, Pablo Picasso Binoche et Godeau, Paris, 30 Nov 1989	£33,123,028 (F.Fr315,000,000)
9 **Irises**, Vincent van Gogh Sotheby's, New York, 11 Nov 1987	£28,000,000 ($49,000,000)
10 **Femme Assise Dans un Jardin**, Pablo Picasso Sotheby's, New York, 10 Nov 1999	£27,950,310 ($45,000,000)

🅞 Doctor in the auction house

In the final months of his troubled life, Vincent van Gogh was cared for by Doctor Paul Gachet (1828–1909) and painted this distinctive portrait of him. It was sold at auction to Japanese collector Ryoei Saito for a record price in 1990 but – following Saito's death in 1996 – has mysteriously disappeared.

top 10 MOST STOLEN PAINTERS

ARTIST / NO. OF WORKS STOLEN

1 Pablo Picasso
551

2 Joan Miró
356

3 Marc Chagall
309

4 Salvador Dalí
231

5 Pierre-Auguste Renoir
209

6 Albrecht Dürer
203

7 Rembrandt van Rijn
174

159
8 Andy Warhol

9 David Teniers
127

10 Henri Matisse
108

Source: Art Loss Register

The Art Loss Register is the largest international database of stolen paintings, antiques, and collectables. It monitors thefts on behalf of private collectors, auction houses, museums, dealers, insurance companies, and the law enforcement agencies that aim to recover them.

top 10 BEST-ATTENDED ART EXHIBITIONS IN THE UK, 2004

EXHIBITION / VENUE	TOTAL ATTENDANCE*
1 Edward Hopper, Tate Modern	429,909
2 El Greco, National Gallery	219,000
3 BP Portrait Award 2004, National Portrait Gallery	182,009
4 Bosch and Brueghel, National Gallery	181,455
5 Vivienne Westwood, Victoria and Albert Museum	170,834
6 Women Travellers, National Portrait Gallery	162,457
7 Tamara de Lempicka: Art Deco Icon, Royal Academy of Arts	162,000
8 Vuillard, Royal Academy of Arts	159,900
9 The Silk Road: Trade, Travel, War and Faith, British Library	154,796
10 Dürer and The Virgin in the Garden, National Gallery	153,000

* Approximate totals provided by museums; excludes exhibitions that began in 2003

Source: *The Art Newspaper*

top 10 albums of all time: page 114

Chapter

5 6 7 8 9

top 10 singles of all time in the UK: page 110

top 10 singles of all time: page 112

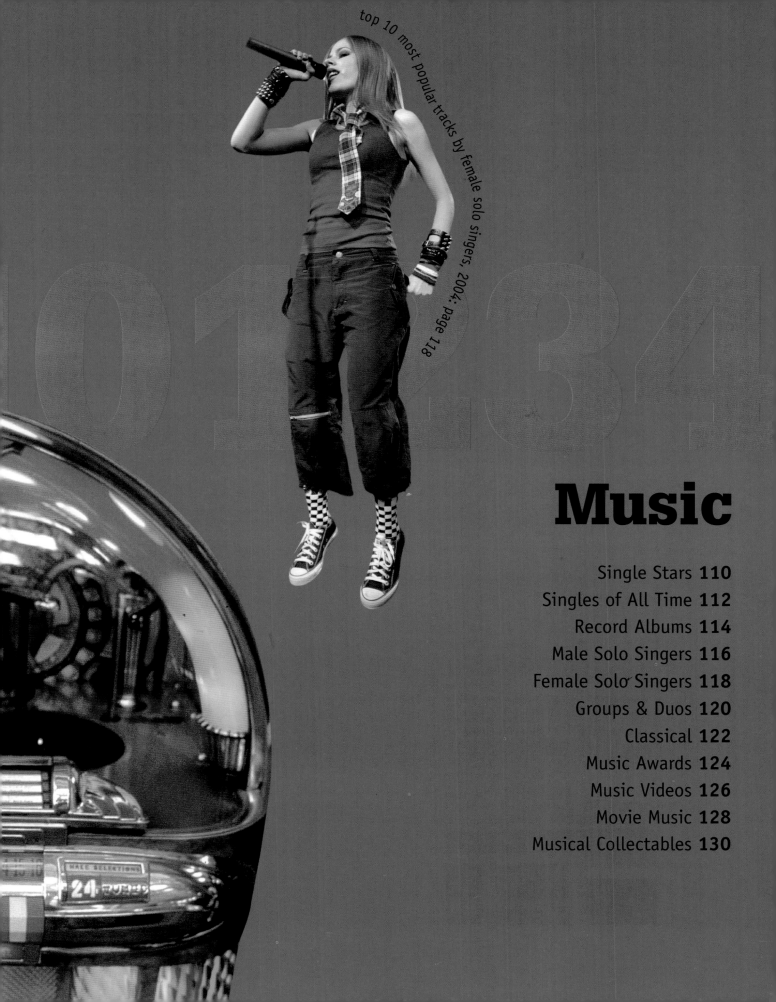

top 10 most popular tracks by female solo singers, 2004: page 118

Music

Single Stars

top 10 SINGLES OF **ALL TIME** IN THE UK

TITLE / ARTIST OR GROUP / YEAR OF ENTRY	EST. UK SALES
1 **Candle in the Wind (1997)/Something About the Way You Look Tonight**, Elton John, 1997	4,864,611
2 **Do They Know It's Christmas?**, Band Aid, 1984	3,550,000
3 **Bohemian Rhapsody**, Queen, 1975/91	2,130,000
4 **Mull of Kintyre/Girls' School**, Wings, 1977	2,050,000
5 **Rivers of Babylon/Brown Girl in the Ring**, Boney M, 1978	1,985,000
6 **You're the One that I Want**, John Travolta and Olivia Newton-John, 1978	1,975,000
7 **Relax**, Frankie Goes to Hollywood, 1984	1,910,000
8 **She Loves You**, The Beatles, 1963	1,890,000
9 **Unchained Melody**, Robson Green and Jerome Flynn, 1995	1,843,701
10 **Mary's Boy Child/Oh My Lord**, Boney M, 1978	1,790,000

Source: The Official UK Charts Company

Seventy-six singles have sold over 1 million copies apiece in the UK during the last 50 years, and these are the cream of that crop. The Band Aid single had a host of special circumstances surrounding it, and it took the remarkable response to the death of Diana, Princess of Wales, to generate sales capable of overtaking it. Two years – 1978 and 1984 – were the all-time strongest for million-selling singles, and this list fittingly has three representatives from each, though the only act to appear twice is Boney M, a group masterminded by German producer Frank Farian. They had a string of UK chart singles, but no others came close to the sales achieved by their two big 1978 hits. These figures were updated in 2002 at the time of the 50th anniversary of the introduction of the pop charts in November 1952.

the 10 FIRST **MILLION-SELLING** SINGLES IN THE UK

TITLE / ARTIST OR GROUP	YEAR
1 **Rock Around the Clock**, Bill Haley & His Comets	1955
2 **Mary's Boy Child**, Harry Belafonte	1957
3 **Diana**, Paul Anka	1957
4 **It's Now or Never**, Elvis Presley	1960
5 **Stranger on the Shore**, Mr. Acker Bilk	1961
6 **The Young Ones**, Cliff Richard	1962
7 **I Remember You**, Frank Ifield	1962
8 **She Loves You**, The Beatles	1963
9 **I Want to Hold Your Hand**, The Beatles	1963
10 **Can't Buy Me Love**, The Beatles	1964

Bill Haley had already achieved success in the USA with *Shake, Rattle and Roll*, but it was his influential *Rock Around the Clock*, featured in the 1955 film *Blackboard Jungle*, that established his status as the UK's first million-seller. The Beatles' appearance with the UK's 10th million-selling single was a foretaste of their all-time pre-eminence. They went on to amass five platinum singles during the 1960s, while John Lennon added one with *Imagine* and Paul McCartney another with *Wings' Mull of Kintyre/Girls' School*.

⬅ Elton John
With sales of almost five million in the UK, 11 million in the USA, and 37 million worldwide, Elton John's *Candle in the Wind (1997)* is the bestselling single ever.

top 10 SINGLES THAT **STAYED LONGEST AT NO. 1** IN THE UK

	TITLE / ARTIST OR GROUP / YEAR OF ENTRY	WEEKS AT NO. 1
1	**I Believe**, Frankie Laine, 1953	18
2	**(Everything I Do) I Do it For You**, Bryan Adams, 1991	16
3	**Love is all Around**, Wet Wet Wet, 1994	15
4	**Bohemian Rhapsody**, Queen, 1975/1991	14
5	**Rose Marie**, Slim Whitman, 1955	11
6	= **Cara Mia**, David Whitfield, 1954	10
	= **I Will Always Love You**, Whitney Houston, 1993	10
8	= **Diana**, Paul Anka, 1957	9
	= **Here in My Heart**, Al Martino, 1952	9
	= **Mull of Kintyre**, Wings, 1977	9
	= **Oh Mein Papa**, Eddie Calvert, 1954	9
	= **Secret Love**, Doris Day, 1954	9
	= **Two Tribes**, Frankie Goes to Hollywood, 1984	9
	= **You're the One that I Want**, John Travolta and Olivia Newton-John, 1978	9

Source: Music Information Database

The totals for *I Believe* and *Bohemian Rhapsody* are cumulative of more than one run at the top, in the former case because the single dropped to No. 2 for two weeks in what otherwise would have been a 20-week spell at No. 1, and in the latter case through a return to the top for a second lengthy run 16 years after its first. All other totals are for consecutive chart-topping weeks, which means Bryan Adams is the champion in terms of an unbroken No. 1 run.

⬆ Usher into the charts
In the 10 years since the release of his first album, Usher (Raymond) has achieved phenomenal success, with *Yeah* topping the USA, UK, and other charts around the world.

top 10 **DOWNLOADED SINGLES** IN THE UK, 2004

	TITLE	ARTIST OR GROUP
1	Vertigo	U2
2	What You Waiting For?	Gwen Stefani
3	Lose My Breath	Destiny's Child
4	American Idiot	Green Day
5	Do They Know It's Christmas?	Band Aid 20
6	These Words	Natasha Bedingfield
7	She Will Be Loved	Maroon 5
8	Just Lose It	Eminem
9	I Believe In You	Kylie Minogue
10	Car Wash	Christina Aguilera

Source: The Official UK Charts Company

top 10 **SINGLES** IN THE UK, 2004

	TITLE	ARTIST OR GROUP
1	Do They Know It's Christmas?	Band Aid 20
2	F**k It (I Don't Want You Back)	Eamon
3	Cha Cha Slide	DJ Casper
4	Call On Me	Eric Prydz
5	Yeah	Usher featuring Lil' Jon & Ludacris
6	All This Time	Michelle
7	Left Outside Alone	Anastacia
8	Mysterious Girl	Peter Andre
9	Toxic	Britney Spears
10	F.U.R.B. (F U Right Back)	Frankee

Source: The Official UK Charts Company

top 10 **SINGLES OF ALL TIME**

	TITLE / ARTIST OR GROUP	RELEASED	SALES EXCEED
1	**Candle in the Wind (1997)/Something About the Way You Look Tonight**, Elton John	1997	37,000,000
2	**White Christmas**, Bing Crosby	1942	30,000,000
3	**Rock Around the Clock**, Bill Haley and His Comets	1954	17,000,000
4	**I Want to Hold Your Hand**, The Beatles	1963	12,000,000
5	=**It's Now or Never**, Elvis Presley	1960	10,000,000
	=**Hey Jude**, The Beatles	1968	10,000,000
	=**I Will Always Love You**, Whitney Houston	1992	10,000,000
8	=**Diana**, Paul Anka	1957	9,000,000
	=**Hound Dog/Don't Be Cruel**, Elvis Presley	1956	9,000,000
10	=**(Everything I Do) I Do it for You**, Bryan Adams	1991	8,000,000
	=**I'm a Believer**, The Monkees	1966	8,000,000

➔ Christmas gift

Originally sung in *Holiday Inn* (1942), Bing Crosby (left, with Rosemary Clooney, Vera Ellen, and Danny Kaye) reprised his hit song *White Christmas* in the 1954 film of the same name.

Global sales are notoriously difficult to calculate, since for many decades, little statistical research on record sales was done in a large part of the world. "Worldwide" is thus usually taken to mean the known minimum "Western world" sales. It took 55 years for a record to overtake Bing Crosby's 1942 *White Christmas*, although the song (also recorded by others and sold as sheet music) has achieved such enormous total sales that it would still appear in first position in any list of bestselling songs.

⊕ **Beatlemania**
Worldwide, over six million copies of the Beatles' *Hey Jude* (1968) were sold within the year of its release.

Record Albums

top 10 ALBUMS **OF ALL TIME**

TITLE / ARTIST OR GROUP	YEAR OF ENTRY
1 **Thriller**, Michael Jackson	1982
2 **Dark Side of the Moon**, Pink Floyd	1973
3 **Their Greatest Hits 1971–1975**, The Eagles	1976
4 **The Bodyguard**, Soundtrack	1992
5 **Rumours**, Fleetwood Mac	1977
6 **Sgt. Pepper's Lonely Hearts Club Band**, The Beatles	1967
7 **Led Zeppelin IV**, Led Zeppelin	1971
8 **Greatest Hits**, Elton John	1974
9 **Come On Over**, Shania Twain	1997
10 **Jagged Little Pill**, Alanis Morissette	1995

Total worldwide sales of albums have traditionally been notoriously hard to gauge, but even with the huge expansion of the album market during the 1980s, and multiple million sales of many major releases, this Top 10 is still élite territory.

⬇ ➡ **Over the moon**
With world sales estimated at some 35 million, Pink Floyd's concept album *Dark Side of the Moon* has maintained its perennial appeal for over 30 years.

top 10 ALBUMS THAT **STAYED LONGEST AT NO. 1** IN THE UK

TITLE / ARTIST OR GROUP	WEEKS AT NO. 1
1 **South Pacific**, Soundtrack	115
2 **The Sound of Music**, Soundtrack	·70
3 **Bridge Over Troubled Water**, Simon & Garfunkel	41
4 **Please Please Me**, The Beatles	30*
5 **Sgt. Pepper's Lonely Hearts Club Band**, The Beatles	27
6 **G.I. Blues**, Elvis Presley/Soundtrack	22
7 = **With The Beatles**, The Beatles	21*
= **A Hard Day's Night**, The Beatles/Soundtrack	21*
9 = **Blue Hawaii**, Elvis Presley/Soundtrack	18
= **Saturday Night Fever**, Soundtrack	18*

* Continuous run

Source: Music Information Database

top 10 ALBUMS THAT STAYED LONGEST IN THE UK CHART

	TITLE / ARTIST OR GROUP	YEAR OF ENTRY	TOTAL WEEKS
1	**Rumours**, Fleetwood Mac	1977	477
2	**Bat Out of Hell**, Meat Loaf	1978	473
3	**Greatest Hits**, Queen	1981	439
4	=**The Sound of Music**, Soundtrack	1965	363
	=**Dark Side of the Moon**, Pink Floyd	1973	363
6	**Legend**, Bob Marley & the Wailers	1984	339
7	**Bridge Over Troubled Water**, Simon & Garfunkel	1970	307
8	**South Pacific**, Soundtrack	1958	288
9	**Greatest Hits**, Simon & Garfunkel	1972	283
10	**Tubular Bells**, Mike Oldfield	1973	276

Source: Music Information Database

The 10 longest-staying records virtually took up residence in the album charts (the Top 50, 75, or 100, depending on the years during which the charts were compiled), remaining there for periods ranging from over five years for *Tubular Bells* to the astonishing nine-year occupation of Meat Loaf's *Bat Out of Hell*.

⬆ **Strong rumours**
Fleetwood Mac's *Rumours* has sold over 26 million copies worldwide. Stevie Nicks (pictured here) wrote "Dreams", a track on the album and the group's only US No. 1 single.

top 10 ALBUMS IN THE UK

	TITLE / ARTIST OR GROUP	YEAR
1	**Sgt. Pepper's Lonely Hearts Club Band**, The Beatles	1967
2	**(What's the Story) Morning Glory?**, Oasis	1995
3	**Bad**, Michael Jackson	1987
4	**Brothers in Arms**, Dire Straits	1985
5	**Stars**, Simply Red	1991
6	**Abba Gold Greatest Hits**, Abba	1990
7	**Thriller**, Michael Jackson	1982
8	**Greatest Hits (Volume One)**, Queen	1981
9	**Spice**, The Spice Girls	1996
10	**Come On Over**, Shania Twain	1998

Source: Music Information Database

With UK sales alone of over 4.5 million copies, the Beatles' *Sgt. Pepper's Lonely Hearts Club Band* album was both a commercial success and a critical triumph, considered by many as the most influential rock album ever and hailed by *Rolling Stone* magazine as "the greatest album of all time".

top 10 ALBUMS IN THE UK, 2004

	TITLE	ARTIST OR GROUP
1	**Scissor Sisters**	Scissor Sisters
2	**Hopes and Fears**	Keane
3	**Greatest Hits**	Robbie Williams
4	**Songs About Jane**	Maroon 5
5	**Call Off the Search**	Katie Melua
6	**Anastacia**	Anastacia
7	**Confessions**	Usher
8	**Feels Like Home**	Norah Jones
9	**Final Straw**	Snow Patrol
10	**Il Divo**	Il Divo

Source: The Official UK Charts Company

Formed in 2001, Scissor Sisters' meteoric rise to fame was based largely on their success in the UK and Europe, rather than their native US, where they are less well-known. Their eponymous album became 2004's bestselling (beating Keane's *Hopes and Fears* by a margin of just 582 copies), and they went on to achieve a unique treble victory in the BRIT Awards with wins in the categories of "Best International Group", "International Breakthrough", and "International Album".

Male Solo Singers

top 10 ALBUMS BY MALE SOLO SINGERS, 2004

ALBUM / SINGER	EST. GLOBAL SALES, 2004
1 **Confessions**, Usher	11,867,000
2 **Encore**, Eminem	6,013,000
3 **Greatest Hits**, Robbie Williams	4,270,000
4 **Genius Loves Company**, Ray Charles	3,018,000
5 **Musicology**, Prince	2,781,000
6 **Suit**, Nelly	2,676,000
7 **Live Like You Were Dying**, Tim McGraw	2,616,000
8 **The College Dropout**, Kanye West	2,356,000
9 **Patience**, George Michael	2,120,000
10 **Stardust...The Great American Songbook, Vol. III**, Rod Stewart	2,027,000

Source: *United World Chart*, mediatraffic

Usher's *Confessions* topped the charts in the USA, UK, and Canada and reached No. 2 in Australia, achieving the greatest first week sale by any artist for three years and the most ever by an R&B artist.

top 10 SINGLES BY MALE SOLO SINGERS IN THE UK

TITLE / SINGER	YEAR
1 **Candle in the Wind (1997)/Something About the Way You Look Tonight**, Elton John	1997
2 **Anything is Possible/Evergreen**, Will Young	2002
3 **I Just Called to Say I Love You**, Stevie Wonder	1984
4 **(Everything I Do) I Do It For You**, Bryan Adams	1991
5 **Tears**, Ken Dodd	1965
6 **Imagine**, John Lennon	1975
7 **Careless Whisper**, George Michael	1984
8 **Release Me**, Engelbert Humperdinck	1967
9 **Unchained Melody**, Gareth Gates	2002
10 **Diana**, Paul Anka	1957

Source: The Official UK Charts Company

This list represents a timeshaft through the history of British popular music, with singles from each decade reflecting the sometimes unpredictable taste of the British public.

⊙ Robbie Williams
With the bestselling album by a non-US singer, Robbie Williams consolidated his international success in 2004 with the release of his *Greatest Hits*, which spans the previous seven years of his chart successes.

top 10 MALE SOLO SINGERS WITH THE **MOST NO. 1 SINGLES** IN THE UK

	SINGER	NO. 1 SINGLES
1	**Elvis Presley**	19
2	**Cliff Richard**	14
3	**Michael Jackson**	7
4	**Rod Stewart**	6
5	=**Eminem**	5
	=**Robbie Williams**	5
7	=**Frank Ifield**	4
	=**Frankie Laine**	4
	=**George Michael**	4
	=**Guy Mitchell**	4
	=**Will Young**	4

Source: Music Information Database

top 10 **MALE SOLO SINGERS** IN THE UK

	SINGER	TOTAL CHART HITS
1	**Elvis Presley**	137
2	**Cliff Richard**	121
3	**Elton John**	66
4	**David Bowie**	62
5	**Rod Stewart**	56
6	**Prince**	52
7	**Stevie Wonder**	47
8	**Michael Jackson**	46
9	=**Tom Jones**	37
	=**Frank Sinatra**	37

Source: Music Information Database

Elvis Presley's UK chart career has spanned nearly 50 years and includes several posthumous hits. His first records were all No. 1 hits in the USA, but he had 15 chart entries (including re-entries) before he achieved the first of his 18 UK No. 1s with *All Shook Up*, in 1957.

➲ The King rules
Elvis Presley's remarkable chart hit tally is unlikely ever to be overtaken.

top 10 **YOUNGEST** MALE SOLO SINGERS TO HAVE A **NO. 1 SINGLE** IN THE UK

	SINGER / TITLE	YEAR	AGE* (YRS	MTHS	DAYS)
1	**Little Jimmy Osmond**, Long Haired Lover from Liverpool	1972	9	8	7
2	**Donny Osmond**, Puppy Love	1972	14	6	30
3	**Paul Anka**, Diana	1957	16	1	1
4	**Gareth Gates**#, Unchained Melody	2002	17	8	18
5	**Gareth Gates**, Anyone of Us (Stupid Mistake)	2002	18	0	8
6	**Glenn Medeiros**, Nothing's Gonna Change My Love	1988	18	0	15
7	**Craig Douglas**, Only Sixteen	1959	18	0	27
8	**Gareth Gates**, Suspicious Minds	2002	18	2	23
9	**Cliff Richard**, Living Doll	1959	18	9	18
10	**Craig David**, Fill Me In	2000	18	11	0

* During first week of debut No. 1 UK single

Youngest British solo No. 1

Source: Music Information Database

Female Solo Singers

top 10 MOST POPULAR TRACKS BY FEMALE SOLO SINGERS, 2004

TRACK / SINGER	POINTS*, 2004
1 **Toxic**, Britney Spears	5,355,000
2 **Left Outside Alone**, Anastacia	4,631,000
3 **Everytime**, Britney Spears	4,118,000
4 **My Happy Ending**, Avril Lavigne	3,960,000
5 **Sick and Tired**, Avril Lavigne	3,805,000
6 **Leave (Get Out)**, JoJo	3,271,000
7 **Don't Tell Me**, Avril Lavigne	2,910,000
8 **Trick Me**, Kelis	2,894,000
9 **Superstar**, Jamelia	2,827,000
10 **Naughty Girl**, Beyoncé	2,768,000

* Points awarded according to global airplay, single-sales data, paid download, and vote

Source: *United World Chart*, mediatraffic

top 10 ALBUMS BY FEMALE SOLO SINGERS, 2004

ALBUM / SINGER	EST. GLOBAL SALES, 2004
1 **Feels Like Home**, Norah Jones	9,020,000
2 **Under My Skin**, Avril Lavigne	6,390,000
3 **Anastacia**, Anastacia	4,442,000
4 **Life for Rent**, Dido	3,528,000
5 **Greatest Hits**, Shania Twain	3,520,000
6 **The Diary of Alicia Keys**, Alicia Keys	3,362,000
7 **Greatest Hits: My Prerogative**, Britney Spears	2,994,000
8 **In the Zone**, Britney Spears	2,754,000
9 **Come Away with Me**, Norah Jones	2,623,000
10 **Single Collection Vol. 1**, Hikaru Utadu	2,313,000

Source: *United World Chart*, mediatraffic

top 10 FEMALE SOLO SINGERS IN THE UK

SINGER / TOTAL CHART HITS

1 Madonna 60　**2** Diana Ross 58　**3** Donna Summer 40　**4** Kylie Minogue 35　**5=** Janet Jackson 32

5= Tina Turner 32　**7** Cher 29　**8** Shirley Bassey 27　**9** Gloria Estefan 26　**10** Whitney Houston 25

Source: Music Information Database

Girl power
In 2004 Canadian singer Avril Lavigne, whose *Under My Skin* hit No. 1 in the USA, Canada, UK, and Australia, vied with US pop singer Anastacia (Newkirk). Her album *Anastacia* attained substantial sales despite not being released in her homeland.

top 10 SINGLES BY FEMALE SOLO SINGERS IN THE UK

TITLE / SINGER	YEAR
1 Believe, Cher	1998
2 Baby One More Time, Britney Spears	1999
3 I Will Always Love You, Whitney Houston	1992
4 My Heart Will Go On, Celine Dion	1998
5 The Power of Love, Jennifer Rush	1985
6 Think Twice, Celine Dion	1994
7 Saturday Night, Whigfield	1994
8 Can't Get You Out of My Head, Kylie Minogue	2001
9 Don't Cry For Me Argentina, Julie Covington	1976

Source: Music Information Database

Perhaps the most significant aspect of this list is how comparatively recent most of its entries are. Only one of these singles was released before 1980. Statistically, therefore, a female artist has stood a better chance of major chart success since the 1980s than in any of pop music's earlier eras.

top 10 YOUNGEST FEMALE SOLO SINGERS TO HAVE A NO. 1 SINGLE IN THE UK

SINGER / TITLE / YEAR	AGE (YRS MTHS DAYS)		
1 Helen Shapiro, You Don't Know, 1961	14	10	13
2 Billie, Because We Want To, 1998	15	9	20
3 Billie, Girlfriend, 1998	16	0	25
4 Tiffany, I Think We're Alone Now, 1988	16	3	28
5 Nicole, A Little Peace, 1982	17	0	0
6 Britney Spears, ...Baby One More Time, 1999	17	2	25
7 Sandie Shaw, (There's) Always Something There to Remind Me, 1964	17	7	26
8 LeAnn Rimes, Can't Fight the Moonlight, 2000	18	2	29
9 Mary Hopkin, Those Were the Days, 1968	18	4	22
10 Sonia, You'll Never Stop Me Loving You, 1989	18	5	9

Source: Music Information Database

The ages shown are those of each artist on the publication date of the chart in which she achieved her first No. 1 single. All ten of these girls were still in their teens when they had their first taste of chart-topping glory.

Groups & Duos

⬆ **Worldbeater** Maroon 5's first album and global smash *Songs About Jane* topped the charts in the USA, UK, and Australia.

top 10 **ALBUMS** BY GROUPS AND DUOS, 2004

ALBUM / GROUP OR DUO	EST. GLOBAL SALES, 2004
1 Songs About Jane, Maroon 5	5,795,000
2 Fallen, Evanescence	5,531,000
3 Elephunk, Black Eyed Peas	5,294,000
4 How to Dismantle an Atomic Bomb, U2	5,289,000
5 Greatest Hits, Guns N' Roses	4,661,000
6 American Idiot, Green Day	3,638,000
7 D12 World, D12	3,533,000
8 Destiny Fulfilled, Destiny's Child	3,299,000
9 Speakerboxxx/The Love Below, Outkast*	3,061,000
10 Hopes and Fears, Keane	2,850,000

* Two discs: *Speakerboxxx* features Big Boi, *The Love Below* features Andre 3000

Source: *United World Chart*, mediatraffic

top 10 **MOST POPULAR** TRACKS BY GROUPS AND DUOS, 2004

TRACK / GROUP OR DUO	POINTS*, 2004
1 This Love, Maroon 5	7,791,000
2 Hey Ya!, Outkast	6,167,000
3 The Reason, Hoobastank	6,044,000
4 It's My Life, No Doubt	4,827,000
5 Shut Up, Black Eyed Peas	4,642,000
6 She Will Be Loved, Maroon 5	4,503,000
7 My Immortal, Evanescence	4,635,000
8 Lose My Breath, Destiny's Child	3,970,000
9 Dragostea Din Tei, O-Zone	3,795,000
10 Let's Get It Started, Black Eyed Peas	3,282,000

* Points awarded according to global airplay, single-sales data, paid download, and vote

Source: *United World Chart*, mediatraffic

top 10 **GROUPS** IN THE UK

	GROUP	TOTAL CHART HITS
1	Status Quo	58
2	The Rolling Stones	51
3	Queen	46
4	UB40	42
5	Depeche Mode	40
6	The Bee Gees	37
7	The Stranglers	36
8	=Hot Chocolate	35
	=Iron Maiden	35
	=Slade	35

Source: Music Information Database

With hits spanning every decade since the 1960s, both Status Quo and the Rolling Stones have clocked up a back catalogue of chart successes that is unlikely ever to be replicated. The Stones have scored eight No. 1s compared with the Quo's single chart-topper.

top 10 **DUOS** IN THE UK

	DUO	TOTAL CHART HITS
1	Pet Shop Boys	36
2	Erasure	31
3	Everly Brothers	30
4	T.Rex	28
5	Eurythmics	27
6	Roxette	25
7	=Everything But the Girl	22
	=Carpenters	22
9	Tears For Fears	20
10	=Daryl Hall & John Oates	16
	=Orbital	16

Source: Music Information Database

Pet Shop Boys started their chart career hesitantly: *West End Girls* was released in 1984 without charting, and it was not until a re-recorded version appeared over a year later that they began their glittering career, with four UK No. 1s.

⬆ **Fallen rise** Amy Lee fronts Evanescence, whose album *Fallen* provided tracks for the film *Daredevil*.

top 10 **SINGLES BY GROUPS** IN THE UK

	TITLE / GROUP	YEAR
1	**Bohemian Rhapsody**, Queen	1975
2	**Mull of Kintyre/Girls' School**, Wings	1977
3	**Rivers of Babylon/Brown Girl in the Ring**, Boney M	1978
4	**Relax**, Frankie Goes To Hollywood	1984
5	**She Loves You**, The Beatles	1963
6	**Mary's Boy Child/Oh My Lord**, Boney M	1978
7	**Love is All Around**, Wet Wet Wet	1994
8	**I Want to Hold Your Hand**, The Beatles	1963
9	**Barbie Girl**, Aqua	1997
10	**Can't Buy Me Love**, The Beatles	1964

Source: The Official UK Charts Company

Not only was Queen's *Bohemian Rhapsody* the biggest-selling single by a group in the UK, but more than one poll has ranked it at the top 10 of a list of "100 Greatest Singles" of all time. Its total sales in the UK alone are over 2.13 million.

Classical

the 10 LATEST WINNERS OF THE "BEST CLASSICAL ALBUM" GRAMMY AWARD

YEAR	COMPOSER / TITLE / CONDUCTOR / SOLOIST(S) / ORCHESTRA
2004	**John Adams**, *On the Transmigration of Souls* Lorin Maazel, Brooklyn Youth Chorus and New Choral Artists, New York Philharmonic
2003	**Gustav Mahler**, *Symphony No. 3; Kindertotenlieder* Michael Tilson Thomas, Michelle DeYoung, San Francisco Symphony Orchestra
2002	**Vaughan Williams**, *A Sea Symphony (Symphony No. 1)* Robert Spano, Norman Mackenzie, Brett Polegato, Christine Goerke, Atlanta Symphony Orchestra
2001	**Hector Belioz**, *Les Troyens* Sir Colin Davis, Ben Heppner, Kenneth Tarver, Michelle De Young, Peter Mattei, Petra Lang, Sara Mingardo, Stephen Milling, London Symphony Orchestra
2000	**Dmitri Shostakovich**, *The String Quartets* Emerson String Quartet
1999	**Igor Stravinsky**, *Firebird; The Rite of Spring; Perséphone* Michael Tilson Thomas, Stuart Neill, San Francisco Symphony Orchestra
1998	**Samuel Barber**, *Prayers of Kierkegaard* / **Vaughan Williams**, *Dona Nobis Pacem* / **Béla Bartók**, *Cantata Profana* Robert Shaw, Richard Clement, Nathan Gunn, Carmen Pelton, Atlanta Symphony Orchestra and chorus
1997	**Richard Danielpour, Leon Kirchner, Christopher Rouse**, *Premieres – Cello Concertos* Yo-Yo Ma, David Zinman, Philadelphia Orchestra
1996	**John Corigliano**, *Of Rage and Remembrance* Leonard Slatkin, National Symphony Orchestra
1995	**Claude Debussy**, *La Mer* Pierre Boulez, Cleveland Orchestra

Source: NARAS

top 10 CLASSICAL ALBUMS IN THE UK

	TITLE / PERFORMER(S) OR ORCHESTRA	YEAR
1	**The Three Tenors In Concert** José Carreras, Placido Domingo, Luciano Pavarotti	1990
2	**The Essential Pavarotti** Luciano Pavarotti	1990
3	**Vivaldi: The Four Seasons** Nigel Kennedy/English Chamber Orchestra	1989
4	**The Three Tenors In Concert 1994** José Carreras, Placido Domingo, Luciano Pavarotti, Zubin Mehta	1994
5	**The Voice** Russell Watson	2000
6	**Voice of an Angel** Charlotte Church	1998
7	**Pure** Hayley Westenra	2003
8	**Encore** Russell Watson	2002
9	**The Essential Pavarotti, 2** Luciano Pavarotti	1991
10	**The Pavarotti Collection** Luciano Pavarotti	1986

Source: Music Information Database

the 10 LATEST WINNERS OF THE "BEST OPERA RECORDING" GRAMMY AWARD

YEAR	COMPOSER / TITLE / PRINCIPAL SOLOIST(S) / ORCHESTRA
2004	**Wolfgang Amadeus Mozart**, *Le Nozze di Figaro* Patrizia Ciofi, Véronique Gens, Simon Keenlyside, Angelika Kirchschlager, and Lorenzo Regazzo, Concerto Köln
2003	**Leos Janácek**, *Jenufa* Jerry Hadley, Karita Mattila, Eva Randová, Anja Silja, Jorma Silvasti, Orchestra of the Royal Opera House, Covent Garden
2002	**Richard Wagner**, *Tannhäuser* Jane Eaglen, Peter Seiffert, Rene Pape, Thomas Hampson, Waltraud Meier, Staatskapelle Berlin
2001	**Hector Berlioz**, *Les Troyens* Sir Colin Davis, Michelle De Young, Ben Heppner, Petra Lang, Peter Mattei, Stephen Milling, Sara Mingardo, Kenneth Tarver, London Symphony Orchestra
2000	**Ferruccio Busoni**, *Doktor Faust* Kent Nagano, Kim Begley, Dietrich Fischer-Dieskau, Dietrich Henschel, Markus Hollop, Torsten Kerl, Eva Jenis, Orchestre de l'Opera Nationale de Lyon
1999	**Igor Stravinsky**, *The Rake's Progress* Ian Bostridge, Bryn Terfel, Anne Sofie von Otter, Deborah York, Monteverdi Choir, London Symphony Orchestra
1998	**Béla Bartók**, *Bluebeard's Castle* Jessye Norman, Laszlo Polgar, Karl-August Naegler, Chicago Symphony Orchestra
1997	**Richard Wagner**, *Die Meistersinger Von Nürnberg* Ben Heppner, Herbert Lippert Karita Mattila, Alan Opie, Rene Pape, Jose van Dam, Iris Vermillion, Chicago Symphony Chorus, Chicago Symphony Orchestra
1996	**Benjamin Britten**, *Peter Grimes* Philip Langridge, Alan Opie, Janice Watson, Opera London, London Symphony Chorus, City of London Sinfonia
1995	**Hector Berlioz**, *Les Troyens* Charles Dutoit, Orchestra Symphonie de Montreal

Source: NARAS

⏴ **Triple triumph**
Selling in numbers comparable to those of rock stars, the recording of the Rome concert by the "Three Tenors" José Carreras, Placido Domingo, and Luciano Pavarotti that opened the 1990 World Cup became the bestselling classical album ever worldwide.

top 10 LARGEST OPERA THEATRES

	THEATRE	LOCATION	CAPACITY*
1	**Arena di Verona**[#]	Verona, Italy	15,000
2	**Municipal Opera Theatre**[#]	St. Louis, USA	10,000
3	**Metropolitan Opera House**	New York, USA	3,800
4	**NHK Hall**	Tokyo, Japan	3,677
5	**Civic Opera House**	Chicago, USA	3,563
6	**Music Hall**	Cincinnati, USA	3,516
7	**The Hummingbird Centre**	Toronto, Canada	3,223
8	**War Memorial Opera House**	San Francisco, USA	3,146
9	**Dorothy Chandler Pavilion**	Los Angeles, USA	3,086
10	**Halle aux Grains**	Toulouse, France	3,000

* Seating capacity only given, although capacity is often larger when standing capacity is included

[#] Open-air venue

Although there are many more venues in the world where opera is regularly performed, the above list is limited to those where the principal performances are opera.

top 10 OPERAS MOST FREQUENTLY PERFORMED AT THE ROYAL OPERA HOUSE, COVENT GARDEN, 1833–2005

	OPERA / COMPOSER	FIRST PERFORMANCE	TOTAL*
1	**La Bohème**, Giacomo Puccini	2 Oct 1897	545
2	**Carmen**, Georges Bizet	27 May 1882	495
3	**Aïda**, Giuseppi Verdi	22 June 1876	481
4	**Rigoletto**, Giuseppi Verdi	14 May 1853	465
5	**Faust**, Charles Gounod	18 July 1863	442
6	**Tosca**, Giacomo Puccini	12 July 1900	415
7	**Don Giovanni**, Wolfgang Amadeus Mozart	17 Apr 1834	414
8	**La Traviata**, Giuseppi Verdi	25 May 1858	391
9	**Madama Butterfly**, Giacomo Puccini	10 July 1905	366
10	**Norma**, Vincenzo Bellini	12 July 1833	355

* To 1 Jan 2005

Most of the works listed were first performed at Covent Garden within a few years of their world premieres (in the case of *Tosca*, in the same year). Although some were considered controversial at the time, all of them are now regarded as important components of the classic opera repertoire.

Music Awards

the 10 LATEST WINNERS OF THE BRIT AWARD FOR **BEST BRITISH ALBUM***

YEAR	ALBUM	ARTIST OR GROUP
2005	Hopes and Fears	Keane
2004	Permission to Land	The Darkness
2003	A Rush of Blood to the Head	Coldplay
2002	No Angel	Dido
2001	Parachutes	Coldplay
2000	The Man Who	Travis
1999	This is My Truth, Tell Me Yours	Oasis
1998	Urban Hymns	The Verve
1997	Everything Must Go	Manic Street Preachers
1996	(What's The Story) Morning Glory?	Oasis

* Previously "Best Album"

the 10 LATEST GRAMMY **ALBUMS OF THE YEAR**

YEAR	ALBUM	ARTIST(S) OR GROUP
2004	Genius Loves Company	Ray Charles and various artists
2003	Speakerboxxx/The Love Below	OutKast
2002	Come Away with Me	Norah Jones
2001	O Brother, Where Art Thou? (Soundtrack)	Various artists
2000	Two Against Nature	Steely Dan
1999	Supernatural	Santana
1998	The Miseducation of Lauryn Hill	Lauryn Hill
1997	Time Out of Mind	Bob Dylan
1996	Falling into You	Celine Dion
1995	Jagged Little Pill	Alanis Morisette

the 10 LATEST WINNERS OF THE BRIT AWARD FOR **BEST BRITISH FEMALE SOLO ARTIST**

YEAR	ARTIST
2005	Joss Stone
2004	Dido
2003	Ms. Dynamite
2002	Dido
2001	Sonique
2000	Beth Orton
1999	Des'ree
1998	Shola Ama
1997	Gabrielle
1996	Annie Lennox

Young British soul sensation Joss Stone (born 1987), whose first album *The Soul Sessions* had appeared in 2003, won a BRIT award not only in this category, but also for "Best British Urban Act". She was additionally nominated for "Best British Breakthrough Act" as well as for three Grammy awards.

the 10 LATEST WINNERS OF THE BRIT AWARD FOR **BEST BRITISH MALE SOLO ARTIST**

YEAR	ARTIST
2005	The Streets
2004	Daniel Bedingfield
2003	Robbie Williams
2002	Robbie Williams
2001	Robbie Williams
2000	Tom Jones
1999	Robbie Williams
1998	Finlay Quaye
1997	George Michael
1996	Paul Weller

Cliff Richard was the first ever winner in this category. Robbie Williams's three consecutive wins and a total of four wins are both records: Phil Collins is the only other male solo artist to receive the award on three occasions.

the 10 LATEST WINNERS OF THE BRIT AWARD FOR **BEST BRITISH GROUP**

YEAR	GROUP
2005	Franz Ferdinand
2004	The Darkness
2003	Coldplay
2002	Travis
2001	Coldplay
2000	Travis
1999	Manic Street Preachers
1998	The Verve
1997	Manic Street Preachers
1996	Oasis

Even though the group had split up in 1970, the Beatles were the first winners in this category in 1977. Subsequent winners have ranged from such acts as Dire Straits to Five Star in 1987, whose dramatic fall from fame compelled them to sell their award trophy.

the 10 LATEST GRAMMY
RECORDS OF THE YEAR

YEAR	RECORD / ARTIST(S) OR GROUP
2004	**Here We Go Again** Ray Charles and Norah Jones
2003	**Clocks** Coldplay
2002	**Don't Know Why** Norah Jones
2001	**Walk On** U2
2000	**Beautiful Day** U2
1999	**Smooth** Santana featuring Rob Thomas
1998	**My Heart Will Go On** Celine Dion
1997	**Sunny Came Home** Shawn Colvin
1996	**Change the World** Eric Clapton
1995	**Kiss From a Rose** Seal

◉ ⬆ Winning team
Norah Jones accepts the award in the category "Best Pop Collaboration with Vocals" at the 47th Grammy Awards ceremony. Her duo with Ray Charles (who died in 2004) also won "Record of the Year".

The Grammys are awarded retrospectively. Thus the 47th awards were presented in 2005 in recognition of musical accomplishment during 2004.

Music Videos

the 10 LATEST RECIPIENTS OF THE MTV VMA "BEST VIDEO OF THE YEAR" AWARD

YEAR	ARTIST OR GROUP	TITLE
2004	OutKast	Hey Ya
2003	Missy "Misdemeanor" Elliott	Work It
2002	Eminem	Without Me
2001	Christina Aguilera, Lil' Kim, Mya, Pink (featuring Missy "Misdeameanor" Elliott)	Lady Marmalade
2000	Eminem	The Real Slim Shady
1999	Lauryn Hill	Doo Wop (That Thing)
1998	Madonna	Ray of Light
1997	Jamiroquai	Virtual Insanity
1996	The Smashing Pumpkins	Tonight, Tonight
1995	TLC	Waterfalls

⬇ Missy's hit

Prior to her award-winning *Work It*, US rap superstar Missy "Misdemeanor" Elliott (Melissa Arnette Elliott) scored a UK No. 1 in 1998 with her Mel B collaboration *I Want You Back*.

the 10 LATEST RECIPIENTS OF THE MTV VMA "BEST FEMALE VIDEO" AWARD

YEAR	ARTIST	TITLE
2004	Beyoncé	Naughty Girl
2003	Beyoncé (featuring Jay-Z)	Crazy in Love
2002	Pink	Get the Party Started
2001	Eve (featuring Gwen Stefani)	Let Me Blow Ya Mind
2000	Aaliyah	Try Again
1999	Lauryn Hill	Doo Wop (That Thing)
1998	Madonna	Ray of Light
1997	Jewel	You Were Meant for Me
1996	Alanis Morissette	Ironic
1995	Madonna	Take a Bow

MTV was launched in the USA on 1 August 1981. The inaugural MTV Video Music Awards (VMA) took place on 14 September 1984 at Radio City Music Hall, New York. At the debut ceremony, Cyndi Lauper was the winner for *Girls Just Want to Have Fun*. Subsequent female winners have included such megastars as Tina Turner, Whitney Houston, and Annie Lennox. To date, and in addition to numerous other MTV awards, Madonna has received the most nominations in this category, a total of 11 from 1985 to 2001, and is the only triple winner (1987, 1995, and 1998).

the 10 LATEST RECIPIENTS OF THE MTV VMA "BEST GROUP VIDEO" AWARD

YEAR	GROUP	TITLE
2004	No Doubt	It's My Life
2003	Coldplay	The Scientist
2002	No Doubt (featuring Bounty Killer)	Hey Baby
2001	*NSYNC	POP
2000	Blink 182	All the Small Things
1999	TLC	No Scrubs
1998	Backstreet Boys	Everybody (Backstreet's Back)
1997	No Doubt	Don't Speak
1996	Foo Fighters	Big Me
1995	TLC	Waterfalls

No Doubt and TLC, both represented in the Top 10 with double wins, are the only groups to have won twice in this award's 20-year history. It has principally honoured US groups, but British bands Dire Straits (1986) and Coldplay (2003), Ireland's U2 (1992), and Australia's INXS (1988) have also won awards in this category.

top 10 BESTSELLING MUSIC DVDS IN THE UK, 2004

TITLE	ARTIST OR GROUP
1 Live Aid	Various
2 On Fire – Live at the Bowl	Queen
3 Definitely Maybe	Oasis
4 Dream Cast – Les Misérables in Concert	Cast recording
5 What We Did Last Summer	Robbie Williams
6 Castles in the Air	Cliff Richard
7 Welcome to the Videos	Guns N' Roses
8 Live at Wembley Stadium	Queen
9 '68 Comeback Special	Elvis Presley
10 Aloha From Hawaii	Elvis Presley

Source: The Official UK Charts Company

Although certain acts declined to be included and it was not released until November 2004, the DVD of the 1985 Live Aid concert achieved remarkable sales, the Government waiving the VAT to enable it to maximize its revenue for the charity.

the 10 LATEST RECIPIENTS OF THE MTV VMA "BEST MALE VIDEO" AWARD

YEAR	ARTIST OR GROUP	TITLE
2004	Usher (featuring Lil Jon and Ludacris)	Yeah
2003	Justin Timberlake	Cry Me a River
2002	Eminem	Without Me
2001	Moby (featuring Gwen Stefani)	South Side
2000	Eminem	The Real Slim Shady
1999	Will Smith	Miami
1998	Will Smith	Just the Two of Us
1997	Beck	The Devil's Haircut
1996	Beck	Where It's At
1995	Tom Petty and the Heartbreakers	You Don't Know How it Feels

the 10 LATEST RECIPIENTS OF THE MTV VMA "BEST BREAKTHROUGH VIDEO" AWARD

YEAR	ARTIST OR GROUP / TITLE
2004	Franz Ferdinand, Take Me Out
2003	Coldplay, The Scientist
2002	The White Stripes, Fell in Love with a Girl
2001	Fatboy Slim, Weapon of Choice
2000	Björk, All is Full of Love
1999	Fatboy Slim, Praise You
1998	Prodigy, Smack My Bitch Up
1997	Jamiroquai, Virtual Insanity
1996	Smashing Pumpkins, Tonight, Tonight
1995	Weezer, Buddy Holly

⊃ Rap beat
As well as his two MTV "Best Male Video" awards, Eminem has won seven other MTV Video Music Awards and six MTV Europe awards.

Movie Music

top 10 MUSICAL FILMS

FILM	YEAR
1 Grease	1978
2 Chicago	2002
3 Saturday Night Fever	1977
4 8 Mile	2002
5 Moulin Rouge!	2001
6 The Sound of Music	1965
7 Evita	1996
8 The Rocky Horror Picture Show	1975
9 Staying Alive	1983
10 Mary Poppins	1964

Traditional musicals (films in which the cast actually sing) and films in which a musical soundtrack is a key component are included here. After suffering a decline in the 1990s, the success of *Chicago* shows that the blockbuster musical retains its appeal almost 80 years after the genre was created.

➡ **Sweet success**
With global earnings of over $180 million, *Sweet Home Alabama* is one of the top films named after a song.

top 10 MUSICAL BIOGRAPHIES

FILM	SUBJECT	YEAR
1 The Sound of Music	The von Trapp family	1965
2 Shine	David Hefgott	1996
3 Coal Miner's Daughter	Loretta Lynn	1980
4 Ray	Ray Charles	2004
5 La Bamba	Ritchie Valens	1987
6 Amadeus	Wolfgang Amadeus Mozart	1984
7 What's Love Got to Do With It?	Tina Turner	1993
8 Selena	Selena Pérez	1997
9 The Doors	The Doors	1991
10 Lady Sings the Blues	Billie Holiday	1972

Biopics on the often troubled lives of famous composers and musicians in both classical and popular genres have long inspired Hollywood. Despite having been released over 40 years ago, blockbuster *The Sound of Music* tops the list, having earned almost twice as much as the second-ranked film, while the recent release of *Ray* indicates the enduring popularity of such subjects. Outside the Top 10 musical biographies have encompassed artists from rock star Buddy Holly (*The Buddy Holly Story*, 1978) to cellist Jacqueline du Pré (*Hilary and Jackie*, 1998) and composer Cole Porter (*De-Lovely*, 2004).

top 10 FILMS WITH TITLES DERIVED FROM SONG TITLES

FILM	SONG*	FILM
1 American Pie	1972	1999
2 Sweet Home Alabama	1976	2002
3 Bad Boys	1983	1995
4 Sea of Love	1959	1989
5 One Fine Day	1963	1996
6 My Girl	1965	1991
7 Something to Talk About	1991	1995
8 When a Man Loves a Woman	1966	1994
9 The Crying Game	1964	1992
10 Addicted to Love	1986	1997

* Release of first hit version

Remarkably, the history of films with titles derived from those of songs dates back more than 100 years, beginning with *How Would You Like to Be the Ice Man?*, a popular song before being appropriated for a film released on 21 April 1899! *White Christmas*, one of the most successful songs of all time, appeared in the film *Holiday Inn* (1942) before in turn becoming the title of the 1954 film.

the 10 LATEST 'BEST SONG' OSCAR WINNERS

YEAR	SONG	FILM
2004	**Al Otro Lado del Río**	The Motorcycle Diaries
2003	**Into the West**	The Lord of the Rings: The Return of the King
2002	**Lose Yourself**	8 Mile
2001	**If I Didn't Have You**	Monsters, Inc.
2000	**Things Have Changed**	Wonder Boys
1999	**You'll Be in My Heart**	Tarzan
1998	**When You Believe**	The Prince of Egypt
1997	**My Heart Will Go On**	Titanic
1996	**You Must Love Me**	Evita
1995	**Colors of the Wind**	Pocahontas

Al Otro Lado Del Río is the first-ever Spanish-language song to win an Oscar. It was written and sung by Uruguayan Jorge Drexler, who was sidelined at the awards ceremony in favour of a version sung by Antonio Banderas.

top 10 ORIGINAL SOUNDTRACK ALBUMS IN THE UK

	ALBUM	YEAR
1	**The Bodyguard**	1992
2	**Dirty Dancing**	1998
3	**Titanic**	1997
4	**Bridget Jones's Diary**	2001
5	**Trainspotting**	1996
6	**The Commitments**	1991
7	**The Full Monty**	1997
8	**Buster**	1988
9	**Top Gun**	1986
10	**Evita**	1996

Source: Music Information Database

Predominantly a vehicle for the film's star, Whitney Houston, the all-time bestselling soundtrack album *The Bodyguard* includes her massive Dolly Parton-penned hit *I Will Always Love You*.

⊙ **Winning track**
The Motorcycle Diaries song *Al Otro Lado Del Río (On the Other Side of the River)* won the "Best Song" Oscar in 2004.

Musical Collectables

top 10 MOST EXPENSIVE GUITARS*

GUITAR / AUCTION / SALE PRICE#

1 Jerry Garcia's "Tiger" guitar
Guernsey's at Studio 54, New York, 9 May 2002
£657,850 ($957,500)

2 Jerry Garcia's "Wolf" guitar
Guernsey's at Studio 54, New York, 9 May 2002
£542,425 ($789,500)

3 Eric Clapton's 1956–57 "Blackie" Fender Stratocaster
Christie's, New York, 25 June 2004
£527,918 ($959,500)

4 Eric Clapton's 1964 Gibson acoustic ES-335
Christie's, New York, 25 June 2004
£465,659 ($847,500)

5 Eric Clapton's 1939 Martin acoustic
Christie's, New York, 25 June 2004
£434,890 ($791,500)

6 Stevie Ray Vaughan's/Eric Clapton's "Lenny" Fender Stratocaster
Christie's, New York, 25 June 2004
£342,582 ($623,500)

7 "Brownie", one of Eric Clapton's favourite electric guitars
Christie's, New York, 24 June 1999
£313,425 ($497,500)

8 George Harrison's 1964 Gibson SG, played by both George Harrison and John Lennon
Christie's, New York, 17 Dec 2004
£294,041 ($567,500)

9 George Harrison's first guitar, a Spanish-style Egmond "Firewood" model
Cooper Owen/Hard Rock Café, London, 21 Nov 2003
£276,000

10 George Harrison's rosewood Telecaster
Odyssey, Los Angeles, 13 Sept 2003
£271,244 ($434,750)

* Sold at auction

Including buyer's premium where appropriate; price conversion calculated on rate prevailing at time of sale

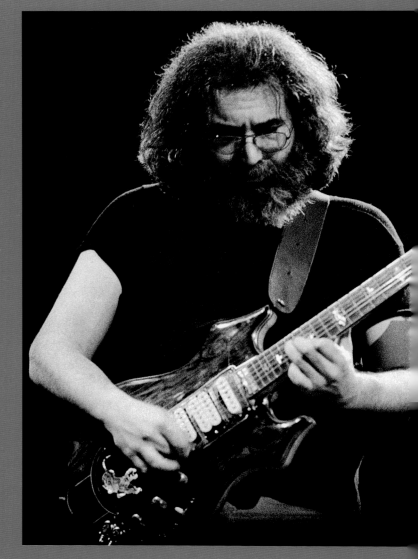

⬆ **Jerry's tiger**
So-called because of the inlaid motif on the front, Jerry Garcia's "Tiger" achieved a new world record when it was sold in 2002, along with "Wolf". Both instruments were made by guitar craftsman Doug Irwin who subsequently inherited them following Garcia's death in 1995.

top 10 MOST EXPENSIVE MUSICAL INSTRUMENTS*

1 John Lennon's Steinway Model Z upright piano
Fleetwood-Owen online auction, Hard Rock Café,
London and New York, 17 Oct 2000
£1,450,000

2 "Kreutzer" violin by Antonio Stradivari, 1727
Christie's, London, 1 Apr 1998
£946,000

3 "Cholmondeley" violincello by Antonio Stradivari
Sotheby's, London, 22 June 1998
£682,000

4 Italian cello by Giovanni Battista, Guadagnini, Parma, 1760
Christie's, London, 3 Nov 2004
£341,250

5 Single-manual harpsichord by Joseph Joannes Couchet, Antwerp, 1679
Sotheby's, London, 21 Nov 2001
£267,500

6 Steinway grand piano, decorated by Lawrence Alma-Tadema and Edward Poynter for Henry Marquand, 1884–87
Sotheby Parke Bernet, New York, 26 Mar 1980
£163,000 ($390,000)

7 Double bass by Domenico Montagnana
Sotheby's, London, 16 Mar 1999
£155,500

8 Viola by Giovanni Paolo Maggini
Christie's, London, 20 Nov 1984
£129,000

9 Verne Powell's platinum flute
Christie's, New York, 18 Oct 1986
£126,200 ($187,000)

10 Charlie Parker's saxophone
Christie's, London, 8 Sept 1994
£93,000

* Sold at auction; excluding guitars

Most expensive example only for each type of instrument

† Including buyer's premium where appropriate; price conversion calculated on rate prevailing at time of sale

top 10 MOST EXPENSIVE POP LYRICS*

1 Bernie Taupin's handwritten lyrics for the rewritten *Candle in the Wind* (1997)
Christie's, Los Angeles, 11 Feb 1998
£278,512 ($400,000)

2 John Lennon's handwritten lyrics for *Nowhere Man* (1965)
Christie's, New York, 18 Nov 2003
£269,526 ($455,000)

3 Paul McCartney's handwritten lyrics for *Getting Better* (1967)
Sotheby's, London, 14 Sept 1995
£161,000

4 John Lennon's handwritten lyrics for *If I Fell* (1964) written on the back of a Valentine's card
Christie's, Los Angeles, 20 Sept 2001
£116,445 ($171,000)

5 Mal Evans' notebook, compiled 1967–68, which includes a draft by Paul McCartney of the lyrics for *Hey Jude* (1968)
Sotheby's, London, 15 Sept 1998
£111,500

6 Page of John Lennon's handwritten lyrics for *I Am the Walrus* (1967)
Christie's, London, 30 Sept 1999
£78,500

7 Twelve pages of John Lennon's handwritten lyrics for the *Plastic Ono Band* album, inscribed to his therapist, Dr. Arthur Janov, creator of "primal scream" therapy (1970)
Christie's, Los Angeles, 15 Nov 2000
£71,857 ($102,800)

8 John Lennon's handwritten lyrics for *Being for the Benefit of Mr. Kite* (1967)
Sotheby's, London, 18 Sept 1996
£66,400

9 Paul McCartney's handwritten lyrics for *She's Leaving Home* (1967)
Sotheby's, London, 27 Aug 1992
£45,100

10 John Lennon's handwritten lyrics for *A Day in the Life* (1967)
Sotheby's, London, 27 Aug 1992
£44,000

* Sold at auction

Including buyer's premium where appropriate; price conversion calculated on rate prevailing at time of sale

Chapter

7

top 10 films to win the most Oscars: page 145

top 10 superhero films: page 139

SCENE 24 TAKE

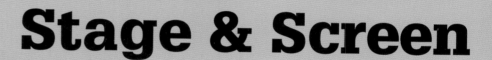

top 10 animated film budgets: page 156

Stage & Screen

eatre

top 10 LONGEST-RUNNING MUSICALS IN THE UK

SHOW / RUN	PERFORMANCES*
1 Cats, 1981–2002	8,949
2 Les Misérables, 1985–	7,916#
3 The Phantom of the Opera, 1986–	7,582#
4 Starlight Express, 1984–2002	7,406
5 Miss Saigon, 1989–99	4,263
6 Jesus Christ Superstar, 1972–80	3,357
7 Evita, 1978–86	2,900
8 Oliver!, 1960–66	2,618
9 The Sound of Music, 1961–67	2,386
10 Salad Days, 1954–60	2,283

* Continuous runs only
\# Still running; total as at 1 Jan 2005

Cats closed on 12 May 2002 – its 21st birthday – having held the record as the UK's longest continuously running musical since 12 May 1989 when, with its 3,358th performance, it overtook *Jesus Christ Superstar*.

top 10 LONGEST-RUNNING NON-MUSICALS IN THE UK

SHOW / RUN	PERFORMANCES
1 The Mousetrap, 1952–	21,708*
2 No Sex, Please – We're British, 1971–81; 1982–86; 1986–87	6,761
3 The Woman in Black, 1989–	6,401*
4 The Complete Works of William Shakespeare (abridged), 1996–2005	4,266
5 Oh! Calcutta!, 1970–74; 1974–80	3,918
6 Run for Your Wife, 1983–91	2,638
7 There's a Girl in My Soup, 1966–69; 1969–72	2,547
8 Pyjama Tops, 1969–75	2,498
9 Sleuth, 1970; 1972; 1973–75	2,359
10 Worm's Eye View, 1945–51	2,245

* Still running; total as at 1 Jan 2005

Oh! Calcutta! is included here as it is regarded as a revue with music, rather than a musical.

top 10 OLDEST LONDON THEATRES

THEATRE / LOCATION	DATE OPENED
1 Theatre Royal, Drury Lane	7 May 1663
2 Sadler's Wells, Rosebery Avenue	3 June 1683
3 The Haymarket (Theatre Royal), Haymarket	29 Dec 1720
4 Royal Opera House, Covent Garden	7 Dec 1732
5 The Adelphi (originally Sans Pareil), Strand	27 Nov 1806
6 The Old Vic (originally Royal Coburg), Waterloo Road	11 May 1818
7 The Vaudeville, Strand	16 Apr 1870
8 The Criterion, Piccadilly Circus	21 Mar 1874
9 The Savoy, Strand	10 Oct 1881
10 The Comedy, Panton Street	15 Oct 1881

These are London's 10 oldest theatres still operating on their original sites – although most of them have been rebuilt, some several times. The Lyceum, built in 1771 as "a place of entertainment", was not originally licensed as a theatre and in its early years was used for such events as circuses and exhibitions, with only occasional theatrical performances. The Savoy was gutted by fire in 1990, but was completely rebuilt and reopened in 1993.

the 10 LATEST WINNERS OF THE LAURENCE OLIVIER AWARD FOR BEST NEW PLAY*

YEAR	PLAY	PLAYWRIGHT
2005	The History Boys	Alan Bennett
2004	The Pillowman	Martin McDonagh
2003	Vincent in Brixton	Nicholas Wright
2002	Jitney	August Wilson
2001	Blue/Orange	Marie Jones
2000	Goodnight Children Everywhere	Richard Nelson
1999	The Weir	Conor McPherson
1998	Closer	Patrick Marber
1997	Stanley	Pam Gems
1996	Skylight	David Hare

* "BBC Award for Best Play" until 1996; "Best New Play" thereafter; awards are for previous season

Presented by The Society of London Theatres (founded 1908), the award itself depicts Laurence (later Lord) Olivier (1907–89), after whom it is named, in his celebrated role as Henry V at the Old Vic in 1937. Several earlier winners went on to become successful films, among them *Children of a Lesser God* (1981/86), *Glengarry Glen Ross* (1983/92), and *Les Liaisons Dangereuses* (1986/88 – as *Dangerous Liaisons*).

⏷ See how it runs
Richard Attenborough, a member of the original
cast of *The Mousetrap*, celebrates the 50th
anniversary of the world's longest-running play.

THE **LONGEST-RUNNING** SHOWS OF ALL TIME

SHOW / LOCATION / RUN	PERFORMANCES
1 **The Golden Horseshoe Revue**, Disneyland, California, 1955–86	47,250
2 **The Mousetrap**, London, 1952–	21,708*
3 **The Fantasticks**, New York, 1960–2002	17,162
4 **La Cantatrice Chauve (The Bald Soprano)**, Paris, 1957–	14,863*
5 **Shear Madness**, Boston, 1980–	10,367*
6 **The Drunkard**, Los Angeles, 1933–59	9,477
7 **The Mousetrap**, Toronto, 1977–2004	9,000
8 **Cats**, London, 1981–2002	8,949
9 **Les Misérables**, London, 1985–	7,916*
10 **Cats**, New York, 1982–2000	7,485

* Still running; total as at 1 Jan 2005

top 10 MOST PRODUCED PLAYS BY **SHAKESPEARE**, 1878–2004

PLAY	PRODUCTIONS
1 **As You Like It**	78
2 = **Hamlet**	76
= **The Taming of the Shrew**	76
= **Twelfth Night**	76
5 = **A Midsummer Night's Dream**	71
= **Much Ado About Nothing**	71
7 **The Merchant of Venice**	70
8 **Macbeth**	65
9 **The Merry Wives of Windsor**	61
10 **Romeo and Juliet**	59

Source: Shakespeare Centre

This list is based on an analysis of Shakespearean productions
(rather than individual performances) from 31 December 1878
to 31 December 2004 at Stratford-upon-Avon and by the Royal
Shakespeare Company in London and on tour.

Film Hits

top 10 HIGHEST-GROSSING FILMS OF ALL TIME IN THE US (ADJUSTED FOR INFLATION)

FILM	YEAR	US BOX OFFICE INCOME ($) (ACTUAL US GROSS)	(ADJUSTED FOR INFLATION*)
1 Gone With the Wind	1939	198,676,459	2,730,013,223
2 Snow White and the Seven Dwarfs#	1937	187,670,866	2,489,247,600
3 Star Wars†	1977	460,998,007	1,452,973,518
4 Bambi#	1942	102,797,000	1,204,554,687
5 Pinocchio#	1940	84,254,167	1,149,471,175
6 Fantasia#	1940	76,408,097	1,042,428,027
7 The Exorcist	1973	232,671,011	1,000,094,155
8 The Sound of Music	1965	163,214,286	989,649,823
9 One Hundred and One Dalmatians#	1961	153,000,000	977,364,000
10 Jaws	1975	260,000,000	923,052,000

* As at 1 Jan 2005

\# Animated

† Later retitled *Star Wars: Episode IV – A New Hope*

Frankly, my dear...
Clark Gable and Vivien Leigh co-star in *Gone with the Wind*, the inflation-adjusted top-earning film of all time.

Unless inflation is factored in, the escalating price of cinema tickets – and hence the total income that films generate – makes the list of all-time blockbusters biased toward recent releases: box office income of $1 million earned 50 years ago (1955), for example, would be worth over $7 million today. However, any inflation-indexing inevitably assumes that the bulk of a film's income was earned in its release year, which is clearly not the case, since the total gross of any film is cumulative often over many years from its release (and, with re-releases, may even increase decades later). The ranking indicated by this list must therefore be taken only as a guide and an impressionistic answer to the question, "If the box office income of film X had been earned today, how much would it be worth?", rather than a precise reflection of the inflation-adjusted earning of every dollar ever earned by each film.

top 10 FILMS IN THE UK

FILM	YEAR	TOTAL UK BOX OFFICE GROSS (£)
1 Titanic	1998	69,025,646
2 Harry Potter and the Philosopher's Stone	2001	66,096,060
3 The Lord of the Rings: The Fellowship of the Ring	2001	63,009,288
4 The Lord of the Rings: The Return of the King	2003	60,880,923
5 The Lord of the Rings: The Two Towers	2002	57,600,094
6 Harry Potter and the Chamber of Secrets	2002	54,780,731
7 The Full Monty	1997	52,232,058
8 Star Wars: Episode I – The Phantom Menace	1999	51,063,811
9 Shrek 2*	2004	48,104,138
10 Jurassic Park	1993	47,886,423

* Animated

↑ **World wide web** Globally, *Spider-Man 2* was the highest-earning live-action film of 2004 and the 9th of all time.

top 10 FILMS **WORLDWIDE**, 2004

FILM	WORLDWIDE GROSS ($)*
1 Shrek 2#	918,506,048
2 Harry Potter and the Prisoner of Azkaban	789,791,069
3 Spider-Man 2	783,964,497
4 The Incredibles#	631,068,449
5 The Passion of the Christ	623,489,009
6 The Day After Tomorrow	542,545,811
7 Meet the Fockers	507,392,324
8 Troy	497,378,256
9 Ocean's Twelve	362,144,280
10 I, Robot	338,780,585

* Including income from ongoing US and overseas releases through 2005

\# Animated

top 10 **FILMS** IN THE UK, 2004

FILM	UK GROSS (£)
1 Shrek 2*	48,104,138
2 Harry Potter and the Prisoner of Azkaban	46,077,489
3 Bridget Jones: The Edge of Reason	35,612,127
4 The Incredibles*	30,264,650
5 Spider-Man 2	26,716,429
6 The Day After Tomorrow	25,212,419
7 Shark Tale*	22,820,804
8 Troy	18,002,561
9 I, Robot	17,981,834
10 Scooby Doo 2: Monsters Unleashed	16,490,226

* Animated

top 10 **TRILOGIES**

FILMS / YEARS	WORLDWIDE TOTAL GROSS ($)*
1 The Lord of the Rings, 2001–03	2,916,544,743
2 Harry Potter, 2001–2004	2,652,297,210
3 Jurassic Park, 1993–2002	1,902,110,926
4 The Matrix, 1999–2003	1,623,924,804
5 Terminator, 1984–2003	1,212,019,531

FILMS / YEARS	WORLDWIDE TOTAL GROSS ($)*
6 Indiana Jones, 1981–89	1,211,716,531
7 Back to the Future, 1985–90	927,715,544
8 The Silence of the Lambs, 1991–2001	833,916,591
9 American Pie, 1999–2003	754,039,152
10 Die Hard, 1988–95	743,562,298

* Cumulative global earnings of all three parts

Film Genres

top 10 WAR FILMS

FILM / SETTING	YEAR
1 Troy, Trojan Wars	2004
2 Saving Private Ryan, World War II	1998
3 Pearl Harbor, World War II	2001
4 The Last Samurai, Japanese Emperor vs. samurai	2003
5 Gone With the Wind, US Civil War	1939
6 Schindler's List, World War II	1993
7 The English Patient, World War II	1996
8 Life is Beautiful (La Vita è bella), World War II	1997
9 Master and Commander: The Far Side of the World, Napoleonic Wars	2003
10 The Patriot, American Revolutionary War	2000

This list excludes successful films that are not technically "war" films but which have military themes, such as *Top Gun* (1986), *Rambo: First Blood Part II* (1985), and *A Few Good Men* (1992), which would otherwise appear in the Top 10, all of which have earned more than $200 million each at the world box office.

⬆ War chest
Starring Brad Pitt as Achilles, *Troy* earned almost $3.7 billion at the world box office.

top 10 BIOGRAPHICAL FILMS*

FILM	SUBJECT	YEAR
1 Catch Me if You Can	Frank Abagnale Jr.	2002
2 Pocahontas#	Pocahontas	1995
3 Schindler's List	Oskar Schindler	1993
4 A Beautiful Mind	John Nash	2001
5 Erin Brockovich	Erin Brockovich	2000
6 Out of Africa	Karen Blixen	1985
7 Braveheart	William Wallace	1995
8 The Aviator	Howard Hughes	2004
9 Patch Adams	Hunter "Patch" Adams	1998
10 Born on the Fourth of July	Ron Kovic	1989

* Excluding musical biographies

Animated

top 10 DOCUMENTARY FILMS

	FILM	SUBJECT	YEAR
1	Fahrenheit 9/11	War on terrorism	2004
2	The Dream is Alive	Space shuttle	1985
3	Everest	Exploration	1998
4	Grand Canyon: The Hidden Secrets	Exploration	1984
5	To Fly	History of flying	1976
6	Jackass: The Movie	Comedy stunts	2002
7	Space Station 3-D	International space station	2002
8	Blue Planet	Earth from space	1990
9	Mysteries of Egypt	Historical	1998
10 =	Antarctica	Exploration/nature	1991
=	Into the Deep	Underwater exploration	1994

➔ **Hot date**
Michael Moore and friend in the all-time documentary hit and Cannes Film Festival "Palme d'Or" winner *Fahrenheit 9/11*.

CONTROVERSY...WHAT CONTROVERSY?

MICHAEL MOORE

FAHRENHEIT 9/11

WINNER / BEST PICTURE 2004 CANNES FILM FESTIVAL

IFCFilms   FELLOWSHIP ADVENTURE GROUP   THIS FILM HAS NOT YET BEEN RATED   LGF LIONS GATE

---

top 10 ROBOT FILMS

	FILM	YEAR
1	Star Wars: Episode I – The Phantom Menace	1999
2	Star Wars*	1977
3	Star Wars: Episode VI – Return of the Jedi	1983
4	Star Wars: Episode V – The Empire Strikes Back	1980
5	Terminator 2: Judgment Day	1991
6	Terminator 3: Rise of the Machines	2003
7	I, Robot	2004
8	Lara Croft: Tomb Raider	2001
9	A.I.: Artificial Intelligence	2001
10	Wild Wild West	1999

* Later retitled *Star Wars: Episode IV – A New Hope*

These are the most successful films in which robots or cyborgs play central or significant roles. All of those in the Top 10 earned upwards of $220 million each worldwide.

---

top 10 HORROR FILMS

	FILM	YEAR
1	Jurassic Park	1993
2	The Sixth Sense	1999
3	The Lost World: Jurassic Park	1997
4	Jaws	1975
5	The Mummy Returns	2001
6	The Mummy	1999
7	Signs	2002
8	Godzilla	1998
9	Jurassic Park III	2001
10	Hannibal	2001

This list encompasses supernatural and science-fiction horror and monster creatures such as dinosaurs and oversized sharks. It has long been a successful genre: each of the films listed has earned $350 million or more at the world box office.

---

top 10 SUPERHERO FILMS

	FILM	YEAR
1	Spider-Man	2002
2	Spider-Man 2	2004
3	The Incredibles*	2004
4	Batman	1989
5	X2: X-Men United	2003
6	Batman Forever	1995
7	The Mask	1994
8	Superman	1978
9	X-Men	2000
10	Batman Returns	1992

* Animated

Superman makes a single showing in this Top 10, since it is in the unusual situation where the first film made a large amount (over $300 million) at the world box office while each of its three sequels made progressively less.

Oscar-Winning Actors

top 10 OLDEST OSCAR-WINNING ACTORS

	ACTOR	FILM	YEAR	AGE*(YRS)	MTHS	DAYS)
1	George Burns	The Sunshine Boys	1975	80	2	9
2	Melvyn Douglas	Being There	1979	79	0	9
3	John Gielgud	Arthur	1981	77	11	15
4	Don Ameche	Cocoon	1985	77	9	24
5	Henry Fonda	On Golden Pond	1981	76	10	13
6	Edmund Gwenn	Miracle on 34th Street	1947	72	5	24
7	Jack Palance	City Slickers	1991	72	0	1
8	John Houseman	The Paperchase	1973	71	6	0
9	Morgan Freeman	Million Dollar Baby	2004	67	8	27
10	Charles Coburn	The More the Merrier	1943	66	8	13

* Age at time of award ceremony

All of the Academy Awards listed here are for "Best Supporting Actor", apart from Henry Fonda's award for "Best Actor" in *On Golden Pond*. The oldest person to win the "Best Actor" award prior to Henry Fonda was John Wayne who was 62 when he received his 1969 award for *True Grit*.

"And the winner is..."

the 10 LATEST "BEST ACTOR" OSCAR WINNERS

YEAR	ACTOR	FILM
2004	Jamie Foxx	Ray
2003	Sean Penn	Mystic River
2002	Adrien Brody	The Pianist
2001	Denzel Washington	Training Day
2000	Russell Crowe	Gladiator*
1999	Kevin Spacey	American Beauty*
1998	Roberto Benigni	Life is Beautiful
1997	Jack Nicholson	As Good As It Gets
1996	Geoffrey Rush	Shine
1995	Nicolas Cage	Leaving Las Vegas

* Won "Best Picture" Academy Award

🔊 **Piano man**
Jamie Foxx played the title role in *Ray*. Like previous Oscar-winner Holly Hunter in *The Pianist*, he played the piano himself in the film.

top 10 **ACTORS** WITH THE MOST NOMINATIONS*

	ACTOR	WINS (SUPPORTING)	(BEST)	NOMINATIONS
1	Jack Nicholson	1	2	12
2	Laurence Olivier	0	1	10
3	= Paul Newman	0	1	9
	= Spencer Tracy	0	2	9
5	= Marlon Brando	0	2	8
	= Jack Lemmon	1	1	8
	= Al Pacino	0	1	8
8	= Richard Burton	0	0	7
	= Dustin Hoffman	0	2	7
	= Peter O'Toole	0	0	7

* In all acting categories

⬅ **Wild about Oscar**
Jack Nicholson's Academy Award nominations span 33 years from *Easy Rider* (1969) to *About Schmidt* (2002). He won the "Best Actor" award for *One Flew Over the Cuckoo's Nest* (1975) and *As Good as It Gets* (1997), and "Best Supporting Actor" for *Terms of Endearment* (1983).

top 10 **YOUNGEST** OSCAR-WINNING ACTORS

	ACTOR	AWARD / FILM	YEAR	AGE* (YRS	MTHS	DAYS)
1	Vincent Winter	Honorary Award: Outstanding Juvenile Performance, *The Little Kidnappers*	1954	7	3	1
2	Jon Whiteley	Honorary Award: Outstanding Juvenile Performance, *The Little Kidnappers*	1954	10	1	11
3	Ivan Jandl	Special Award: Outstanding Juvenile Performance of 1948, *The Search*	1948	12	2	0
4	Claude Jarman Jr.	Special Award: Outstanding Child Actor of 1946, *The Yearling*	1946	12	4	14
5	Bobby Driscoll	Special Award: Outstanding Juvenile Actor of 1949, *The Window*	1949	13	0	20
6	Mickey Rooney	Special Award for juvenile players setting a high standard of ability and achievement[#]	1938	18	5	0
7	Timothy Hutton	Best Supporting Actor, *Ordinary People*	1980	20	7	15
8	George Chakiris	Best Supporting Actor, *West Side Story*	1961	26	7	1
9	Cuba Gooding Jr.	Best Supporting Actor, *Jerry Maguire*	1996	29	3	22
10	Adrien Brody	Best Actor, *The Pianist*	2002	29	11	9

* Age at time of award ceremony
[#] Shared with fellow teen star Deanna Durbin

Oscar-Winning Actresses

the 10 LATEST ACTRESSES TO WIN TWO "BEST ACTRESS" OSCARS

	ACTRESS	FIRST WIN	YEAR	SECOND WIN	YEAR
1	Hilary Swank	Boys Don't Cry	1999	Million Dollar Baby	2004
2	Jodie Foster	The Accused	1988	The Silence of the Lambs	1991
3	Sally Field	Norma Rae	1979	Places in the Heart	1984
4	Jane Fonda	Klute	1971	Coming Home	1978
5	Glenda Jackson	Women in Love	1970	A Touch of Class	1973
6	Katharine Hepburn	The Lion in Winter	1968	On Golden Pond	1981
7	Katharine Hepburn	Morning Glory	1932/33	Guess Who's Coming to Dinner?	1967
8	Elizabeth Taylor	Butterfield 8	1960	Who's Afraid of Virginia Woolf?	1966
9	Ingrid Bergman	Gaslight	1944	Anastasia	1956
10	Vivien Leigh	Gone With the Wind	1939	A Streetcar Named Desire	1951

top 10 OLDEST OSCAR-WINNING ACTRESSES

	ACTRESS	FILM	YEAR	AGE* (YRS	MTHS	DAYS)
1	Jessica Tandy	Driving Miss Daisy	1989	80	9	21
2	Peggy Ashcroft	A Passage to India	1984	77	3	3
3	Katharine Hepburn	On Golden Pond	1981	74	4	11
4	Ruth Gordon	Rosemary's Baby	1968	72	5	15
5	Margaret Rutherford	The VIPs	1963	71	11	2
6	Helen Hayes	Airport	1970	70	5	25
7	Ethel Barrymore	None But the Lonely Heart	1944	65	7	0
8	Josephine Hull	Harvey	1950	65	1	26
9	Judi Dench	Shakespeare in Love	1998	64	3	12
10	Beatrice Straight	Network	1976	62	7	26

* Age at time of award ceremony

🔵 **Veteran winner**
Two years after becoming the most senior recipient of an Oscar – and almost 60 years after making her first film – Jessica Tandy was again nominated for "Best Supporting Actress" for her role in *Fried Green Tomatoes* (1991), but lost out to Mercedes Ruehl in *The Fisher King*.

All of the Academy Awards listed here are for "Best Supporting Actress", apart from Jessica Tandy in *Driving Miss Daisy* and Katharine Hepburn in *On Golden Pond*, who both won "Best Actress" awards. Jessica Tandy holds the record as both the oldest nominee and oldest winner of a "Best Actor" or "Best Actress" Academy Award. Among those female senior citizens who received nominations but did not win Oscars are Gloria Stuart, aged 87, for "Best Supporting Actress" in *Titanic* (1997), and May Robson who was 75 when she was nominated as "Best Actress" in *Lady for a Day* (1933).

the 10 LATEST "BEST ACTRESS" OSCAR WINNERS

YEAR	ACTRESS	FILM
2004	**Hilary Swank**	Million Dollar Baby*
2003	**Charlize Theron**	Monster
2002	**Nicole Kidman**	The Hours
2001	**Halle Berry**	Monster's Ball
2000	**Julia Roberts**	Erin Brockovich
1999	**Hilary Swank**	Boys Don't Cry
1998	**Gwyneth Paltrow**	Shakespeare in Love*
1997	**Helen Hunt**	As Good As It Gets
1996	**Frances McDormand**	Fargo
1995	**Susan Sarandon**	Dead Man Walking

* Won "Best Picture" Academy Award

Hilary Swank's second win is unique in that both her wins were for roles in films that also won "Best Picture" Oscars. She was the second youngest (after Jodie Foster) to win two Oscars. The youngest "Best Actress" winner was Marlee Matlin, aged 21, for *Children of a Lesser God* (1986), and the youngest nominee Keisha Castle-Hughes, who was 13 when nominated for her role in *Whale Rider* (2002).

➔ Top dollar
Hilary Swank's Oscar for *Million Dollar Baby* was matched by a Golden Globe and other major awards.

Oscar-Winning Films

the 10 LATEST "BEST PICTURE" OSCAR-WINNERS

YEAR	FILM	DIRECTOR
2004	**Million Dollar Baby**	Clint Eastwood
2003	**The Lord of the Rings: The Return of the King**	Peter Jackson
2002	**Chicago**	Rob Marshall*
2001	**A Beautiful Mind**	Ron Howard
2000	**Gladiator**	Ridley Scott*
1999	**American Beauty**	Sam Mendes
1998	**Shakespeare in Love**	John Madden*
1997	**Titanic**	James Cameron
1996	**The English Patient**	Anthony Minghella
1995	**Braveheart**	Mel Gibson

* Did not also win "Best Director" Academy Award

top 10 HIGHEST-EARNING "BEST PICTURE" OSCAR WINNERS

	FILM	YEAR*	WORLD BOX OFFICE ($)
1	**Titanic**	1997	1,845,000,000
2	**The Lord of the Rings: The Return of the King**	2003	1,118,900,000
3	**Forrest Gump**	1994	677,400,000
4	**Gladiator**	2000	457,600,000
5	**Dances With Wolves**	1990	424,200,000
6	**Rain Man**	1988	416,000,000
7	**Gone With the Wind**	1939	400,200,000
8	**American Beauty**	1999	356,300,000
9	**Schindler's List**	1993	321,300,000
10	**A Beautiful Mind**	2001	313,500,000

* Of release; Academy Awards are made the following year

◉ For a few million dollars more
With his latest Oscar wins, actor-director Clint Eastwood repeated the "Best Picture" and "Best Director" double victory of *Unforgiven* (1992).

Although since equalled by two recent blockbusters, *Ben-Hur* was the first film to win more than 10 Oscars. Based on the 1880 book by Lew Wallace, *Ben-Hur* was directed by William Wyler who had worked as an assistant director on the original 1925 silent version of the film, and had two previous Oscars to his credit. Had it won in the one other category in which it was nominated – "Best Writing, Screenplay Based on Material from Another Medium" – it would have secured a record 12 wins.

➲ **Racing ahead**
Ben-Hur's amazing haul of 11 Oscars set a record that remained unbeaten for almost 40 years.

top 10 FILMS TO WIN THE MOST OSCARS

	FILM	YEAR	NOMINATIONS	AWARDS
1	=Ben-Hur	1959	12	11
	=Titanic	1997	14	11
	=The Lord of the Rings: The Return of the King	2003	11	11
4	West Side Story	1961	11	10
5	=Gigi	1958	9	9
	=The Last Emperor	1987	9	9
	=The English Patient	1996	12	9
8	=Gone With the Wind	1939	13	8*
	=From Here to Eternity	1953	13	8
	=On the Waterfront	1954	12	8
	=My Fair Lady	1964	12	8
	=Cabaret	1972	10	8
	=Gandhi	1982	11	8
	=Amadeus	1984	11	8

* Plus two special awards

Ten other films have won seven Oscars each: *Going My Way* (1944), *The Best years of Our Lives* (1946), *The Bridge on the River Kwai* (1957), *Lawrence of Arabia* (1962), *Patton* (1970), *The Sting* (1973), *Out of Africa* (1985), *Dances With Wolves* (1991), *Schindler's List* (1993), and *Shakespeare in Love* (1998). *Titanic* (1997) matched the previous record of 14 nominations of *All About Eve* (1950), but outshone it by winning 11, compared with the latter's six.

top 10 FILMS NOMINATED FOR THE MOST OSCARS

	FILM	YEAR	NOMINATIONS	AWARDS
1	=All About Eve	1950	14	6
	=Titanic	1997	14	11
3	=Gone With the Wind	1939	13	8*
	=From Here to Eternity	1953	13	8
	=Shakespeare in Love	1998	13	7
	=Mary Poppins#	1964	13	5
	=Who's Afraid of Virginia Woolf?#	1966	13	5
	=Forrest Gump	1994	13	6
	=The Lord of the Rings: The Fellowship of the Ring	2001	13	4
	=Chicago	2002	13	6

* Plus two special awards
# Did not win "Best Picture" Academy Award

A total of eight films have received 13 Oscar nominations. They, and the two films with 14, have received the greatest share of votes from Academy members (currently over 5,500 in total), using a system that creates a shortlist of five nominees in each of 24 categories. Eliminating certain specialist categories reduces the potential number of awards for which a film may be nominated, and they may be nominated in one category that excludes another – screenplays, for example, are divided into two awards according to whether they are based on material previously produced or published, or written directly for the screen.

TOP 10 FILMS OF ALL TIME

FILM	YEAR	(USA)	GROSS INCOME ($) (OVERSEAS)	(WORLD TOTAL)
1 Titanic*	1997	600,788,188	1,244,246,000	1,845,034,188
2 The Lord of the Rings: The Return of the King	2003	377,027,325	741,861,654	1,118,888,979
3 Harry Potter and the Philosopher's Stone	2001	317,575,550	668,242,109	985,817,659
4 The Lord of the Rings: The Two Towers	2002	341,784,377	584,500,642	926,287,400
5 Star Wars: Episode I – The Phantom Menace	1999	431,088,297	494,511,703	925,600,000
6 Shrek 2#	2004	441,226,247	470,823,405	918,506,048
7 Jurassic Park	1993	357,067,947	557,623,171	914,691,118
8 Harry Potter and the Chamber of Secrets	2002	261,988,482	614,700,000	876,688,482
9 The Lord of the Rings: The Fellowship of the Ring	2001	314,776,170	556,592,194	871,368,364
10 Finding Nemo#	2003	339,714,978	524,911,000	864,625,978

* Winner of "Best Picture" Academy Award

Animated

Prior to the release of *Star Wars* in 1977, no film had ever made more than $500 million worldwide. Since then, some 35 films have done so. *Titanic* remains the only film to have made more than this amount in the USA alone, and just 10 films have exceeded this total outside the USA. To date, those in the Top 10, along with *Spider-Man 2* (2004), *Spider-Man* (2002) and *Independence Day* (1996) are the only films to earn more than $800 million globally.

← Titanic prowess
Leonardo DiCaprio and Kate Winslet co-star as ill-fated *Titanic* passengers Jack Dawson and Rose DeWitt Bukater in the USA and world's highest-earning film.

⊕ Golden Rings
Each of the *Lord of the Rings* films
earned progressively more than its
predecessor. Cumulatively, the trilogy
has earned almost $3 billion worldwide.

Film Actors

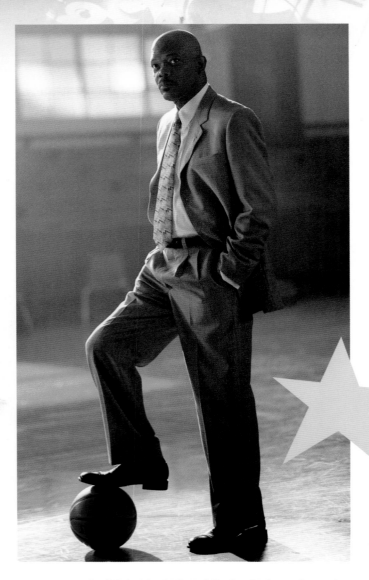

top 10 TOM CRUISE FILMS

FILM	YEAR
1 Mission: Impossible II	2000
2 Mission: Impossible	1996
3 The Last Samurai	2003
4 Rain Man	1988
5 Minority Report	2002
6 Top Gun	1986
7 Jerry Maguire	1996
8 The Firm	1993
9 A Few Good Men	1992
10 Interview with the Vampire: The Vampire Chronicles	1994

Tom Cruise (real name Thomas Cruise Mapother IV) built his career on playing a combination of handsome all-American heroes, military, and light comedy roles, but has shown himself equally at home with dramatic parts, for which he has been nominated for Oscars on three occasions. Few actors have matched his commercial success: every one of his Top 10 films has earned more than $220 million worldwide, a total of more than $3.6 billion. Cruise appeared as himself in *Austin Powers in Goldmember*, which if included in this list, would be ranked 7th.

⊙ On the ball
Samuel L. Jackson in the title role of *Coach Carter* (2005). His prolific filmography includes so many high-earning films that he heads the list of box office total earnings.

top 10 ACTORS BY US BOX OFFICE TOTALS

	ACTOR	FILMS	US TOTAL ($)
1	Samuel L. Jackson	60	3,316,546,256
2	Harrison Ford	33	3,255,071,377
3	Tom Hanks	33	3,083,738,308
4	Eddie Murphy	30	2,916,492,624
5	Tom Cruise	28	2,673,139,642
6	Bruce Willis	45	2,475,454,726
7	James Earl Jones	40	2,343,822,050
8	Mel Gibson	35	2,316,662,303
9	Gene Hackman	59	2,253,788,994
10	Jim Cummings	26	2,250,222,445

top 10 JIM CARREY FILMS

FILM	YEAR
1 Bruce Almighty	2003
2 Dr. Seuss's How the Grinch Stole Christmas	2000
3 Batman Forever	1995
4 The Mask	1994
5 Liar Liar	1997
6 The Truman Show	1998
7 Dumb & Dumber	1994
8 Ace Ventura: When Nature Calls	1995
9 Lemony Snicket's A Series of Unfortunate Events	2004
10 Me, Myself & Irene	2000

Jim Carrey is a member of an élite club of actors all of whose Top 10 films have earned more than $100 million worldwide. In fact, such is his international appeal that the average for the films in this list is over $250 million.

⊕ **High flier** Leonardo DiCaprio as Howard Hughes in *The Aviator*, one of his highest-earning films.

top 10 **LEONARDO DICAPRIO** FILMS

FILM	YEAR
1 Titanic	1997
2 Catch Me If You Can	2002
3 The Aviator	2004
4 Gangs of New York	2002
5 The Man in the Iron Mask	1998
6 Romeo + Juliet	1996
7 The Beach	2000
8 The Quick and the Dead	1995
9 Marvin's Room	1996
10 What's Eating Gilbert Grape?	1993

top 10 **JOHNNY DEPP** FILMS

FILM	YEAR
1 Pirates of the Caribbean: The Curse of the Black Pearl	2003
2 Sleepy Hollow	1999
3 Platoon	1986
4 Chocolat	2000
5 Donnie Brasco	1997
6 Desperado II: Once Upon a Time in Mexico	2003
7 Secret Window	2004
8 Edward Scissorhands	1990
9 Blow	2001
10 From Hell	2001

top 10 **BRAD PITT** FILMS

FILM	YEAR
1 Troy	2004
2 Ocean's Eleven	2001
3 Ocean's Twelve	2004
4 Se7en	1995
5 Interview with the Vampire: The Vampire Chronicles	1994
6 Twelve Monkeys	1995
7 Sleepers	1996
8 Legends of the Fall	1994
9 The Mexican	2001
10 Spy Game	2001

Film Actresses

top 10 ACTRESSES BY US BOX OFFICE TOTALS

	ACTRESS	FILMS	US TOTAL ($)
1	Julia Roberts	31	2,100,225,877
2	Carrie Fisher	28	1,862,987,964
3	Cameron Diaz	23	1,829,146,650
4	Whoopi Goldberg	41	1,705,812,987
5	Maggie Smith	26	1,582,143,126
6	Drew Barrymore	30	1,539,958,383
7	Kathy Bates	33	1,496,552,561
8	Kirsten Dunst	25	1,466,237,842
9	Bonnie Hunt	17	1,409,452,306
10	Sally Field	24	1,389,128,778

Julia Roberts' place at the head of this list derives from a career in which it is almost impossible to identify a film in which she has starred that has not enjoyed success ranging from moderate to spectacular. *Pretty Woman* (1990), her seventh film, is still her highest-earning at some £463 million worldwide.

🔅 **Star earner**
Carrie Fisher (and wookie Chewbacca) at the MTV Movie Awards. Her role as Princess Leia in three of the *Star Wars* films has contributed to her overall tally.

top 10 RENEE ZELLWEGER FILMS

	FILM	YEAR
1	Chicago	2002
2	Bridget Jones's Diary	2001
3	Jerry Maguire	1996
4	Bridget Jones: The Edge of Reason	2004
5	Cold Mountain	2003
6	Me, Myself & Irene	2000
7	Down with Love	2003
8	Nurse Betty	2000
9	The Bachelor	1999
10	Reality Bites	1994

Aside from some unmemorable early roles in films such as *The Return of the Texas Chainsaw Massacre* (1994), Renée Zellweger has followed an ever-upward trajectory in her film career, gaining consecutive Best Actress Oscar nominations for *Bridget Jones's Diary* (2001) and *Chicago* (2002), and winning Best Actress in a Supporting Role for *Cold Mountain* (2003). Although discounted here, the animated *Shark Tale*, for which she provided the voice of Angie, has outearned all the films in which she has appeared.

top 10 KATE WINSLET FILMS

	FILM	YEAR
1	Titanic	1997
2	Sense and Sensibility	1995
3	Finding Neverland	2004
4	Eternal Sunshine of the Spotless Mind	2004
5	The Life of David Gale	2003
6	Quills	2000
7	Iris	2001
8	Enigma	2001
9	A Kid in King Arthur's Court	1995
10	Hamlet	1996

Elf queen
Cate Blanchett as elf queen Galadriel in the *Lord of the Rings* trilogy.

top 10 CATE BLANCHETT FILMS

FILM	YEAR
1 The Lord of the Rings: The Return of the King	2003
2 The Lord of the Rings: The Two Towers	2002
3 The Lord of the Rings: The Fellowship of the Ring	2001
4 The Aviator	2004
5 The Talented Mr. Ripley	1999
6 Bandits	2001
7 Elizabeth	1998
8 The Gift	2000
9 The Missing	2003
10 The Life Aquatic with Steve Zissou	2004

top 10 UMA THURMAN FILMS

FILM	YEAR
1 Batman & Robin	1997
2 Pulp Fiction	1994
3 Kill Bill: Vol. 1	2003
4 Kill Bill: Vol. 2	2004
5 Paycheck	2003
6 The Truth About Cats & Dogs	1996
7 The Avengers	1998
8 Final Analysis	1992
9 Dangerous Liaisons	1988
10 Beautiful Girls	1996

Although featuring in her Top 10 by virtue of its global box office income, *The Avengers* did not earn back its substantial production budget, and may thus be regarded as a flop. Conversely, *Pulp Fiction* had a budget of some $8 million, but went on to make more than $200 million worldwide.

top 10 NICOLE KIDMAN FILMS

FILM	YEAR
1 Batman Forever	1995
2 The Others	2001
3 Moulin Rouge!	2001
4 Cold Mountain	2003
5 Days of Thunder	1990
6 Eyes Wide Shut	1999
7 Far and Away	1992
8 The Peacemaker	1997
9 The Hours*	2002
10 The Stepford Wives	2004

* Won Academy Award for "Best Actress"

Honolulu-born Nicole Kidman was raised in Australia, where she acted on TV before her break into film, in which she has pursued a highly successful career: her Top 10 films have each earned upwards of $100 million worldwide.

Film Directors

⬆ **Express delivery** Robert Zemeckis-directed *Polar Express* was a pioneering exercise in 3D motion capture technology.

top 10 DIRECTORS

	DIRECTOR	FILMS	HIGHEST-EARNING FILM	TOTAL US GROSS OF ALL FILMS ($)
1	Steven Spielberg	22	ET the Extra-Terrestrial	3,223,585,018
2	Robert Zemeckis	13	Forrest Gump	1,696,212,782
3	Chris Columbus	11	Harry Potter and the Philosopher's Stone	1,530,121,285
4	Ron Howard	15	Dr. Seuss's How the Grinch Stole Christmas	1,316,036,170
5	George Lucas	5	Star Wars*	1,309,272,429
6	Richard Donner	16	Lethal Weapon 2	1,194,703,637
7	James Cameron	7	Titanic	1,142,636,142
8	Peter Jackson	5	The Lord of the Rings: The Return of the King	1,052,251,914
9	Ivan Reitman	12	Ghostbusters	974,005,978
10	Tim Burton	10	Batman	973,377,367

* Later retitled Star Wars: Episode IV – A New Hope

While the cumulative total US box office income of all the films of these directors provides a comparative view of the overall earning power of the group, the most impressive representative is George Lucas, with relatively few but extremely high-grossing releases, a per-picture average of $264 million.

top 10 FILMS DIRECTED BY ROBERT ZEMECKIS

	FILM	YEAR
1	Forrest Gump*	1994
2	Cast Away	2000
3	Back to the Future	1985
4	Who Framed Roger Rabbit?	1988
5	Back to the Future Part II	1989
6	What Lies Beneath	2000
7	The Polar Express	2004
8	Back to the Future Part III	1990
9	Contact	1997
10	Death Becomes Her	1992

* Won Academy Award for "Best Director"; film won Academy Award for "Best Picture"

top 10 FILMS DIRECTED BY PETER WEIR

FILM	YEAR
1 The Truman Show	1998
2 Dead Poets Society	1989
3 Master and Commander: The Far Side of the World	2003
4 Witness	1985
5 Green Card	1990
6 The Mosquito Coast	1986
7 The Year of Living Dangerously	1982
8 Fearless	1993
9 Gallipoli	1981
10 Picnic at Hanging Rock	1975

top 10 FILMS DIRECTED BY MARTIN SCORSESE

FILM	YEAR
1 The Aviator	2004
2 Gangs of New York	2002
3 Cape Fear	1991
4 Casino	1995
5 The Color of Money	1986
6 Goodfellas	1990
7 The Age of Innocence	1993
8 Taxi Driver	1976
9 Raging Bull	1980
10 Bringing Out the Dead	1999

top 10 FILMS DIRECTED BY CLINT EASTWOOD

FILM	YEAR
1 The Bridges of Madison County	1995
2 Million Dollar Baby*	2004
3 Unforgiven*	1992
4 Mystic River	2003
5 A Perfect World	1993
6 Space Cowboys	2000
7 Absolute Power	1997
8 The Rookie	1990
9 Sudden Impact	1983
10 Firefox	1982

* Won Academy Award for "Best Director"; film won Academy Award for "Best Picture"

◐ Commanding presence
Fellow Australian Russell Crowe as Jack Aubrey in Peter Weir-directed *Master and Commander*.

top 10 FILMS DIRECTED BY WOMEN

FILM	DIRECTOR	YEAR
1 Shrek*	Victoria Jenson#	2001
2 What Women Want	Nancy Meyers	2000
3 Deep Impact	Mimi Leder	1998
4 Look Who's Talking	Amy Heckerling	1989
5 Doctor Dolittle	Betty Thomas	1998
6 Bridget Jones's Diary	Sharon Maguire	2001
7 Something's Gotta Give	Nancy Meyers	2003
8 You've Got M@il	Nora Ephron	1998
9 Sleepless in Seattle	Nora Ephron	1993
10 The Prince of Egypt*	Brenda Chapman†	1998

* Animated

\# Co-director with Andrew Adamson

† Co-director with Steve Hickner and Simon Wells

Bridget Jones: The Edge of Reason (2004), directed by Beeban Kidron, the highest-earning film by a British woman director, just fails to find a place in this Top 10. Kelly Asbury directed segments of *Shrek 2* (2004); if included, it would easily top this list.

Film Studios

A small group of studios once controlled the entire film industry, owning all production facilities and acting as producers, distributors and, before the 1950s, through their ownership of cinema chains, exhibitors. Some of the original studios no longer exist, while as a result of mergers and takeovers, most of the leading names are now components of large global media conglomerates operating alongside some newer independent studios, such as Artisan and Dimension, the specialist studio within Miramax. Today the studios are primarily financial and distribution organizations with the actual production undertaken by independent production companies – often more than one may be involved in a co-production. The films listed here represent the Top 10 productions distributed by each of the major studios based on US revenue. In many instances other companies acted as distributors outside the USA.

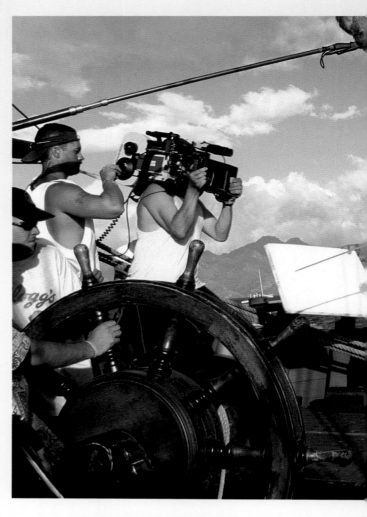

top 10 STUDIOS 2004

STUDIO	MARKET SHARE (PERCENTAGE)	TOTAL US GROSS 2004 ($)
1 Sony	14.3	1,342,300,000
2 Warner Bros.	13.0	1,223,500,000
3 Buena Vista	12.4	1,165,700,000
4 DreamWorks	9.9	935,300,000
5 20th Century Fox	9.9	929,500,000
6 Universal	9.8	918,700,000
7 Paramount	6.8	635,100,000
8 New Line	4.5	418,800,000
9 Newmarket	4.3	406,700,000
10 Miramax	4.0	373,800,000

top 10 20TH CENTURY FOX FILMS

FILM	YEAR
1 Star Wars*	1977
2 Star Wars: Episode I – The Phantom Menace	1999
3 Star Wars: Episode II – Attack of the Clones	2002
4 Star Wars: Episode VI – Return of the Jedi	1983
5 Independence Day	1996
6 Star Wars: Episode V – The Empire Strikes Back	1980
7 Home Alone	1990
8 Cast Away	2000
9 Mrs. Doubtfire	1993
10 X2: X-Men United	2003

* Later retitled *Star Wars: Episode IV – A New Hope*

William Fox, a New York nickelodeon owner, founded a film production company in 1912. At his California studios he created a number of popular movies, pioneering the use of sound, especially through the medium of Fox Movietone newsreels. The company was merged with 20th Century Pictures in 1935, and under the control of Darryl F. Zanuck and Joseph M. Schenck achieved some of its greatest successes in the 1940s, later producing *The Sound of Music* (1965) and *Star Wars* (1977).

top 10 SONY FILMS*

FILM	YEAR
1 Spider-Man	2002
2 Spider-Man 2	2004
3 Men in Black	1997
4 Ghostbusters	1984
5 Terminator 2: Judgment Day	1991
6 Men in Black II	2002
7 Tootsie	1982
8 Air Force One	1997
9 Big Daddy	1999
10 Jerry Maguire	1997

* Including Columbia and TriStar

top 10 BUENA VISTA FILMS

FILM*		YEAR
1	Pirates of the Caribbean: The Curse of the Black Pearl	2003
2	The Sixth Sense	1999
3	Signs	2002
4	Armageddon	1998
5	Pearl Harbor	2001
6	Pretty Woman	1990
7	Three Men and a Baby	1987
8	The Waterboy	1998
9	Who Framed Roger Rabbit?	1988
10	The Santa Clause	1994

* Excluding animated Disney features

Following Walt Disney's death in 1966, a new management team launched the company in novel directions, establishing Touchstone Pictures, a production company concentrating on films aimed at a more adult audience, with Buena Vista acting as the distributor for these and for Disney's animated films.

top 10 MIRAMAX FILMS

FILM*		YEAR
1	Chicago	2002
2	Scary Movie	2000
3	Good Will Hunting	1997
4	Spy Kids	2001
5	Pulp Fiction	1994
6	Shakespeare in Love	1998
7	The Others	2001
8	Cold Mountain	2003
9	The Talented Mr. Ripley	1999
10	The English Patient	1996

* Excluding Dimension films

Founded in 1979 by brothers Harvey and Bob Weinstein, Miramax is a production and distribution company that has been part of the Walt Disney Company since 1993. It continues to operate as a major force in achieving both critical acclaim and commercial success for releases that might otherwise have been disregarded as "art" films.

⬆ **Pirate treasure**
Pirates of the Caribbean is Buena Vista's most successful film.

➡ **Funny money**
DreamWorks' comedy *Meet the Fockers* is among its top earners.

top 10 DREAMWORKS FILMS

FILM		YEAR
1	Shrek 2*	2004
2	Shrek*	2001
3	Saving Private Ryan	1998
4	Meet the Fockers	2004
5	Gladiator	2000
6	Meet the Parents	2000
7	Catch Me if You Can	2003
8	Shark Tale*	2004
9	What Lies Beneath	2000
10	American Beauty	1999

* Animated

Animation

⬆ **Just incredible** Disney's latest smash hit *The Incredibles* has earned some $628 million around the world.

top 10 ANIMATED **OPENING WEEKENDS** IN THE UK

	FILM	UK RELEASE	OPENING WEEKEND GROSS (£)
1	Shrek 2	2 July 2004	16,220,752
2	The Incredibles	26 Nov 2004	9,874,782
3	Monsters, Inc.	8 Feb 2002	9,200,257
4	Toy Story 2	11 Feb 2000	7,971,539
5	Finding Nemo	10 Oct 2003	7,590,845
6	Shark Tale	15 Oct 2004	7,545,074
7	Shrek	29 June 2001	4,686,210
8	A Bug's Life	5 Feb 1999	4,204,678
9	Chicken Run	30 June 2000	3,488,755
10	Toy Story	22 Mar 1996	3,387,160

top 10 ANIMATED **FILM BUDGETS**

	FILM	YEAR	BUDGET ($)
1	The Polar Express	2004	150,000,000
2	Tarzan	1999	145,000,000
3	Treasure Planet	2002	140,000,000
4	Final Fantasy: The Spirits Within	2001	137,000,000
5	Dinosaur	2000	128,000,000
6	Monsters, Inc.	2001	115,000,000
7	Home on the Range	2004	110,000,000
8	The Emperor's New Groove	2000	100,000,000
9	The Road to El Dorado	2000	95,000,000
10	Finding Nemo	2003	94,000,000

Animated film budgets have risen progressively since *Snow White and the Seven Dwarfs* (1937) set a then record of $1.49 million. Budgets of $50 million or more have been commonplace since the 1990s, while *Tarzan* became the first to break through the $100 million barrier.

top 10 **WALT DISNEY** ANIMATED FEATURE FILMS

FILM	YEAR
1 Finding Nemo	2003
2 The Lion King	1994
3 The Incredibles	2004
4 Monsters, Inc.	2001
5 Aladdin	1992
6 Toy Story 2	1999
7 Tarzan	1999
8 Beauty and the Beast	1991
9 A Bug's Life	1998
10 Toy Story	1995

Within just a month of its 30 May 2003 release, *Finding Nemo* had earned more than $256 million at the US box office, and has more than trebled that figure since its international release. In addition to these high-earners (all of which have earned over $350 million worldwide), some of the studio's earlier productions, including *Bambi* (1942) and *Snow White and the Seven Dwarfs* (1937), are close runners-up.

the 10 **LATEST OSCAR-WINNING** ANIMATED FILMS*

YEAR	FILM	DIRECTOR / COUNTRY
2004	Ryan	Chris Landreth, USA
2003	Harvie Krumpet	Adam Elliot, Australia
2002	The ChubbChubbs!	Eric Armstrong, Canada
2001	For the Birds	Ralph Eggleston, USA
2000	Father and Daughter	Michael Dudok de Wit, Netherlands
1999	The Old Man and the Sea	Aleksandr Petrov, USA
1998	Bunny	Chris Wedge, USA
1997	Geri's Game	Jan Pinkava, USA
1996	Quest	Tyron Montgomery, UK
1995	Wallace & Gromit: A Close Shave	Nick Park, UK

* In the category "Short Films (Animated)"

Latest winner 14-minute short *Ryan* is the story of Canadian film animator Ryan Larkin, who himself won an Oscar in the same category for his *En Marchant* (1969).

⬇ On the line
Computer-animated DreamWorks film *Shark Tale* has earned over $337 million.

top 10 **NON-DISNEY** ANIMATED FEATURE FILMS

FILM	PRODUCTION COMPANY	YEAR
1 Shrek 2	DreamWorks	2004
2 Shrek	DreamWorks	2001
3 Ice Age	Fox Animation	2002
4 Shark Tale	DreamWorks	2004
5 Casper*	Amblin Entertainment	1995
6 The Polar Express	Castle Rock	2004
7 Spirited Away (Sento Chihiro no Kamikakushi)	Studio Ghibli	2001
8 Space Jam*	Warner Bros.	1996
9 Chicken Run	DreamWorks	2000
10 The Prince of Egypt	DreamWorks	1998

* Part animated, part live action

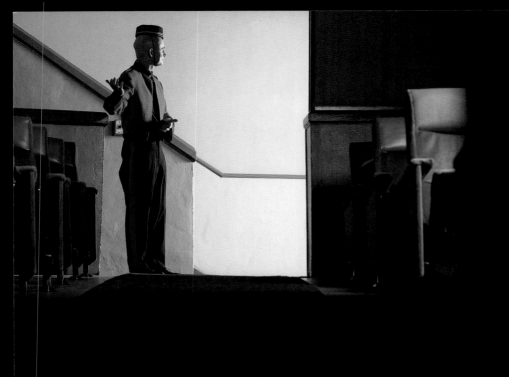

Movie Mosts

top 10 COUNTRIES WITH THE **MOST CINEMA ADMISSIONS** PER CAPITA

COUNTRY	ADMISSIONS PER CAPITA, 2003
1 USA	5.53
2 Iceland	5.40
3 Singapore	4.75
4 Ireland	4.56
5 New Zealand	4.49
6 Australia	4.45
7 Canada	3.83
8 Spain	3.43
9 India	3.15
10 Luxembourg	2.98
UK	*2.78*
World average	*1.14*

Source: *Screen Digest*

top 10 **CINEMA-GOING COUNTRIES** (TOTAL)

COUNTRY	TOTAL ATTENDANCE, 2003
1 India	3,420,000,000
2 USA	1,570,000,000
3 France	174,100,000
4 UK	167,200,000
5 Japan	162,300,000
6 Germany	149,000,000
7 Mexico	139,000,000
8 Spain	137,420,000
9 Canada	124,600,000
10 China	117,000,000
World	*7,261,070,000*

Source: *Screen Digest*

top 10 COUNTRIES WITH MOST **CINEMA SCREENS**

COUNTRY	SCREENS PER MILLION, 2003
1 Iceland	154.8
2 Sweden	130.8
3 USA	126.1
4 Spain	106.1
5 Australia	94.6
6 France	89.2
7 Norway	88.5
8 Canada	86.6
9 Ireland	86.0
10 Malta	84.4
UK	*57.0*
World average	*24.4*

Source: *Screen Digest*

top 10 **FILM-PRODUCING** COUNTRIES

	COUNTRY	FILMS PRODUCED, 2003
1	India	1,100
2	USA	593
3	Japan	287
4	France	212
5	UK	175
6	China	140
7	Italy	117
8	Spain	110
9	Germany	107
10	Bangladesh	96

Source: *Screen Digest*

Based on the number of full-length feature films produced, Hollywood's "golden age" was the 1920s and 1930s, with a peak of 854 films made in 1921, and its nadir reached in 1978 with just 354.

⊖ Hooray for Bollywood!
The Indian film industry's output overtook that of Hollywood as early as 1954, and – 50 years on – Bollywood produces almost twice as many feature films.

top 10 FILM **BUDGETS**

	FILM	YEAR	BUDGET ($)
1	The Chronicles of Narnia: The Lion, the Witch and the Wardrobe	2005	216,000,000*
2	= Battle Angel	2007#	200,000,000
	= Spider-Man 2	2004	200,000,000
	= Titanic	1997	200,000,000
5	Troy	2004	185,000,000
6	Waterworld	1995	175,000,000
7	= Terminator 3: Rise of the Machines	2003	170,000,000
	= Wild, Wild West	1999	170,000,000
9	Van Helsing	2004	160,000,000
10	Pearl Harbor	2001	152,700,000

* Budget reputedly NZ$292 million

\# Scheduled release

Battle Angel is *Titanic* director James Cameron's latest blockbuster, a science-fiction epic based on a graphic novel and containing an unprecedented array of state-of-the art CGI effects.

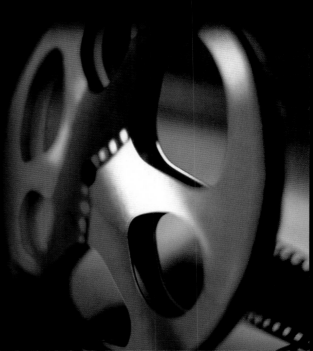

TV & Radio Listings

top 10 TELEVISION AUDIENCES IN THE UK, 2004

PROGRAMME*	CHANNEL	DATE	AUDIENCE
1 Euro 2004: Portugal v England	BBC1	24 June	20,664,000
2 Coronation Street	ITV1	16 Feb	16,328,000
3 I'm a Celebrity – Get Me Out of Here	ITV1	9 Feb	14,993,000
4 Eastenders	BBC1	5 Jan	14,797,000
5 A Touch of Frost	ITV1	22 Feb	12,965,000
6 The Vicar of Dibley	BBC1	25 Dec	12,524,000
7 Emmerdale	ITV1	2 Jan	11,760,000
8 Strictly Come Dancing	BBC1	11 Dec	11,595,000
9 Christmas Lights	ITV1	20 Dec	11,208,000
10 Heartbeat	ITV1	22 Feb	11,118,000

* Based on highest-rated episode only

Source: BARB/TNS Infosys

As with comparable world lists of the most-watched programmes, a crucial sporting event grabbed the year's biggest audience. Tragically, for the majority of its almost 21 million viewers, Portugal beat England 6-5 after a penalty shoot-out.

top 10 TELEVISION-OWNING COUNTRIES

COUNTRY	TVS PER 1,000 POPULATION, 2000
1 Qatar	869
2 USA	854
3 Denmark	807
4 Latvia	789
5 Australia	738
6 Japan	725
7 Canada	715
8 Finland	692
9 Norway	669
10 UK	653
World average	*270*

Source: International Telecommunication Union, *World Telecommunication Development Report 2002*

top 10 BBC RADIO 1 PROGRAMMES, 2004

SHOW

1 Chris Moyles
2 Jo Whiley
3 Colin and Edith
4 Scott Mills
5 Zane Lowe
6 Vernon Kaye
7 Nemone
8 Spoony
9 Radio 1 Chart Show
10 Pete Tong

Radio 1 attracts an 8.2 per cent share of listeners. Although individual presenter figures are not published, it is claimed that *The Chris Moyles Show* audience of those aged 4-plus is 7.6 million.

top 10 MOST POPULAR PROGRAMMES ON BBC RADIO 4

SHOW

1 Today
2 The Archers
3 PM
4 Six o'clock News
5 You and Yours
6 The World at One
7 Woman's Hour
8 Daily Service
9 Afternoon Play
10 Front Row

Radio 4's most popular programmes include several of its longest runners: *Today* was first broadcast on 28 October 1957, and *The Archers* on 1 January 1951.

top 10 RADIO-OWNING COUNTRIES

COUNTRY	RADIOS PER 1,000 POPULATION, 2001
1 Norway	3,324
2 Sweden	2,811
3 USA	2,117
4 Australia	1,999
5 Finland	1,624
6 UK	1,446
7 Denmark	1,400
8 Estonia	1,136
9 Canada	1,047
10 South Korea	1,034
World average	*419*

Source: World Bank, *World Development Indicators 2003*

top 10 **SATELLITE TELEVISION** COUNTRIES

COUNTRY	HOME SATELLITE ANTENNAE, 2002 (% OF TV-OWNING HOMES)
1 Algeria	92.2
2 Palestine	86.1
3 Burkina Faso	83.3
4 Bahrain	65.3
5 Saudi Arabia	64.3
6 Austria	48.0
7 Lebanon	45.0
8 Syria	44.8
9 Slovenia	43.5
10 Jordan	40.1
UK	*28.8*
World	*14.6*

Source: International Telecommunication Union, *World Telecommunication Development Report 2003*

➲ **Satellite country**
Algeria has adopted satellite TV with unrivalled enthusiasm, as the proliferation of receivers on this typical Algiers apartment block testifies.

top 10 **RADIO STATIONS** IN THE UK

STATION	AVERAGE WEEKLY LISTENER HOURS*
1 BBC Radio 2	172,139
2 BBC Radio 4	121,347
3 BBC Radio 1	85,895
4 Classic FM	46,527
5 BBC Radio FIVE LIVE	45,534
6 talkSPORT (Talk Radio)	17,221
7 BBC Radio 3	13,483
8 95.8 Capital FM	13,144
9 Magic 105.4	12,930
10 Heart 106.2 FM	11,243
All UK radio	*1, 051,075*

* Estimated total number of hours spent by all adults (over 15) listening to the station in an average week, based on sample audience for period 13 September to 12 December 2004

Source: RAJAR

DVD & Video

⬆ **Monster hit** The DVD release of *Shrek 2* mirrored the popularity of the film release, and earned almost twice as much as *Shrek*.

top 10 **DVDS RENTED** IN THE UK, 2004

TITLE

1 **Love Actually**
2 **Kill Bill: Volume 1**
3 **The Day After Tomorrow**
4 **The Last Samurai**
5 **Troy**
6 **The League of Extraordinary Gentlemen**
7 **Starsky & Hutch**
8 **Master and Commander: The Far Side of the World**
9 **Lost In Translation**
10 **Shaun of the Dead**

Source: British Video Association/MRIB

Love Actually's DVD release followed the box office success of the film, which had earned over £36 million.

top 10 **BESTSELLING DVDS** IN THE UK, 2004

TITLE

1 **The Lord of the Rings: The Return of the King**
2 **Shrek 2**
3 **Finding Nemo**
4 **Harry Potter and the Prisoner of Azkhaban**
5 **Love Actually**
6 **The Day After Tomorrow**
7 **Little Britain: Complete First Series**
8 **I Robot**
9 **Pirates of the Caribbean: The Curse of the Black Pearl**
10 **Star Wars Trilogy**

Source: British Video Association/The Official UK Charts Company

Each successive DVD release of *The Lord of the Rings* trilogy has topped the UK's annual chart.

top 10 **MOST-RENTED VIDEOS** IN THE UK*

TITLE / YEAR OF RELEASE

1 **Four Weddings and a Funeral**, 1994
2 **Dirty Dancing**, 1987
3 **Basic Instinct**, 1992
4 **Crocodile Dundee**, 1986
5 **Gladiator**, 1992
6 **Sister Act**, 1992
7 **Forrest Gump**, 1994
8 **The Sixth Sense**, 1999
9 **Home Alone**, 1990
10 **Ghost**, 1990

* To 1 Jan 2005; includes VHS and DVD

Source: British Video Association/MRIB

Following its international box office success, the British comedy *Four Weddings and a Funeral* was hugely popular on video at the end of 1994 and through much of 1995, when it overtook *Dirty Dancing*. The latter and *Crocodile Dundee* are the only pre-1990 films to have maintained a place in this list.

GAME /
PUBLISHER

1 **Grand Theft Auto: San Andreas**
Take 2

2 **FIFA 2005**
Electronic Arts

3 **Need For Speed: Underground 2**
Electronic Arts

4 **The Simpsons: Hit & Run**
Vivendi Universal Games

5 **Pro Evolution Soccer 4**
Konami

6 **Sonic Heroes**
Sega UK

7 **Spider-Man 2**
Activision

8 **Need For Speed: Underground**
Electronic Arts

9 **Halo 2**
Microsoft

10 **Driv3r**
Atari

Source: Entertainment and
Leisure Software Publishers
Association (ELSPA)

top 10 **BESTSELLING VIDEOS** IN THE UK*

TITLE / YEAR OF RELEASE

1 The Lord of the Rings: The Return of the King, 2004

2 Titanic, 1998

3 Shrek, 2001

4 The Lord of the Rings: The Two Towers, 2003

5 The Lion King, 1995

6 The Jungle Book, 1993

7 The Matrix, 1999

8 Snow White and the Seven Dwarfs, 1992

9 Toy Story, 1999

10 Gladiator, 2000

* To 1 Jan 2005; includes VHS and DVD formats

Source: British Video Association/The Official UK Charts Company

⬆ Game winners
The global success of video
game *Grand Theft Auto: San
Andreas* owes much to its
film-based style, featuring
the images and voices of
real stars, including Ice T.
and Samuel L. Jackson.

Chapter

78910

the 10 countries
consuming the most
energy: page 182

123456

Commercial World

top 10 richest countries: page 169

BANQUE

Workers

top 10 COMPANIES WITH THE MOST WORKERS

	COMPANY / BASE	INDUSTRY	EMPLOYEES*
1	**Wal-Mart Stores**, USA	Retail	1,400,000
2	**PetroChina**, China	Oil and gas	422,554
3	**China Petroleum and Chemical**, China	Oil and gas	418,871
4	**Siemens**, Germany	Conglomerates	417,000
5	**McDonald's**, USA	Fast food restaurants	413,000
6	**Carrefour**, France	Food markets	396,662
7	**DaimlerChrysler**, Germany	Automotives	370,677
8	**United Parcel Service**, USA	Transportation	360,000
9	**Ford Motor**, USA	Automotives	350,321
10	**General Motors**, USA	Automotives	350,000

* As at 13 Feb 2004

Source: *Forbes 2000*

This list excludes public-sector organizations and hence discounts the 1.6 million employed by the Indian railway network, the 1.3 million who work for the British National Health Service, and the almost 800,000 employees of the US Postal Service.

top 10 COUNTRIES WITH THE MOST WORKERS

	COUNTRY	WORKERS*, 2004 EST.
1	**China**	778,100,000
2	**India**	472,000,000
3	**USA**	146,500,000
4	**Indonesia**	105,700,000
5	**Brazil**	82,590,000
6	**Russia**	71,680,000
7	**Japan**	66,660,000
8	**Bangladesh**	64,020,000
9	**Nigeria**	54,360,000
10	**Vietnam**	45,740,000
	UK	*29,600,000*

* Based on people aged 15–64 who are currently employed; unpaid groups are not included

Source: Central Intelligence Agency

The International Labour Organization defines the "labour force" as people between the ages of 15 and 64 who are currently employed (excluding unpaid groups) or unemployed but seeking employment. In practice, it is difficult to count the unemployed accurately, especially in developing countries, so it may be just as difficult to know who is fully employed.

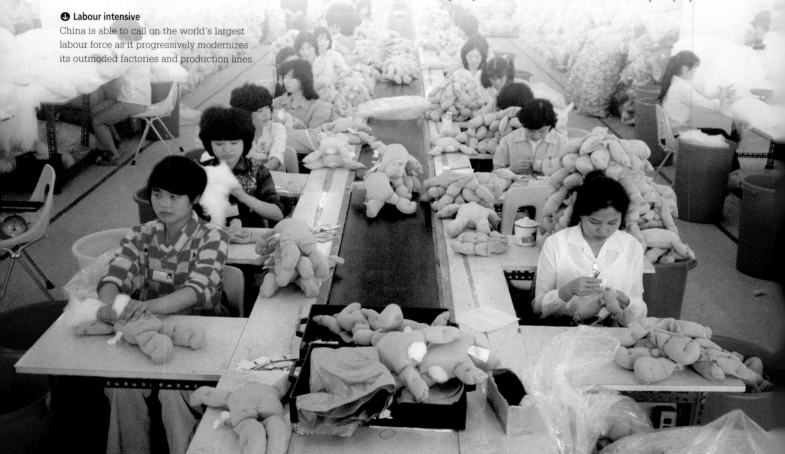

⬇ **Labour intensive**
China is able to call on the world's largest labour force as it progressively modernizes its outmoded factories and production lines.

Work force
Almost half the total world population – some 3 billion in total – are identified as economically productive workers.

top 10 COUNTRIES WITH **LOWEST** PROPORTION OF **ELDERLY PEOPLE** AT WORK

	COUNTRY	EST. PERCENTAGE OF OVER-74-YEAR-OLDS ECONOMICALLY ACTIVE*
1	Spain	0.2
2	Slovakia	0.4
3	France	0.5
4	Belgium	0.6
5	Germany	0.9
6	= Lithuania	1.1
	= Netherlands	1.1
8	Greece	1.2
9	Italy	1.4
10	Latvia	1.5
	UK (50 years and over)	*38.0*

* Excludes unpaid work; 2003 or latest for which data are available (some countries excluded because data are not collected for this age group)

Source: International Labour Organization

the 10 COUNTRIES WITH **HIGHEST** PROPORTION OF **ELDERLY PEOPLE** AT WORK

	COUNTRY	EST. PERCENTAGE OF OVER-74-YEAR-OLDS ECONOMICALLY ACTIVE*
1	Malawi	84.2
2	Ghana	52.9
3	Madagascar	52.1
4	Philippines	42.4
5	Papua New Guinea	40.5
6	Sudan	39.6
7	Rwanda	38.6
8	Dominican Republic	35.9
9	Bolivia	35.1
10	Georgia	31.7

* Excludes unpaid work; 2003 or latest for which data are available (some countries excluded because data are not collected for this age group)

Source: International Labour Organization

Cross-country comparisons of workers in terms of their ages are difficult because methods of collecting data vary from country-to-country.

top 10 COUNTRIES WITH THE **HIGHEST** PROPORTION OF **CHILD WORKERS**

	COUNTRY	PERCENTAGE OF 10–14-YEAR-OLDS AT WORK*, 2000
1	Mali	51.14
2	Bhutan	51.10
3	Burundi	48.50
4	Uganda	43.79
5	Niger	43.62
6	Burkina Faso	43.45
7	Ethiopia	42.45
8	Nepal	42.05
9	Rwanda	41.35
10	Kenya	39.15
	World average	*11.24*

* Excludes unpaid work

Source: International Labour Organization (ILO)

The ILO's International Programme on the Elimination of Child Labour (IPEC) estimates that some 29 per cent of children in Africa and 19 per cent in Asia are working.

The Global Economy

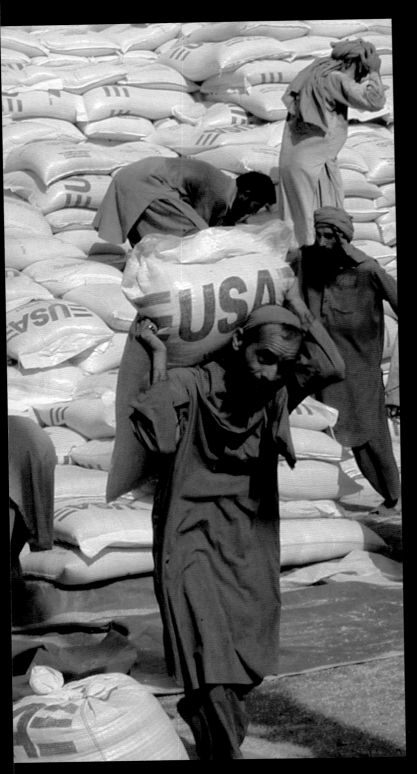

top 10 **AID** DONORS

	COUNTRY	NET ODA*, 2004 (% OF GNI#)	(TOTAL, $)
1	USA	0.16	18,999,000,000
2	Japan	0.19	8,859,000,000
3	France	0.42	8,475,000,000
4	UK	0.36	7,836,000,000
5	Germany	0.28	7,497,000,000
6	Netherlands	0.74	4,235,000,000
7	Sweden	0.77	2,704,000,000
8	Spain	0.26	2,547,000,000
9	Canada	0.26	2,537,000,000
10	Italy	0.15	2,484,000,000

* ODA = Official Development Assistance

GNI = Gross National Income

Source: Organisation for Economic Co-operation and Development (OECD)

The amounts the 30 full members of the OECD give in aid
ranges in terms both of overall totals and as a percentage
of each country's Gross National Income: Italy's and the
USA's contributions are the lowest and Norway (which
provided $2.2 billion in 2004) the highest at 0.87 per cent.

the 10 COUNTRIES **MOST IN DEBT**

	COUNTRY	EXTERNAL DEBT, 2002 (TOTAL, $)	(% OF GNI*)
1	Congo	5,152,000,000	228
2	Dem. Rep. of Congo	8,726,000,000	171
3	Zambia	5,969,000,000	127
4	Angola	10,134,000,000	120
5	Syria	21,504,000,000	117
6	Burundi	1,204,000,000	110
7	Sierra Leone	1,448,000,000	103
8	= Lebanon	17,077,000,000	102
	= Serbia and Montenegro	12,688,000,000	102
10	Ecuador	16,452,000,000	95

* GNI = Gross National Income

Source: World Bank, *World Development Indicators 2005*

Expressed as a percentage of their Gross National Income,
these countries stand out, but in terms of total external
debt (the amount owed to foreign agencies, rather than
their domestic banking sector), certain countries have even
higher levels, among them Brazil at $228 billion, China
$168 billion, Russia $147 billion, and Mexico $141 billion.

top 10 FASTEST-GROWING ECONOMIES

	COUNTRY	GDP* PER CAPITA, 2002 ($)	ANNUAL GROWTH RATE, 1990–2002 (%)
1	Equatorial Guinea	4,394	20.8
2	Bosnia and Herzegovina	1,362	18.0
3	China	989	8.6
4	Ireland	30,982	6.8
5	Albania	1,535	6.0
6	Vietnam	436	5.9
7 =	Maldives	2,182	4.7
=	South Korea	10,006	4.7
9	Mozambique	195	4.5
10	Chile	4,115	4.4
	UK	*26,444*	*2.4*
	World average	*5,174*	*1.2*

* Gross Domestic Product

Source: United Nations, *Human Development Indicators 2004*

top 10 AREAS OF UK GOVERNMENT EXPENDITURE

	DEPARTMENT	ESTIMATED EXPENDITURE, 2004–05 (£)
1	Health	69,118,000,000
2	Local Government	43,351,000,000
3	Defence	32,591,000,000
4	Education and Skills	24,613,000,000
5	Scotland	19,961,000,000
6	Home Office	12,293,000,000
7	Wales	10,689,000,000
8	Work and Pensions	8,391,000,000
9	Transport	8,277,000,000
10	Northern Ireland Executive	6,977,000,000
	Total estimated expenditure	*268,687,000,000*

Source: HM Treasury

the 10 POOREST COUNTRIES

	COUNTRY	GDP* PER CAPITA, 2002 ($)
1	Sierra Leone	520
2 =	Malawi	580
=	Tanzania	580
4	Burundi	630
5	Dem. Rep. of Congo	650
6	Guinea-Bissau	710
7	Madagascar	740
8	Ethiopia	780
9	Niger	800
10	Zambia	840

* GDP = Gross Domestic Product

Source: United Nations, *Human Development Indicators 2004*

First Fact The first credit card was issued in 1950 in the USA by Diners Club, the brainchild of Frank X. McNamara. Initially, just 200 cards were issued, allowing holders to use them to pay for meals in 14 New York restaurants. Within a year, the numbers had expanded to 20,000 customers and 1,000 restaurants.

top 10 RICHEST COUNTRIES

	COUNTRY	GDP* PER CAPITA, 2002 ($)
1	Luxembourg	47,354
2	Norway	41,974
3	Switzerland	36,687
4	USA	36,006
5	Denmark	32,179
6	Japan	31,407
7	Ireland	30,982
8	Iceland	29,749
9	Qatar	28,634
10	Sweden	26,929
	UK	*26,444*
	World average	*5,174*

* GDP = Gross Domestic Product

Source: United Nations, *Human Development Indicators 2004*

➲ De Luxe
Despite being one of the world's smallest countries, Luxembourg enjoys enviable economic prosperity.

Personal Wealth

top 10 RICHEST AMERICANS

	NAME	SOURCE	NET WORTH ($)
1	William H. Gates III	Microsoft	46,500,000,000
2	Warren Edward Buffett	Berkshire Hathaway	44,000,000,000
3	Paul Gardner Allen	Microsoft	21,000,000,000
4	Lawrence Joseph Ellison	Oracle	18,400,000,000
5	S. Robson Walton	Wal-Mart	18,300,000,000
6	=Jim C. Walton	Wal-Mart	18,200,000,000
	=John T. Walton	Wal-Mart	18,200,000,000
8	=Alice L. Walton	Wal-Mart	18,000,000,000
	=Helen R. Walton	Wal-Mart	18,000,000,000
10	Michael Dell	Dell	16,000,000,000

Source: *Forbes Billionaires List 2005*

The estimated net worth of the world's richest man William Henry Gates III, the co-founder of Microsoft, has increased by a factor of 18.6 since he entered the Top 10 in 1990 with assets of "only" $2.5 billion. The Bill & Melinda Gates Foundation he set up in 2000 with his wife provides over $1 billion a year to health and other causes, especially in the Third World.

top 10 RICHEST BRITISH PEOPLE

	NAME	SOURCE	NET WORTH ($)
1	Philip and Cristina Green	Retail	6,300,000,000
2	Duke of Westminster and family	Land and property	5,600,000,000
3	Lord Sainsbury and family	Retail	4,300,000,000
4	Bernie Ecclestone and family	Formula One motor racing	3,600,000,000
5	David and Frederick Barclay	Property, retail, and media	3,400,000,000
6	Richard Branson	Travel, retail, and entertainment	3,200,000,000
7	Earl Cadogan and family	Property	2,700,000,000
8	Clive Calder	Record label	2,300,000,000
9	Bruno Schroder and family	Banking	2,000,000,000
10	John Whittaker	Real estate	1,700,000,000

Source: *Forbes Billionaires List 2005*

According to *Forbes* magazine, British Home Stores, and Arcadia Group owners Philip and Cristina Green are the richest people in Britain, but 68th in the world. Like the Gates Foundation in the USA, the Philip Green Memorial Trust aids children with illnesses.

top 10 HIGHEST-EARNING CELEBRITIES

	CELEBRITY	PROFESSION	EARNINGS* ($)
1	=Mel Gibson	Film producer/director	210,000,000
	=Oprah Winfrey	Talk show host/producer	210,000,000
3	J.K. Rowling	Author	147,000,000
4	=Michael Schumacher	Racing driver	80,000,000
	=Tiger Woods	Golfer	80,000,000
6	Steven Spielberg	Film producer/director	75,000,000
7	Jim Carrey	Actor	66,000,000
8	Bruce Springsteen	Musician	64,000,000
9	Nora Roberts (J.D. Robb)	Author	60,000,000
10	David Copperfield	Magician	57,000,000

* June 2003–June 2004

Source: *Forbes, The Celebrity 100*, 2004

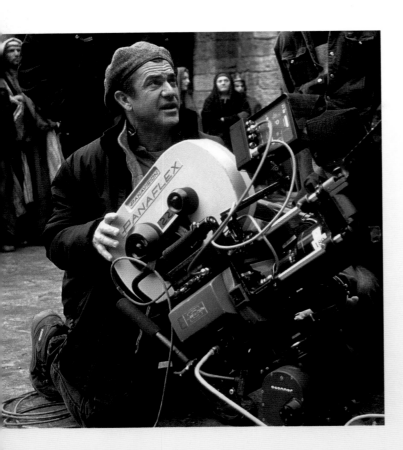

☉ Mel's wealth

Mel Gibson has long figured prominently in the celebrity earnings league table, but the huge success of *The Passion of The Christ* (2004) which he directed propelled him to the top alongside Oprah Winfrey, who has headed the list for many years.

top 10 RICHEST **NON-AMERICANS**

NAME / COUNTRY	SOURCE	NET WORTH ($)
1 **Lakshmi Mittal**, India	Steel	25,000,000,000
2 **Carlos Slim Helu**, Mexico	Telecom	23,800,000,000
3 **Prince Alwaleed Bin Talal Alsaud**, Saudi Arabia	Investments	23,700,000,000
4 **Ingvar Kamprad**, Sweden	Ikea	23,000,000,000
5 **Karl Albrecht**, Germany	Retail	18,500,000,000
6 **Kenneth Thomson and family**, Canada	Publishing	17,900,000,000
7 **Liliane Bettencourt**, France	L'Oréal	17,200,000,000
8 **Bernard Arnault**, France	LVMH	17,000,000,000
9 **Theo Albrecht**, Germany	Retail	15,500,000,000
10 **Roman Abramovich**, Russia	Oil	13,300,000,000

Source: *Forbes Billionaires List 2005*

➔ Roman emperor
The oil and other business interests of Roman Abramovich have made him the richest Russian and 21st richest person in the world.

First Fact John D. Rockefeller (1839–1937) was the first ever billionaire. From modest beginnings, he founded Standard Oil (Esso) and became the world's richest man. Despite giving away over $500 million during his lifetime, at his death Rockefeller was reckoned to be worth $1.4 billion, the equivalent to 1/65th of the entire Gross National Income of the USA. In modern money, such a proportion of the USA's GNI would be worth some $200 billion, dwarfing the fortunes of today's mega-rich.

top 10 RICHEST **RUSSIANS**

NAME	SOURCE	NET WORTH ($)
1 **Roman Abramovich**	Oil	13,300,000,000
2 = **Mikhail Fridman**	Oil and banking	7,000,000,000
= **Vladimir Lisin**	Steel	7,000,000,000
4 **Oleg Deripaska**	Manufacturing	5,500,000,000
5 **Viktor Vekselberg**	Oil and metals	5,000,000,000
6 **Alexei Mordashov**	Steel	4,800,000,000
7 = **Vladimir Potanin**	Metals	4,400,000,000
= **Mikhail Prokhorov**	Metals	4,400,000,000
9 **Vagit Alekperov**	Oil	4,300,000,000
10 **Victor Rashnikov**	Iron and steel	3,600,000,000

Source: *Forbes Billionaires List 2005*

Since the collapse of the Soviet Union and the privatization of its industries, a new breed of Russian oligarchs has emerged. Several of these multi-billionaires, including Abramovich, Deripaska, and Mordahshov, are aged under 40.

Diamonds & Gold

top 10 COUNTRIES WITH THE **MOST GOLD**

COUNTRY	GOLD RESERVES* (TROY OUNCES)	(TONNES)
1 USA	261,584,525	8,136.2
2 Germany	110,389,783	3,433.2
3 France	95,738,354	2,977.8
4 Italy	78,827,086	2,451.8
5 Switzerland	42,827,947	1,332.1
6 Netherlands	24,675,662	767.5
7 Japan	24,601,715	765.2
8 China	19,290,420	600.0
9 Spain	16,824,461	523.3
10 Portugal	14,863,268	462.3

* As at March 2005

Source: World Gold Council

Gold reserves are the government holdings of gold in each country – which are often far greater than the gold owned by private individuals. In the days of the "Gold Standard", this provided a tangible measure of a country's wealth, guaranteeing the convertibility of its currency, and determined such factors as exchange rates. Though less significant today, gold reserves remain a component in calculating a country's international reserves, alongside its holdings of foreign exchange and SDRs (Special Drawing Rights).

top 10 **GOLD-PRODUCING** COUNTRIES

COUNTRY	2003 PRODUCTION (TROY OUNCES)	(TONNES)
1 South Africa	13,316,820	375.8
2 USA	10,108,180	285.2
3 Australia	10,050,308	283.6
4 China	7,552,199	213.1
5 Russia	6,462,290	182.3
6 Peru	6,082,912	171.6
7 Indonesia	5,764,620	162.7
8 Canada	2,835,691	140.5
10 Ghana	2,491,679	70.3
World	*91,828,829*	*2,593.1*

Source: Gold Fields Mineral Services Ltd., Gold Survey 2004

As reported by Gold Fields Mineral Services Ltd., output by world-dominating gold producer South Africa experienced a decline for the tenth consecutive year since its 1993 all-time high of 619.5 tonnes. Australia's output increased again in 2003 for the first time since 1999: the country's record annual production had stood at 119 tonnes since 1903, but in 1988 rocketed to 152 tonnes, peaking at 313.2 tonnes in 1997.

top 10 **DIAMOND PRODUCERS** BY VOLUME

COUNTRY	VALUE, 2003 ($)	VOLUME, 2003 (CARATS)
1 Australia	417,000,000	30,994,000
2 Botswana	2,489,000,000	30,412,000
3 Dem. Rep. of Congo	686,000,000	29,000,000
4 Russia	1,600,000,000	19,000,000
5 South Africa	1,100,000,000	12,400,000
6 Canada	1,240,000,000	11,200,000
7 Angola	1,100,000,000	6,300,000
8 Namibia	474,000,000	1,550,000
9 Ghana	23,000,000	900,000
10 Brazil	83,000,000	700,000

Source: De Beers

top 10 MOST EXPENSIVE SINGLE DIAMONDS*

	DIAMOND / DETAILS	SALE	PRICE
1	Star of the Season, pear-shaped 100.10 carat D# IF† diamond	Sotheby's, Geneva, 17 May 1995	£10,548,444 (SF19,858,500)
2	Star of Happiness, cut cornered rectangular-cut 36 carat D# IF† diamond	Sotheby's, Geneva, 17 Nov 1993	£8,183,425 (SF17,823,500)
3	The Mouawad Splendor, pear-shaped 101.84 carat D# IF† diamond	Sotheby's, Geneva, 14 Nov 1990	£6,510,002 (SF15,950,000)
4	Fancy blue emerald-cut 20.17 carat diamond VS2†	Sotheby's, New York, 18 Oct 1994	£6,145,277 ($9,902,500)
5	Eternal Light, pear-shaped 85.91 carat D# IF† diamond	Sotheby's, New York, 19 Apr 1988	£4,793,909 ($9,130,000)
6	Rectangular-cut fancy deep-blue 13.49 carat diamond IF†	Christie's, New York, 13 Apr 1995	£4,679,487 ($7,482,500)
7	Fancy pink rectangular-cut 19.66 carat diamond VVS2†	Christie's, Geneva, 17 Nov 1994	£4,675,017 (SF9,573,500)
8	The Jeddah Bride, rectangular-cut 80.02 carat D# IF† diamond	Sotheby's, New York, 24 Oct 1991	£4,185,203 ($7,150,000)
9	The Agra Diamond, fancy light pink cushion-shaped 32.24 carat diamond VS1†	Christie's, London, 20 June 1990	£4,070,000
10	Rectangular-cut 52.59 carat D# IF† diamond	Christie's, New York, 20 Apr 1988	£3,953,488 ($7,480,000)

* Sold at auction; price conversion calculated on rate prevailing at time of sale

\# A colour grade given to a diamond for its whiteness, D being the highest grade

† A clarity grade, which gives the relative position of a diamond on a flawless-to-imperfect scale: IF = internally flawless, VS = very slightly flawed, VVS = very, very slightly flawed; the numbers indicate the degree of the flaw

Saudi jeweller Sheikh Ahmed Hassan Fitaihi, also the owner of the Jeddah Bride (named after his home town) at No.8, fought off competing buyers to establish a new world record with his acquisition of the flawless Star of the Season, and has since declined even higher private offers for the unique gem. The 100.10-carat diamond weighs only 8 carats less than the famed Koh-I-Noor of the British Crown Jewels, and is one of few diamonds of over 100 carats ever to be auctioned.

Fast Fact

The Cullinan diamond – the largest ever discovered – was found by Frederick Wells in 1905 at the Premier Mine, South Africa and named after Sir Thomas Cullinan, the President of diamond company De Beers. About 5 inches (12.7 cm) across and weighing 3,106 carats, it was presented to King Edward VII on his 66th birthday in 1907 and the following year was cut by Dutch expert Joseph Asscher – producing 105 separate gems. The most important of these are now among the British Crown Jewels and include the 530.2-carat Great Star of Africa – the largest cut diamond in the world – which is mounted in the royal sceptre, and the 317.40-carat Second Star of Africa, set in the Imperial State Crown beneath the Black Prince's Ruby.

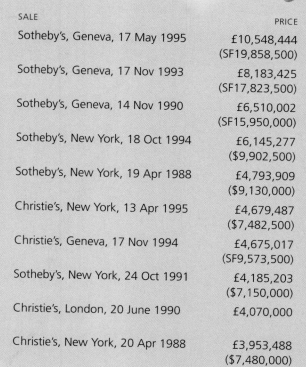

top 10 COUNTRIES THAT
SPEND THE MOST
ON ADVERTISING

($)

1 US $155,000,000,000

2 Japan $37,000,000,000

3 China $23,000,000,000

4 GERMANY $19,000,000,000

5 UK $14,000,000,000

6 France $11,000,000,000

7 Italy $8,000,000,000

8 = Canada $6,000,000,000

= Spain $6,000,000,000

10 = AUSTRALIA $5,000,000,000

= Brazil $5,000,000,000

* BY FORECAST ADVERTISING EXPENDITURE
SOURCE: *INITIATIVE GLOBAL ADEX 2004*

top 10 COUNTRIES IN WHICH COCA-COLA IS THE **TOP COLA BRAND**

	COUNTRY	PERCENTAGE OF TOTAL STANDARD COLA MARKET
1	Morocco	86.5
2	Indonesia	86.3
3	Bulgaria	81.3
4	Greece	77.4
5	Chile	76.2
6	Brazil	75.2
7	Mexico	73.7
8	Singapore	72.2
9	Japan	69.5
10	France	65.2
	UK	*26.1*
	World average	*46.2*

Source: Euromonitor

top 10 **WORLD RETAIL** SECTORS

	SECTOR	NO. OF COMPANIES*
1	Speciality	108
2	Supermarket	96
3	Department	56
4	Convenience	50
5	Discount	48
6	Superstore	40
7	Hypermarket	37
8	Cash and carry	25
9	Drug	23
10	DIY	22

* Of those listed in *Stores' Top 250 Global Retailers*; stores can operate in more than one area

Source: *Stores* magazine

➔ Great Wal-Mart of China
In 1996, American retail giant Wal-Mart opened its first store in China in Shenzen. By 2004 its sales in China were £477.1 million ($917.75 million), and by March 2005 it had opened 44 outlets.

top 10 **GLOBAL** MARKETERS

	COMPANY / BASE	MEASURED ADVERTISING* SPENDING, 2003 ($)
1	Procter & Gamble Company, USA	5,762,000,000
2	Unilever, Netherlands/UK	3,540,000,000
3	General Motors Corporation, USA	3,412,000,000
4	Toyota Motor Corporation, Japan	2,669,000,000
5	Ford Motor Company, USA	2,537,000,000
6	Time Warner, USA	2,378,000,000
7	DaimlerChrysler, Germany/USA	2,230,000,000
8	L'Oréal, France	2,180,000,000
9	Nestlé, Switzerland	1,737,000,000
10	Sony Corporation, Japan	1,684,000,000

* Includes magazine, newspaper, outdoor, television, radio, Internet, and *Yellow Pages* advertising

Source: Ad Age Global

⊖ Brand awareness
Coca-Cola and other high-profile brands represent the very public face of globalization with advertising displays all around the world.

top 10 **GLOBAL** RETAILERS

	COMPANY / BASE	RETAIL SALES, 2003* ($)
1	Wal-Mart Stores, Inc., USA	256,329,000,000
2	Carrefour, France	79,796,000,000
3	Home Depot, Inc., USA	64,816,000,000
4	METRO AG, Germany	60,503,000,000
5	Kroger Co., USA	51,760,000,000
6	Tesco plc, UK	51,535,000,000
7	Target Corp., USA	46,781,000,000
8	Ahold, Netherlands	44,584,000,000
9	Costco Wholesale Corp., USA	41,693,000,000
10	Aldi Einkauf GmbH & Co., Germany	40,060,000,000

* Financial year

Source: *Stores* magazine, *2005 Global Powers of Retailing*

A survey of the Top 250 global retailers, all of which had sales of $2.2 billion or more, showed that 41.6 per cent were based in the USA, 14.0 in Japan, and 9.6 in the UK – although all those in the top 10, other than Kroger and Target, also operate in other countries. The USA took 47.7 per cent of sales by value, Germany 11.0, France 9.7, and the UK 8.5.

TOP 10 MOST VALUABLE GLOBAL BRANDS

BRAND NAME / COUNTRY OF OWNERSHIP*	INDUSTRY	BRAND VALUE 2004 ($)
1 Coca-Cola	Beverages	67,394,000,000
2 Microsoft	Technology	61,372,000,000
3 IBM	Technology	53,791,000,000
4 General Electric	Diversified	44,111,000,000
5 Intel	Technology	33,499,000,000
6 Disney	Leisure	27,113,000,000
7 McDonald's	Food retail	25,001,000,000
8 Nokia, Finland	Technology	24,041,000,000
9 Toyota, Japan	Automobiles	22,673,000,000
10 Marlboro	Tobacco	22,128,000,000

* All US-owned unless otherwise stated

Source: Interbrand/*BusinessWeek*

Brand consultants Interbrand use a method of estimating value that takes account of the profitability of individual brands within a business (rather than the companies that own them – thus a parent company such as Procter & Gamble does not figure), as well as such factors as their potential for growth. Airlines are also disqualified from the Interbrand rankings. The year 2004 saw several accessions to the Top 100, including Siemens, eBay, Audi, Cartier, and Armani, while Apple experienced a rise in its ranking as a result of the global success of the iPod digital music player. Some 58 of the 100 most valuable global brands surveyed are US-owned, with Europe accounting for 34, Japan seven, and South Korea just one.

➔ **Multi-national brands**
Finnish electronics giant Nokia sponsors curling in Canada, Coca-Cola is promoted in Poland, and McDonalds conquers the Japanese market, illustrating the global diversity of the world's most powerful brands.

Food

top 10 EGG CONSUMERS

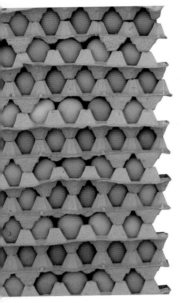

	COUNTRY	AVERAGE CONSUMPTION PER CAPITA, 2002 (KG)	(LB / OZ)	
1	Japan	19.1	42	1
2	China	17.4	38	5
3	Hungary	17.0	37	7
4	Denmark	16.4	36	2
5	Brunei	16.3	35	14
6	Mexico	16.0	35	4
7	Netherlands	15.6	34	6
8	France	15.3	33	11
9	USA	14.6	32	2
10	Spain	14.3	31	8
	UK	*11.6*	*25*	*9*
	World average	*8.4*	*18*	*8*

Source: Food and Agriculture Organization of the United Nations

top 10 VEGETABLE CONSUMERS

	COUNTRY	AVERAGE CONSUMPTION PER CAPITA, 2002 (KG)	(LB / OZ)	
1	Cuba	266.6	587	12
2	China	254.1	560	3
3	Greece	245.5	541	3
4	Israel	227.8	502	3
5	Turkey	224.3	494	7
6	Lebanon	224.1	494	0
7	Libya	222.9	491	6
8	United Arab Emirates	217.7	479	15
9	Macedonia	215.3	474	10
10	South Korea	209.2	461	3
	UK	*89.2*	*196*	*10*
	World average	*114.1*	*251*	*8*

Source: Food and Agriculture Organization of the United Nations

top 10 MEAT CONSUMERS

	COUNTRY	AVERAGE CONSUMPTION PER CAPITA, 2002 (KG)	(LB / OZ)	
1	USA	124.1	273	9
2	Spain	118.5	261	3
3	Denmark	114.1	251	8
4	Austria	111.2	245	2
5 =	Australia	108.8	239	13
=	Mongolia	108.8	239	13
7	New Zealand	106.7	235	3
8	Cyprus	104.1	229	8
9	France	102.3	225	8
10	Canada	100.5	221	9
	UK	*80.7*	*177*	*14*
	World average	*39.3*	*86*	*10*

Source: Food and Agriculture Organization of the United Nations

top 10 FISH CONSUMERS

	COUNTRY	AVERAGE CONSUMPTION PER CAPITA*, 2002 (KG)	(LB / OZ)	
1	Maldives	185.9	409	13
2	Samoa	91.6	201	15
3	Iceland	91.0	200	9
4	Kiribati	75.2	165	12
5	Japan	66.3	146	2
6	Seychelles	62.0	136	10
7	Lithuania	59.8	131	13
8	Portugal	59.3	130	11
9	South Korea	58.7	129	6
10	Malaysia	57.0	125	10
	UK	*23.2*	*51*	*2*
	World average	*16.3*	*35*	*14*

* Marine only

Source: Food and Agriculture Organization of the United Nations

The majority of the fish consumed comes from the sea. The average annual consumption of freshwater fish is 4.7 kg (10 lb 5 oz), with the largest consumers being Norway, whose population consume 26 kg (57 lb 5 oz) of freshwater fish per capita per annum.

top 10 **FOODS CONSUMED** IN THE UK*

ITEM / AVERAGE WEEKLY
CONSUMPTION PER HEAD (G / LB OZ)

Milk, cream, and milk products
2,049 g / 4 lb 8 oz

Meat and meat products
1,039 g / 2 lb 4 oz

Fresh fruit 794 g / 1 lb 12 oz

Bread 756 g / 1 lb 10 oz

Fresh vegetables
(excluding potatoes) 736 g / 1 lb 9 oz

Fresh potatoes 617 g / 1 lb 5 oz

Processed vegetables
(including processed potatoes) 613 g / 1 lb 5 oz

8

Flour and other cereals or cereal products#
511 g / 1 lb 2 oz

9

Processed fruit and nuts 413 g / 0 lb 14 oz

10

Cakes and biscuits 337 g / 0 lb 11 oz

* By weight

\# Excluding bread, cakes, and biscuits

Source: Department of Environment,
Food and Rural Affairs (DEFRA),
Expenditure and Food Survey 2002–2003

top 10 **BREAKFAST** CEREAL CONSUMERS

COUNTRY	AVERAGE CONSUMPTION PER CAPITA, 2004 (KG)	(LB / OZ)	
1 **UK**	8.0	17	10
2 **Sweden**	7.7	16	15
3 **Australia**	7.5	16	8
4 **Finland**	6.7	14	12
5 **Canada**	6.1	13	7
6 **Ireland**	5.6	12	5
7 **USA**	5.4	11	14
8 **New Zealand**	5.0	11	0
9 **Denmark**	3.8	8	6
10 **Norway**	3.7	8	2

Source: Euromonitor

top 10 **RICE** CONSUMERS

COUNTRY	AVERAGE CONSUMPTION PER CAPITA*, 2002 (KG)	(LB / OZ)	
1 **Myanmar**	306.9	676	9
2 **Vietnam**	253.3	558	6
3 **Laos**	251.5	554	7
4 **Bangladesh**	245.4	541	0
5 **Cambodia**	223.2	492	1
6 **Indonesia**	222.6	490	11
7 **Philippines**	156.8	345	10
8 **Thailand**	153.8	339	1
9 **Nepal**	152.8	336	13
10 **Madagascar**	143.1	315	7
UK	*4.1*	*9*	*0*
World average	*85.9*	*189*	*6*

* Paddy equivalent

Source: Food and Agriculture Organization of the United Nations

Rice is the staple diet of more than half the world's population. Perhaps surprisingly, given that it has been cultivated since ancient times and the place of rice in its cuisine, China does not figure in the Top 10 – its annual consumption is reckoned at 124.1 kg (273 lb 9 oz) per capita – while that of Japan is only fractionally greater than the world average.

◉ National diet
Despite nutritional concerns, milk continues to feature prominently in the shopping basket of the average British consumer.

Drinks

top 10 COFFEE DRINKERS
COUNTRY / CONSUMPTION PER CAPITA, 2003 (KG / LB OZ / CUPS*)

1 Finland 11.21 kg / 24 lb 11 oz / 1,681 cups

2 Belgium and Luxembourg 9.60 kg / 21 lb 2 oz / 1,440 cups

3 Norway 8.95 kg / 19 lb 11 oz / 1,342 cups

4 Denmark 8.10 kg / 17 lb 13 oz / 1,215 cups

5 Sweden 7.88 kg / 17 lb 6 oz / 1,182 cups

6 Switzerland 6.90 kg / 15 lb 3 oz / 1,035 cups

7 Netherlands 6.76 kg / 14 lb 14 oz / 1,014 cups

8 Germany 6.64 kg / 14 lb 10 oz / 996 cups

9 Greece 6.01 kg / 13 lb 4 oz / 901 cups

10 Italy 5.73 kg / 12 lb 10 oz / 859 cups

UK 2.20 kg / 4 lb 13 oz / 330 cups

* Based on 150 cups per kg (2 lb 3 oz)
Source: International Coffee Organization

top 10 TEA DRINKERS
COUNTRY / ANNUAL CONSUMPTION PER CAPITA* (KG / LB OZ / CUPS#)

1 Ireland 2.96 kg / 6 lb 8 oz / 1,302 cups

2 Libya 2.92 kg / 6 lb 7 oz / 1,284 cups

3 Qatar 2.89 kg / 6 lb 6 oz / 1,271 cups

4 Iraq 2.42 kg / 5 lb 5 oz / 1,064 cups

5 Kuwait 2.29 kg / 5 lb 0 oz / 1,007 cups

6 UK 2.24 kg / 4 lb 15 oz / 985 cups

7 Turkey 1.98 kg / 4 lb 5 oz / 871 cups

8 Afghanistan 1.84 kg / 4 lb 0 oz / 809 cups

9 Syria 1.62 kg / 3 lb 9 oz / 712 cups

10 Morocco 1.42 kg / 3 lb 2 oz / 624 cups

* 2001–2003
# Based on 440 cups per kg (2 lb 3 oz)
Source: International Tea Committee Ltd, London

top 10 **WINE** DRINKERS

COUNTRY	CONSUMPTION PER CAPITA, 2003 (LITRES)	(PINTS)
1 Luxembourg	66.1	116.3*
2 France	48.5	85.3
3 Italy	47.5	83.6
4 Portugal	42.0	73.9*
5 Switzerland	40.9	72.0
6 Hungary	37.4	65.8*
7 Argentina	34.6	60.9
8 Greece	33.8	59.5*
9 Uruguay	33.3	58.6*
10 Denmark	32.6	57.4*
UK	20.1	35.3

* Estimated from wine production data due to lack of consumption data

Source: Commission for Distilled Spirits

Since 1970, wine consumption has increased by almost 600 per cent in the UK. In contrast, in France, people have been drinking less: wine consumption per person peaked at 127.3 litres (224.0 pints) in 1963, since then it has fallen by 62 per cent.

top 10 **BEER** DRINKERS

COUNTRY	CONSUMPTION PER CAPITA, 2003 (LITRES)	(PINTS)
1 Czech Republic	157.0	276.3*
2 Ireland	141.2	248.5
3 Germany	117.5	206.8
4 Austria	110.6	194.6
5 Luxembourg	101.6	178.8
6 UK	101.5	178.6
7 =Belgium	96.2	169.3
=Denmark	96.2	169.3
9 Australia	91.5	161.0*
10 Slovak Republic	88.4	155.6*

* Estimated from beer production data due to lack of consumption data

Source: Commission for Distilled Spirits

Despite its position as the world's leading producer of beer, the USA's consumption is ranked in 12th position. In African countries, many people do drink a lot of beer, but as bottled beer is often prohibitively expensive, they tend to consume home-made beers sold in local markets and hence excluded from national statistics.

top 10 **SOFT DRINK** CONSUMERS

COUNTRY	CONSUMPTION PER CAPITA, 2003* (LITRES)	(PINTS)
1 USA	330.0	580.9
2 Mexico	293.3	516.3
3 Spain	282.1	496.6
4 Belgium	275.2	484.5
5 Germany	261.6	460.5
6 Italy	250.3	440.6
7 Switzerland	249.9	439.9
8 Austria	247.5	435.7
9 France	223.6	393.6
10 Canada	213.7	376.2
UK	158.3	278.6
World	64.4	113.3

* In those countries for which data available

Source: Euromonitor

➲ **Wine growth**
The identities of the world's leading wine consumers have shifted, with three of those outside the Top 10, Japan, Finland, and the UK, experiencing the greatest increases in the past three decades.

top 10 **BOTTLED WATER** DRINKERS

COUNTRY	CONSUMPTION PER CAPITA, 2003 (LITRES)	(PINTS)
1 Italy	177.1	311.7
2 Spain	156.7	275.8
3 France	152.5	268.4
4 Mexico	152.1	267.7
5 Belgium	130.1	229.0
6 Germany	118.6	208.7
7 Switzerland	112.0	197.1
8 Austria	98.0	172.4
9 Portugal	96.8	170.3
10 Argentina	81.4	143.2
UK	28.7	50.5
World average	22.9	40.3

Source: Euromonitor

Worldwide consumption of bottled mineral water has more than doubled in the past decade, hitting a 2003 total of 144.5 billion litres. Although its total consumption of 18.3 billion litres makes it the world's leading overall consumer, on a per capita basis the USA remains unusually absent from the Top 10.

Energy & Environment

the 10 COUNTRIES CONSUMING THE MOST ENERGY

COUNTRY	(OIL)	(GAS)	ENERGY CONSUMPTION, 2003* (COAL)	(NUCLEAR)	(HEP#)	(TOTAL)
1 USA	914.3	566.8	573.9	181.9	60.9	2,297.8
2 China	275.2	29.5	799.7	9.8	64.0	1,178.2
3 Russia	124.7	365.2	111.3	34.0	35.6	670.8
4 Japan	248.7	68.9	112.2	52.2	22.8	504.8
5 India	113.3	27.1	185.3	4.1	15.6	345.4
6 Germany	125.1	77.0	87.1	37.3	5.7	332.2
7 Canada	96.4	78.7	31.0	16.8	68.6	291.5
8 France	94.2	39.4	12.4	99.8	14.8	260.6
9 UK	76.8	85.7	39.1	20.1	1.3	223.0
10 South Korea	105.7	24.4	51.1	27.0	1.6	209.8
World total	3,636.6	2,591.0	2,578.4	598.8	595.4	10,000.2

* Millions of tonnes of oil equivalent

\# HEP = Hydroelectric power

Source: *BP Statistical Review of World Energy 2004*

the 10 COUNTRIES CONSUMING THE MOST OIL

COUNTRY / CONSUMPTION, 2003 (TONNES)

 1 USA 914,300,000

 2 China 275,200,000

 3 Japan 248,700,000

 4 Germany 125,100,000

 5 Russia 124,700,000

 6 India 113,300,000

7 South Korea 105,700,000

8 Canada 96,400,000

9 France 94,200,000

 10 Italy 92,100,000

UK 76,800,000

World total 3,636,600,000

Source: *BP Statistical Review of World Energy 2004*

⬅ **Environmentally unfriendly**
Pollution and its effects on the environment and human health are among the biggest challenges facing the world.

the 10 COUNTRIES EMITTING THE MOST CARBON DIOXIDE

COUNTRY	CO₂ EMISSIONS PER CAPITA, 2002 (TONNES OF CO₂)
1 Qatar	46.08
2 United Arab Emirates	43.53
3 Bahrain	33.07
4 Singapore	27.22
5 Kuwait	25.49
6 Trinidad and Tobago	23.71
7 Luxembourg	22.96
8 Australia	21.00
9 USA	19.97
10 Canada	18.92
UK	*9.36*
World average	*3.93*

Source: Energy Information Administration

CO_2 emissions derive from three principal sources – fossil fuel burning, cement manufacturing, and gas flaring. Since World War II, increasing industrialization in many countries has resulted in huge increases in carbon output, a trend that most countries are now actively trying to reverse, with some degree of success among the former leaders in this Top 10, although the USA remains the worst offender in total, with over 5,749,410,000 tonnes released in 2002. Around the world there are a number of island territories with small populations but a high CO_2 output resulting from such industries as the production of liquid fuels. Among them, Gibraltar (144.11 tonnes per head) and the US Virgin Islands (114.55 tonnes per head) have greater per capita emissions than those countries in the Top 10.

First Fact The first person to suggest the notion of the greenhouse effect was French mathematician Baron Jean-Baptiste-Joseph Fournier, in 1827. In 1908, Swedish chemist and Nobel Prize winner Svante Arrhenius was the first to warn of the danger of global warming as a result of the release of carbon dioxide from the use of fossil fuels.

the 10 LEAST ENVIRONMENTALLY FRIENDLY COUNTRIES

COUNTRY / ESI RANKING*

 North Korea 29.2

 Taiwan 32.7

 Turkmenistan 33.1

 Iraq 33.6

 Uzbekistan 34.4

 Haiti 34.8

 Sudan 35.9

 Trinidad and Tobago 36.3

 Kuwait 36.6

 Yemen 37.3

* Based on calculations of 20 key indicators in five categories: environmental systems, environmental stresses, human vulnerability to environmental risks, a society's institutional capacity to respond to environmental threats, and a nation's stewardship of the shared resources of the global commons

Source: World Economic Forum, *2005 Environmental Sustainability Index*

top 10 ENVIRONMENTALLY FRIENDLY COUNTRIES

COUNTRY / ESI RANKING*

 Finland 75.1

 Norway 73.4

 Uruguay 71.8

 Sweden 71.7

 Iceland 70.8

 Canada 64.4

 Switzerland 63.7

 Guyana 62.9

 = Argentina 62.7
= Austria 62.7

* Based on calculations of 20 key indicators in five categories: environmental systems, environmental stresses, human vulnerability to environmental risks, a society's institutional capacity to respond to environmental threats, and a nation's stewardship of the shared resources of the global commons

Source: World Economic Forum, *2005 Environmental Sustainability Index*

the 10 worst air disasters caused
by terrorism: page 196

Chapter

8 9 10 12

top 10 tourist destinations: page 198

top 10 countries with the
longest road networks: page 188

the 10 latest holders of the water speed record: page 187

34567

Transport & Tourism

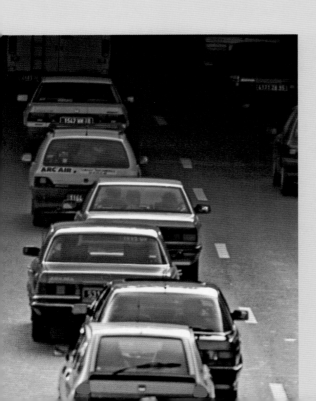

Speed Records

the 10 LATEST HOLDERS OF THE *AIR SPEED* RECORD *BY JETS**

	PILOT(S) / COUNTRY	LOCATION	AIRCRAFT	SPEED (KM/H)	(MPH)	DATE
1	**Eldon W. Joersz**, USA **George T. Morgan Jr.**, USA	Beale AFB, USA	Lockheed SR-71A	3,529.560	2,193.167	28 July 1976
2	**Robert L. Stephens**, USA **Daniel Andre**, USA	Edwards AFB, USA	Lockheed YF-12A	3,331.507	2,070.102	1 May 1965
3	**Georgi Mossolov**, USSR	Podmoskownoe, USSR	Mikoyan E-166	2,681.000	1,665.896	7 July 1962
4	**Robert B. Robinson**, USA	Edwards AFB, USA	McDonnell F4H-1F Phantom II	2,585.425	1,606.509	22 Nov 1961
5	**Joseph W. Rogers**, USA	Edwards AFB, USA	Convair F-106A Delta Dart	2,455.736	1,525.924	15 Dec 1959
6	**Georgi Mossolov**, USSR	Jukowski-Petrowskol, USSR	Mikoyan E-66	2,388.000	1,483.834	31 Oct 1959
7	**Walter W. Irwin**, USA	Edwards AFB, USA	Lockheed YF-104A Starfighter	2,259.538	1,404.012	16 May 1958
8	**Adrian E. Drew**, USA	Edwards AFB, USA	McDonnell F-101A Voodoo	1,943.500	1,207.635	12 Dec 1957
9	**Peter Twiss**, UK	Chichester, UK	Fairey Delta Two	1,822.000	1,132.138	10 Mar 1956
10	**Horace A. Hanes**, USA	Palmdale, USA	North American F-100C Super Sabre	1,323.312	822.268	20 Aug 1955

* Ground-launched only, hence excludes X-15 records

The flight of Horace A. Hanes was the first official supersonic record-holder. The next holder, that of Peter Twiss, was the greatest-ever incremental increase – 498.688 km/h (309.870 mph). It should be noted that although air records are traditionally expressed to three decimal places, few flights have ever been recorded to such a level of accuracy.

top 10 *FASTEST* RAIL JOURNEYS

	JOURNEY* / COUNTRY	TRAIN	DISTANCE (KM)	(MILES)	SPEED (KM/H)	(MPH)
1	**Hiroshima to Kokura**, Japan	15 Nozomi	192.0	119.3	261.8	162.7
2	**Valence TGV to Avignon TGV**, France	TGV 5102	129.7	80.6	259.4	161.2
3	**Brussels Midi to Valence TGV**, International	ThalysSoleil	831.3	516.5	242.1	150.4
4	**Frankfurt Flughafen to Siegburg/Bonn**, Germany	19 ICE trains	143.3	89.0	232.4	144.4
5	**Madrid Atocha to Sevilla (Seville)**, Spain	2 AVE trains	470.5	292.4	209.1	129.9
6	**Alvesta to Hassleholm**, Sweden	X2000 541	98.0	61.0	178.2	111.0
7	**Darlington to York**, UK	6 Voyager trains	71.0	44.1	177.5	110.3
8	**Roma (Rome) Termini to Firenze (Florence) SMN**, Italy	Eurostar 9458	261.0	162.2	166.6	103.5
9	**Wilmington to Baltimore**, USA	Acela Expresses	110.1	68.4	165.1	102.6
10	**Salo to Karjaa**, Finland	2 Pendolinos	53.1	33.0	151.7	94.3

* Fastest journey for each country; all those countries in the Top 10 have other equally or similarly fast services

Source: *Railway Gazette International*

the 10 LATEST HOLDERS OF THE **WATER SPEED** RECORD

DRIVER / BOAT / LOCATION	SPEED (KM/H)	(MPH)	DATE
1 **Dave Villwock**, Miss Budweiser, Lake Oroville, California, USA	354.849	220.493	13 Mar 2004
2 **Russ Wicks**, Miss Freei, Lake Washington, Washington, USA	330.711	205.494	15 June 2000
3 **Roy Duby**, Miss US1, Lake Guntersville, Alabama, USA	322.543	200.419	17 Apr 1962
4 **Bill Muncey**, Miss Thriftaway, Lake Washington, Washington, USA	308.996	192.001	16 Feb 1960
5 **Jack Regas**, Hawaii Kai III, Lake Washington, Washington, USA	301.956	187.627	30 Nov 1957
6 **Art Asbury**, Miss Supertest II, Lake Ontario, Canada	296.988	184.540	1 Nov 1957
7 **Stanley Sayres**, Slo-Mo-Shun IV, Lake Washington, Washington, USA	287.263	178.497	7 July 1952
8 **Stanley Sayres**, Slo-Mo-Shun IV, Lake Washington, Washington, USA	258.015	160.323	26 June 1950
9 **Malcolm Campbell**, Bluebird K4, Coniston Water, UK	228.108	141.740	19 Aug 1939
10 **Malcolm Campbell**, Bluebird K3, Hallwiler See, Switzerland	210.679	130.910	17 Aug 1938

All these record-holders were propeller-driven craft, taking the average of two runs over a measured kilometre or mile course. Since the 1950s, jet-powered boats, which skim over the surface of the water, have achieved consistently faster speeds, with Ken Warby's *Spirit of Australia* setting the jet record of 511.11 km/h (317.58 mph) on *Blowering Dam*, New South Wales, Australia, on 8 October 1978.

⏷ Miss Budweiser
Powered by a 2,650-hp Chinook helicopter engine, hydroplane *Miss Budweiser* set a new world water speed record in 2004.

the 10 LATEST HOLDERS OF THE **LAND SPEED** RECORD

DRIVER / COUNTRY / CAR / SPEED / DATE

1 **Andy Green**, UK, Thrust SSC*, 1,227.99 km/h (763.04 mph), 15 Oct 1997

2 **Richard Noble**, UK, Thrust 2*, 1,013.47 km/h (633.47 mph), 4 Oct 1983

3 **Gary Gabelich**, USA, The Blue Flame, 995.85 km/h (622.41 mph), 23 Oct 1970

4 **Craig Breedlove**, USA, Spirit of America – Sonic 1, 960.96 km/h (600.60 mph), 15 Nov 1965

5 **Art Arfons**, USA, Green Monster, 922.48 km/h (576.55 mph), 7 Nov 1965

6 **Craig Breedlove**, Spirit of America – Sonic 1, 888.76 km/h (555.48 mph), 2 Nov 1965

7 **Art Arfons**, Green Monster, 858.73 km/h (536.71 mph), 27 Oct 1964

8 **Craig Breedlove**, Spirit of America, 842.04 km/h (526.28 mph), 15 Oct 1964

9 **Craig Breedlove**, Spirit of America, 749.95 km/h (468.72 mph), 13 Oct 1964

10 **Art Arfons**, Green Monster, 694.43 km/h (434.02 mph), 5 Oct 1964

* Location Black Rock Desert, US; all other speeds were achieved at Bonneville Salt Flats, USA

On the Road

top 10 CARS IN THE UK

	MODEL	SALES, 2004
1	Ford Focus	141,021
2	Vauxhall Corsa	101,625
3	Ford Fiesta	89,295
4	Peugeot 206	86,605
5	Renault Mégane	86,569
6	Vauxhall Astra	85,087
7	Renault Clio	72,412
8	Volkswagen Golf	69,784
9	Ford Mondeo	60,441
10	Peugeot 307	58,742

Source: Society of Motor Manufacturers and Traders Ltd.

top 10 CAR PRODUCERS

	COUNTRY	CAR PRODUCTION, 2004*
1	Japan	8,720,385
2	Germany	5,192,101
3	USA	4,229,625
4	France	3,220,329
5	South Korea	3,122,600
6	Spain	2,402,103
7	China	2,316,262
8	UK	1,646,881
9	Brazil	1,756,166
10	Canada	1,335,464

* Provisional figures

Source: OICA Correspondents Survey

top 10 COUNTRIES WITH THE LONGEST ROAD NETWORKS

	COUNTRY	LENGTH (KM)	LENGTH (MILES)
1	USA	6,406,296 km	3,980,687 miles
2	India	3,319,644 km	2,062,731 miles
3	Brazil	1,724,929 km	1,071,821 miles
4	Canada	1,408,800 km	875,388 miles
5	China	1,402,698 km	871,596 miles
6	Japan	1,161,894 km	721,967 miles
7	France	894,000 km	555,506 miles
8	Australia	811,603 km	504,307 miles
9	Spain	663,795 km	412,463 miles
10	Russia	532,393 km	330,814 miles
	UK	371,913 km	231,096 miles

Source: Central Intelligence Agency

The CIA's assessment of road lengths includes both paved (mostly tarmac-surfaced) and unpaved (gravel and earth-surfaced) highways. In many developing countries the proportion of unpaved is greater than paved.

top 10 MOTOR VEHICLE **MANUFACTURERS**

MANUFACTURER	MOTOR VEHICLE PRODUCTION*, 2003
1 General Motors	8,185,997
2 Ford	6,566,089
3 Toyota	6,240,526
4 Volkswagen Group	5,024,032
5 DaimlerChrysler	4,231,603
6 PSA Peugeot Citroën	3,310,368
7 Nissan	2,942,306
8 Honda	2,922,526
9 Hyundai-Kia	2,697,435
10 Renault-Dacia-Samsung	2,386,098

* Includes cars, light trucks, lorries, buses, and coaches

Source: OICA Correspondents Survey

top 10 MOTOR VEHICLE **PRODUCERS**

COUNTRY	MOTOR VEHICLE PRODUCTION, 2004*
1 USA	11,989,387
2 Japan	10,511,518
3 Germany	5,569,954
4 China	5,070,527
5 France	3,665,990
6 South Korea	3,469,464
7 Spain	3,011,010
8 Canada	2,710,683
9 Brazil	2,210,062
10 UK	1,856,049

* Provisional figures; includes cars, light trucks, lorries, buses, and coaches

Source: OICA Correspondents Survey

⊕ Traffic jam

In the past 50 years annual motor vehicle production has risen from 13.6 million to over 60 million globally, with more than 500 million cars alone on the world's roads.

Track Records

TOP 10 LONGEST UNDERGROUND RAILWAY NETWORKS

London UK
(1)
1863	
267	
392 km	
244 miles	

New York USA
(2)
1904	
468	
371 km	
231 miles	

Moscow Russia
(3)
1935	
160	
262 km	
163 miles	

Tokyo Japan*
(4)
1927	
241	
256 km	
159 miles	

Paris France#
(5)
1900	
297	
202 km	
126 miles	

CITY   OPENED ▬▬▬   STATIONS ▬▬▬   TOTAL TRACK LENGTH (KM) ▬▬▬   (MILES) ▬▬▬

the 10 FIRST COUNTRIES WITH RAILWAYS

COUNTRY	FIRST RAILWAY ESTABLISHED
1 UK	27 Sept 1825
2 France	7 Nov 1829
3 USA	24 May 1830
4 Ireland	17 Dec 1834
5 Belgium	5 May 1835
6 Germany	7 Dec 1835
7 Canada	21 July 1836
8 Russia	30 Oct 1837
9 Austria	6 Jan 1838
10 Netherlands	24 Sept 1839

Inaugurated with the UK's Stockton & Darlington Railway, the first steam (rather than horse-drawn) services rapidly launched a "golden age" of railway building across the world.

top 10 LONGEST RAIL NETWORKS

LOCATION	TOTAL RAIL LENGTH (KM)	(MILES)
1 USA	228,464	141,961
2 Russia	87,157	54,157
3 China	70,058	43,532
4 India	63,140	39,233
5 Canada	48,909	30,391
6 Germany	46,039	28,607
7 Australia	44,015	27,350
8 Argentina	34,091	21,183
9 France	32,175	19,993
10 Brazil	29,412	18,276
UK	*17,186*	*10,679*
World	*1,115,205*	*692,956*

Source: Central Intelligence Agency

54

⬅ **Early train**
Pioneer passengers in open carriages savour the revolutionary experience of travelling by rail.

exico City Mexico	**San Francisco** USA	**Chicago** USA	**Madrid** Spain	**Washington, DC** USA
6	**7**	**8**	**9**	**10**
1969	1972	1943	1919	1976
175	42	140	201	83
201 km	200 km	173 km	171 km	166 km
125 miles	124 miles	107 miles	106 miles	103 miles

* Includes Toei, Eidan lines   # Metro and RER   Source: Tony Pattison, Centre for Environmental Initiatives Researcher

top 10 BUSIEST RAIL NETWORKS

LOCATION	PASSENGER-KMS PER ANNUM*	PASSENGER-MILES PER ANNUM*
1 Japan	568,036,000,000	354,137,000,000
2 China	390,484,000,000	243,900,000,000
3 India	357,013,000,000	222,994,000,000
4 Russia	170,300,000,000	106,371,000,000
5 France	61,830,000,000	38,620,000,000
6 Egypt	60,100,000,000	37,539,000,000
7 Germany	59,350,000,000	37,071,000,000
8 Ukraine	59,080,000,000	36,902,000,000
9 Italy	51,129,000,000	31,936,000,000
10 UK	31,653,000,000	19,771,000,000

* Number of passengers multiplied by the distance carried; totals include national and local services where applicable

Source: *Railway Gazette International*

Though coming to rail transport later than many other countries, Japan (first railway 1872), China (1880), and India (1853) today have the world's busiest systems.

➔ **Rush hour**
Morning on the Yamanote Line, Tokyo's busiest commuter route: as many as half of all employees in Japan commute to work by train.

Water Ways

top 10 **LARGEST** YACHTS

	YACHT	OWNER / COUNTRY	BUILT / REFITTED	LENGTH (M)	LENGTH (FT IN)	
1	Octopus	Paul Allen, USA	2003	126.1	414	0
2	Savarona	Kahraman Sadikoglu, Turkey (charter)	1931/1992	124.3	408	0
3	Alexander	Latsis family, Greece	1976/1986	122.0	400	2
4	Atlantis II	Niarchos family, Greece	1981	115.6	379	7
5	Pelorus	Roman Abramovich, Russia	2003	114.9	377	3
6	Le Grand Bleu	Roman Abramovich	2000	112.7	370	0
7	Lady Moura	Nasser al-Rashid, Saudi Arabia	1990	104.8	344	0
8	Christina O	John Paul Papanicolaou, Greece	1943/2001	99.1	325	3
9	Carinthia VII	Heidi Horten, Germany	2002	97.9	321	5
10	Limitless	Leslie Wexner, USA	1997	96.1	315	7

Source: *Power & Motoryacht*, August 2004

Owned by Microsoft co-founder Paul Allen, German-built *Octopus* – the world's largest privately-owned yacht – boasts such equipment as an 18-m (60-ft) landing craft and a submarine.

top 10 **BUSIEST** PORTS

	PORT / COUNTRY	CONTAINER TRAFFIC, 2003 (TEUS*)
1	**Hong Kong**, China	20,499,000
2	**Singapore**, Singapore	18,411,000
3	**Shanghai**, China	11,280,000
4	**Shenzhen**, China	10,615,000
5	**Busan**, South Korea	10,408,000
6	**Kaohsiung**, Taiwan	8,843,000
7	**Los Angeles**, USA	7,149,000
8	**Rotterdam**, Netherlands	7,107,000
9	**Hamburg**, Germany	6,138,000
10	**Antwerp**, Belgium	5,445,000

* TEUS = Twenty-foot Equivalent Units

Source: American Association of Port Authorities

A "Twenty-foot Equivalent Unit" is a measurement used in quantifying container traffic, in which Hong Kong is the world leader, although Singapore is the largest in terms of total weight handled, with over 347 million tonnes in 2003, compared with Hong Kong's 207 million.

top 10 **LARGEST** OIL TANKERS*

TANKER / YEAR BUILT / OPERATOR'S COUNTRY / DEADWEIGHT TONNAGE#

5 **Marine Pacific**

1	=**TI Africa** 2002	UK	441,893
	=**TI Asia** 2002	UK	441,893
	=**TI Europe** 2002	UK	441,893

4 **TI Oceania** 2003 UK 441,585

* As at April 2004

Total weight of the vessel, including its cargo, crew, passengers, and supplies

Source: Lloyd's Register-Fairplay Ltd.
www.lrfairplay.com

top 10 LONGEST SHIP CANALS

	CANAL / COUNTRY	OPENED	LENGTH (KM)	(MILES)
1	**Grand Canal**, China	283*	1,795	1,114
2	**Erie Canal**, USA	1825	584	363
3	**Göta Canal**, Sweden	1832	386	240
4	**St. Lawrence Seaway**, Canada/USA	1959	290	180
5	**Canal du Midi**, France	1692	240	149
6	**Main-Danube**, Germany	1992	171	106
7	**Suez**, Egypt	1869	162	101
8	**= Albert**, Belgium	1939	129	80
	= Moscow-Volga, Russia	1937	129	80
10	**Volga-Don**, Russia	1952	101	63

* Extended from 605–10 and rebuilt during 1958–72

Connecting Hang Zhou in the south to Beijing in the north, China's Grand Canal was largely built by manual labour alone, long before the invention of the mechanized digging used in the construction of the other major artificial waterways. The Panama Canal, opened in 1914 (82 km/51 miles), just fails to find a place in the Top 10.

⬆ Slow boats in China
China's Grand, or Jinghang, Canal combines sections of navigable rivers, lakes, and man-made canals to form a major water highway from Beijing to Zhejiang.

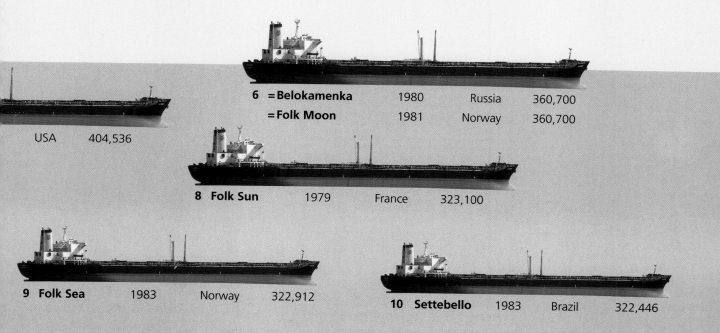

USA   404,536

6   **= Belokamenka**   1980   Russia   360,700

   = Folk Moon   1981   Norway   360,700

8   **Folk Sun**   1979   France   323,100

9   **Folk Sea**   1983   Norway   322,912

10   **Settebello**   1983   Brazil   322,446

Airlines

top 10 BUSIEST AIRPORTS

Source: Airports Council International

	Airport	Location	Country	Passengers, 2003
1	ATLANTA HARTSFIELD INTERNATIONAL	ATLANTA	USA	79,086,792
2	CHICAGO O'HARE	CHICAGO	USA	69,508,672
3	LONDON HEATHROW	LONDON	UK	63,487,136
4	TOKYO INTERNATIONAL	TOKYO	JAPAN	62,876,269
5	LOS ANGELES INTERNATIONAL	LOS ANGELES	USA	54,982,838
6	DFW INTERNATIONAL	DALLAS/FORT WORTH	USA	53,253,607
7	FRANKFURT	FRANKFURT	GERMANY	48,351,664
8	CHARLES DE GAULLE	PARIS	FRANCE	48,220,436
9	SCHIPHOL	AMSTERDAM	NETHERLANDS	39,960,400
10	DENVER INTERNATIONAL	DENVER	USA	37,505,138

top 10 AIRLINES WITH THE MOST AIRCRAFT

AIRLINE / COUNTRY*	MAIN FLEET SIZE, 2004#
1 American Airlines	840
2 Delta Air Lines	587
3 United Airlines	523
4 Northwest Airlines	452
5 Southwest Airlines	417
6 Lufthansa German Airlines, Germany	368
7 Air France, France	363
8 Continental Airlines	358
9 US Airways	279
10 British Airways, UK	220

* All from the US unless otherwise stated

2003 data where 2004 not yet available

American Airlines not only has the largest fleet but also the greatest passenger traffic and employs the largest number of staff. It serves 172 cities, averages 2,600 departures a day, and handles some 80 million passengers a year.

top 10 COUNTRIES WITH THE MOST AIRPORTS

COUNTRY	AIRPORTS, 2003 EST.
1 USA	14,807
2 Brazil	3,803
3 Russia	2,609
4 Mexico	1,827
5 Canada	1,357
6 Argentina	1,335
7 Bolivia	1,067
8 Colombia	980
9 Paraguay	880
10 South Africa	728
UK	471

Source: Central Intelligence Agency

● Runway success
Handling more international traffic than any other airport, London Heathrow is also Europe's busiest for passenger traffic. Its 5th terminal scheduled for 2008–2015 will enable it to handle 90 million passengers a year.

Lost luggage
Some 16 per cent of all complaints to airlines concern mishandled baggage – a greater proportion than for any other issue.

top 10 AIRLINES WITH THE MOST PASSENGER TRAFFIC

AIRLINE / COUNTRY	PASSENGER-KMS FLOWN, 2003*
1 **American Airlines**, USA	193,100,000,000
2 **United Airlines**, USA	163,400,000,000
3 **Delta Airlines**, USA	143,400,000,000
4 **Northwest Airlines**, USA	110,200,000,000
5 **British Airways**, UK	101,600,000,000
6 **Air France**, France	97,600,000,000
7 **Lufthansa German Airlines**, Germany	96,600,000,000
8 **Continental Airlines**, USA	91,500,000,000
9 **Japan Airlines**, Japan	72,900,000,000
10 **Qantas Airways**, Australia	68,900,000,000

* Total distance travelled on scheduled flights by aircraft of these airlines multiplied by the number of passengers carried

Source: International Civil Aviation Organization (ICAO)

British Airways, the largest non-US airline, was created in 1973 by the merging of the British Overseas Airways Corporation and British European Airways. In the 1990s it was proclaimed as "The World's Favourite Airline" and until 2003 was, along with Air France, one of the operators of the supersonic Concorde.

top 10 AIR TRANSPORT COMPLAINTS IN THE UK

TYPE OF COMPLAINT	COMPLAINTS, 2003–2004* (WRITTEN)	(TELEPHONE)	(TOTAL)
1 **Mishandled baggage**	276	625	901
2 **Cancellations**	221	519	740
3 **Delays**	230	330	560
4 **Ticketing issues**	211	269	480
5 **Reservation problems**	114	323	437
6 **Schedule changes**	69	297	364
7 **Overbooking**	87	194	281
8 **Refunds**	–	229	229
9 **Ground services**	115	113	228
10 **Special needs problems**	56	122	178
Total (inc. those not in Top 10)	1,750	3,972	5,722

* 1 Apr 2003–31 Mar 2004

Source: Air Transport Users Council

In the days of Concorde, jokes were told along the lines of "Breakfast in London, lunch in New York, luggage in Jamaica", and the misrouting of and damage to luggage remains the number one cause for complaint. This list represents only those problems that generate written and phoned complaints.

Transport Disasters

the 10 WORST AIR DISASTERS (EXCLUDING TERRORISM)

LOCATION / DATE / INCIDENT	NO. KILLED

1 Tenerife, Canary Islands, 27 Mar 1977 — 583
Two Boeing 747s (Pan Am and KLM, carrying 380 passengers and 16 crew and 234 passengers and 14 crew respectively) collided and caught fire on the runway of Los Rodeos airport after the pilots received incorrect control tower instructions. A total of 61 people escaped.

2 Mt Ogura, Japan, 12 Aug 1985 — 520
A JAL Boeing 747 on an internal flight from Tokyo to Osaka crashed, killing all but four of the 509 passengers and all 15 crew on board.

3 Charkhi Dadri, India, 12 Nov 1996 — 349
Soon after taking off from New Delhi's Indira Gandhi International Airport, a Saudi Airways Boeing 747 collided with a Kazakh Airlines Ilyushin IL-76 cargo aircraft on its descent and exploded, killing all 312 people (289 passengers and 23 crew) on the Boeing and all 37 people (27 passengers and 10 crew) on the Ilyushin in the world's worst mid-air crash.

4 Paris, France, 3 Mar 1974 — 346
Immediately after take-off for London, a Turkish Airlines DC-10 crashed at Ermenonville, north of Paris, killing all 335 passengers, including many England rugby supporters, and its crew of 11.

5 Riyadh, Saudi Arabia, 19 Aug 1980 — 301
A Saudia (Saudi Arabian) Airlines Lockheed TriStar caught fire during an emergency landing, killing all 287 passengers and 14 crew.

6 Off the Iranian coast, 3 July 1988 — 290
An Iran Air A300 airbus was shot down in error by a missile fired by the *USS Vincennes*, with 274 passengers and 16 crew killed.

7 Chicago, USA, 25 May 1979 — 273
The worst air disaster in the US occurred when an engine fell off an American Airlines DC-10 as it took off from Chicago O'Hare airport and the plane plunged out of control, killing all 258 passengers and 13 crew on board and two on the ground.

8 Sakhalin Island, off the Siberian coast, 1 Sept 1983 — 269
A Korean Air Boeing 747 that had strayed into Soviet airspace was shot down by a Soviet fighter.

9 Belle Harbor, New York, USA, 12 Nov 2001 — 265
An American Airlines Airbus A.300B4-605R broke up in mid-air and crashed in a residential area, killing all 260 on board and five on the ground.

10 Nagoya airport, Japan, 26 Apr 1994 — 264
A China Airlines Airbus A300, on a flight from Taipei, Taiwan, stalled at 300 m (980 ft) and crashed while landing, killing all 15 crew and 249 out of the 256 passengers on board.

the 10 WORST AIR DISASTERS CAUSED BY TERRORISM

LOCATION / DATE / INCIDENT	NO. KILLED

1 New York, USA, 11 Sept 2001 — c.1,622
Following a hijacking by terrorists, an American Airlines Boeing 767 was deliberately flown into the North Tower of the World Trade Center, killing all 81 passengers and 11 crew on board and an estimated 1,530 on the ground, both as a direct result of the crash, and the subsequent fire and collapse of the building.

2 New York, USA, 11 Sept 2001 — c.677
As part of the coordinated attack, hijackers commandeered a second Boeing 747 and crashed it into the South Tower of the World Trade Center, killing all 56 passengers and 9 crew on board and approximately 612 on the ground.

3 Off the Irish coast, 23 June 1985 — 329
An Air India Boeing 747 on a flight from Vancouver to Delhi exploded in mid-air, probably as a result of a terrorist bomb, killing all 307 passengers and 22 crew in the worst-ever air disaster over water.

4 Lockerbie, Scotland, 21 Dec 1988 — 270
Pan Am Flight 103 – a Boeing 747 – from London Heathrow to New York exploded in mid-air as a result of a terrorist bomb, killing 243 passengers, 16 crew, and 11 on the ground in the UK's worst-ever air disaster.

5 Pentagon, USA, 11 Sept 2001 — 189
As part of the 9/11 hijackings, a Boeing 757 was deliberately crashed into the Pentagon, killing 64 on board and 125 on the ground.

6 Tenere Desert, Niger, 19 Sept 1989 — 171
A Union de Transports Ariens DC-10 flying out of Ndjamena, Chad, exploded over Niger. French investigators implicated Libyan and Syrian terrorists.

7 Baiyun Airport, China, 2 Oct 1990 — 128
A Xiamen Airlines Boeing 737 was hijacked in flight and, during an enforced landing, crashed into a taxiing Boeing 757.

8 Comoros Islands, Indian Ocean, 23 Nov 1996 — 125
An Ethiopian Airlines Boeing 767 was hijacked and ditched in the sea when it ran out of fuel.

9 Andaman Sea, off Myanmar, 29 Nov 1987 — 115
A Korean Air Boeing 707 exploded in mid-air. Two North Korean terrorists were captured, one of whom committed suicide, while the other was sentenced to death but later pardoned.

10 Near Abu Dhabi, United Arab Emirates, 23 Sept 1983 — 113
A Gulf Air Boeing 737 exploded as it prepared to land. Evidence indicated that it had been caused by a bomb in the cargo hold.

the 10 WORST MARINE DISASTERS

LOCATION / DATE / INCIDENT	APPROXIMATE NO. KILLED
1 Off Gdansk, Poland, 30 Jan 1945 The German liner *Wilhelm Gustloff*, laden with refugees, was torpedoed by a Soviet submarine, *S-13*. The precise death toll remains uncertain, but is in the range of 5,348 to 7,800.	up to 7,800
2 Off Cape Rixhöft (Rozeewie), Poland, 16 Apr 1945 The German ship *Goya* carrying evacuees from Gdansk, was torpedoed in the Baltic.	6,800
3 Off Yingkow, China, 3 Dec 1948 The boilers of an unidentified Chinese troopship carrying Nationalist soldiers from Manchuria exploded, detonating ammunition.	over 6,000
4 Lübeck, Germany, 3 May 1945 The German ship *Cap Arcona*, carrying concentration camp survivors, was bombed and sunk by British Typhoon fighter-bombers.	5,000
5 Off British coast, Aug to Oct 1588 Military conflict and storms combined to destroy the Spanish Armada.	c.4,000
6 Off Stolpmünde (Ustka), Poland, 10 Feb 1945 German war-wounded and refugees were lost when the *General Steuben* was torpedoed by the same Russian submarine that had sunk the *Wilhelm Gustloff* 10 days earlier.	3,500
7 Off St. Nazaire, France, 17 June 1940 The British troop ship *Lancastria* sank.	3,050
8 Tabias Strait, Philippines, 20 Dec 1987 The ferry *Dona Paz* was struck by oil tanker *MV Victor*.	up to 3,000
9 Woosung, China, 3 Dec 1948 The overloaded steamship *Kiangya*, carrying refugees, struck a Japanese mine.	over 2,750
10 Lübeck, Germany, 3 May 1945 The refugee ship *Thielbeck* sank along with the *Cap Arcona* during the British bombardment of Lübeck harbour in the closing weeks of World War II.	2,750

Recent re-assessments of the death tolls in some of the World War II marine disasters means that the most famous marine disaster of all, the *Titanic*, the British liner that struck an iceberg in the North Atlantic and sank on 15 April 1912 with the loss of 1,517 lives, no longer ranks in the Top 10. However, the *Titanic* tragedy remains one of the worst-ever peacetime disasters, along with such notable incidents as that involving the *General Slocum*, an excursion liner that caught fire in the port of New York on 15 June 1904 with the loss of 1,021 lives.

the 10 WORST LAND TRANSPORT DISASTERS

LOCATION / DATE / INCIDENT	NO. KILLED
1 Afghanistan, 3 Nov 1982 Following a collision with a Soviet army truck, a petrol tanker exploded in the 2.7-km (1.7-mile) Salang Tunnel. Some authorities have put the death toll from the explosion, fire, and fumes as high as 3,000.	over 2,000
2 Colombia, 7 Aug 1956 Seven army ammunition trucks exploded at night in the centre of Cali, destroying eight city blocks, including a barracks where 500 soldiers were sleeping.	1,200
3 Bagmati River, India, 6 June 1981 The carriages of a train travelling from Samastipur to Banmukhi in Bihar plunged off a bridge over the river Bagmati near Mansi when the driver braked, apparently to avoid hitting a sacred cow. Although the official death toll was said to have been 268, many authorities have claimed that the train was so massively overcrowded that the actual figure was in excess of 800, making it probably the worst rail disaster of all time.	c.800
4 Chelyabinsk, Russia, 3 June 1989 Two passenger trains, laden with holidaymakers heading to and from Black Sea resorts, were destroyed when liquid gas from a nearby pipeline exploded.	up to 800
5 Guadalajara, Mexico, 18 Jan 1915 A train derailed on a steep incline, but political strife in the country meant that full details of the disaster were suppressed.	over 600
6 Modane, France, 12 Dec 1917 A troop-carrying train ran out of control and was derailed. It has been claimed that it was overloaded and that as many as 1,000 may have died.	573
7 Balvano, Italy, 2 Mar 1944 A heavily laden train stalled in the Armi Tunnel, and many passengers were asphyxiated. Like the disaster at Torre (No. 8), wartime secrecy prevented the full details from being published.	521
8 Torre, Spain, 3 Jan 1944 A double collision and fire in a tunnel resulted in many deaths – some have put the total as high as 800.	over 500
9 Awash, Ethiopia, 13 Jan 1985 A derailment hurled a train laden with some 1,000 passengers into a ravine.	428
10 Cireau, Romania, 7 Jan 1917 An overcrowded passenger train crashed into a military train and was derailed.	374

World Tourism

top 10 TOURIST DESTINATIONS

	COUNTRY	INTERNATIONAL VISITORS, 2003
1	*France*	75,048,000
2	*Spain*	52,477,000
3	*USA*	40,356,000
4	*Italy*	39,604,000
5	*China*	32,970,000
6	*UK*	24,785,000
7	*Austria*	19,078,000
8	*Mexico*	18,665,000
9	*Germany*	18,399,000
10	*Canada*	17,468,000

Source: World Tourism Organization

⬆ Italian treasures
Italy's picturesque towns and villages and the cultural attractions of its cities have been a magnet for tourists since the days of the 18th-century Grand Tour.

⬆ Spanish pleasures
The resorts of Spain and its islands, beaches, and leisure facilities, attract increasing numbers of tourists.

top 10 WORLDWIDE AMUSEMENT AND THEME PARKS

PARK / LOCATION	ESTIMATED ATTENDANCE, 2004
1 The Magic Kingdom at Walt Disney World, Lake Buena Vista, Florida, USA	15,170,000
2 Disneyland, Anaheim, California, USA	13,360,000
3 Tokyo Disneyland, Tokyo, Japan	13,200,000
4 Disneysea, Tokyo, Japan	12,200,000
5 Disneyland Paris, Marne-La-Vallée, France	10,200,000
6 Universal Studios Japan, Osaka, Japan	9,900,000
7 Epcot at Walt Disney World, Lake Buena Vista, Florida, USA	9,400,000
8 Disney-MGM Studios at Walt Disney World, Lake Buena Vista, Florida, USA	8,260,000
9 Lotte World, Seoul, South Korea	8,000,000
10 Disney's Animal Kingdom at Walt Disney World, Lake Buena Vista, Florida, USA	7,820,000

Source: *Amusement Business*

After experiencing flat or declining entrance numbers in recent years, most amusement parks recorded increases in 2004. New parks in Japan, such as Tokyo's Disneysea and Universal Studios and Osaka's Universal Studios, which all opened in 2001, and the enormous Dubai Land scheduled to open in 2006, are shifting the global balance from the USA and to the East and Middle East.

⬆ **Disneyland's domination**
Including Epcot, eight of the world's Top 10 amusement parks are members of The Walt Disney Company. Its pioneering Disneyland, in second place, opened in 1955.

top 10 TOURIST ATTRACTIONS IN THE UK

ATTRACTION / LOCATION	VISITORS, 2004
1 Blackpool Pleasure Beach, Blackpool	6,200,000
2 The National Gallery, London	4,959,946
3 British Museum, London	4,868,176
4 Tate Modern, London	4,441,225
5 British Airways London Eye, London	3,700,000*
6 Natural History Museum, London	3,250,376
7 Science Museum, London	2,886,850
8 Tower of London, London	2,135,204*
9 Victoria & Albert Museum, London	2,010,825
10 National Portrait Gallery, London	1,516,402#

* Charging admission

Part charging admission/part free admission

Source: Association of Leading Visitor Attractions (ALVA)

top 10 COUNTRIES EARNING THE MOST FROM TOURISM

COUNTRY	INTERNATIONAL TOURISM RECEIPTS, 2003 ($)
1 USA	65,100,000,000
2 Spain	41,700,000,000
3 France	36,600,000,000
4 Italy	31,300,000,000
5 Germany	23,000,000,000
6 UK	19,400,000,000
7 China	17,400,000,000
8 Austria	13,600,000,000
9 Turkey	13,200,000,000
10 Greece	10,700,000,000

Source: World Tourism Organization

top 10 **CLOSE-UP**

top 10 *FASTEST* ROLLER COASTERS

	ROLLER COASTER / LOCATION	YEAR OPENED	SPEED (KM/H)	(MPH)
1	**Kingda Ka**, Six Flags Great Adventure, Jackson, New Jersey, USA	2005*	206	128
2	**Top Thrill Dragster**, Cedar Point, Sandusky, Ohio, USA	2003	193	120
3	**Dodonpa**, Fuji-Q Highlands, ShinNishihara, FujiYoshida-shi, Yamanashi, Japan	2001	172	106.9
4	=**Superman The Escape**, Six Flags Magic Mountain, Valencia, California, USA	1997	161	100
	=**Tower of Terror**, Dreamworld, Coomera, Queensland, Australia	1997	161	100
6	**Steel Dragon 2000**, Nagashima Spa Land, Nagashima, Mie, Japan	2000#	153	95
7	**Millennium Force**, Cedar Point, Sandusky, Ohio, USA	2000	149	93
8	=**Goliath**, Six Flags Magic Mountain, Valencia, California, USA	2000	137	85
	=**Titan**, Six Flags Over Texas, Arlington, Texas, USA	2001	137	85
10	=**Phantom's Revenge**, Kennywood Park, West Mifflin, Pennsylvania, USA	2001	132	82
	=**Xcelerator**, Knott's Berry Farm, Buena Park, California, USA	2002	132	82

* Scheduled opening date Spring 2005

Still standing but not operating since 23 Aug 2003

➲ Millennium force
When it was built Cedar Point's 14th roller coaster set new records as the world's fastest and, at 94.5 m (310 ft), the tallest.

Chapter

10

top 10 longest-standing outdoor field athletics world records: page 214

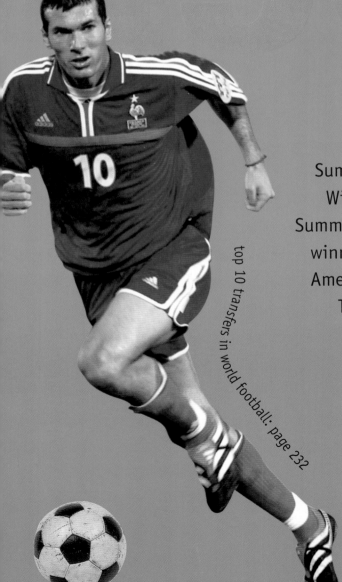

top 10 transfers in world football: page 232

Sport

Summer Olympics

TOP 10 SUMMER OLYMPICS **GOLD MEDAL** WINNERS

	ATHLETE / COUNTRY	SPORT	YEARS	GOLD MEDALS
1	**Ray Ewry**, USA	Athletics	1900–08	10
2	=**Paavo Nurmi**, Finland	Athletics	1920–28	9
	=**Larissa Latynina**, USSR	Gymnastics	1956–64	9
	=**Mark Spitz**, USA	Swimming	1968–72	9
	=**Carl Lewis**, USA	Athletics	1984–96	9
6	=**Sawao Kato**, Japan	Gymnastics	1968–76	8
	=**Matt Biondi**, USA	Swimming	1984–92	8
	=**Jenny Thompson**, USA	Swimming	1992–2000	8
9	=**Aladár Gerevich**, Hungary	Fencing	1932–60	7
	=**Viktor Chukarin**, USSR	Gymnastics	1952–56	7
	=**Boris Shakhlin**, USSR	Gymnastics	1956–64	7
	=**Vera Cáslavská**, Czechoslovakia	Gymnastics	1964–68	7
	=**Nikolay Andrianov**, USSR	Gymnastics	1972–80	7

All Ewry's golds were in the standing jumps – long jump, high jump, and triple jump – that once formed part of the track and field competition. Born in 1873, Ewry contracted polio as a boy and seemed destined to be confined to a wheelchair for life but, through a determined effort to overcome his handicap, he exercised and developed his legs to such a remarkable degree that he went on to become one of the world's greatest athletes. Spitz's seven gold medals in 1972 is a record for medals won at a single celebration. Latynina is the all-time top Olympic medallist, with 18 medals to her credit (9 gold, 5 silver, 4 bronze).

the 10 FIRST ATHLETES TO WIN MEDALS AT **FIVE** SUMMER OLYMPICS

	ATHLETE / COUNTRY	SPORT	YEARS
1	**Heikki Ilmari Savolainen**, Finland	Gymnastics	1928–52
2	**Aladár Gerevich***, Hungary	Fencing	1932–56
3	**Edoardo Mangiarotti**, Italy	Fencing	1936–60
4	**Gustav Fischer**, Switzerland	Dressage	1952–68
5	**Hans Günther Winkler#**, West Germany	Show-jumping	1956–72
6	**Ildikó Ságiné–Rejtö (née Uljaki–Rejtö)**, Hungary	Fencing	1960–76
7	**John Michael Plumb**, USA	Three Day Event	1964–84
8	**Reiner Klimke**, West Germany	Dressage	1964–88
9	=**Teresa Edwards**, USA	Basketball	1984–2000
	=**Birgit Fischer-Schmidt**, East Germany	Canoeing	1980–2000
	=**Stephen Redgrave**, UK	Rowing	1984–2000

* Also won medal at the 1960 Games

Also won medal at the 1976 Games

First Fact The first athlete to win an Olympic medal was James Brendan Connolly (USA, 1868–1957), in the hop, skip, and jump (triple jump) at the Athens Olympic, at 2.00 pm on Monday, 6 April 1896. A student at Harvard University, Connolly had been barred from attending and had to drop out of college in order to compete. The medal he won was silver – gold medals were not awarded in the inaugural games – but such wins are regarded as gold for statistical purposes.

top 10 SUMMER OLYMPICS MEDAL WINNERS (MEN)

	ATHLETE / COUNTRY	SPORT	YEARS	MEDALS* (GOLD)	(SILVER)	(BRONZE)	(TOTAL)
1	**Nikolai Andrianov**, USSR	Gymnastics	1972–80	7	5	3	15
2	**=Edoardo Mangiarotti**, Italy	Fencing	1936–60	6	5	2	13
	=Takashi Ono, Japan	Gymnastics	1952–64	5	4	4	13
	=Boris Shakhlin, USSR	Gymnastics	1956–64	7	4	2	13
5	**=Paavo Nurmi**, Finland	Athletics	1920–28	9	3	0	12
	=Sawao Kato, Japan	Gymnastics	1968–76	8	3	1	12
	=Alexei Nemov, Russia	Gymnastics	1996–2000	4	2	6	12
8	**=Carl Osburn**, USA	Shooting	1912–24	5	4	2	11
	=Viktor Chukarin, USSR	Gymnastics	1952–56	7	3	1	11
	=Mark Spitz, USA	Swimming	1968–72	9	1	1	11
	=Matt Biondi, USA	Swimming	1984–92	8	2	1	11

* 1896–2004 inclusive

Nikolai Andrianov is married to Olympic gymnast Lyubov Burda, who herself won two Olympic gold medals. Fencer Edoardo Mangiarotti won his first gold at the age of 17, making him the youngest male medallist at the 1936 Berlin Games. Although his overall total relegates him to the bottom of this list, Mark Spitz has the distinction of winning the most gold medals at a single Olympics, with seven in 1972.

top 10 SUMMER OLYMPICS MEDAL WINNERS (WOMEN)

	ATHLETE / COUNTRY	SPORT	YEARS	MEDALS* (GOLD)	(SILVER)	(BRONZE)	(TOTAL)
1	**Larissa Latynina**, USSR	Gymnastics	1956–64	9	5	4	18
2	**Birgit Fischer-Schmidt**, East Germany	Canoeing	1980–2004	8	4	0	12
3	**Vera Cáslavská**, Czechoslovakia	Gymnastics	1960–68	7	4	0	11
4	**=Agnes Keleti**, Hungary	Gymnastics	1952–56	5	3	2	10
	=Polina Astakhova, USSR	Gymnastics	1956–64	5	2	3	10
	=Jenny Thompson, USA	Swimming	1992–2000	8	1	1	10
7	**=Lyudmila Turishcheva**, USSR	Gymnastics	1968–76	4	3	2	9
	=Nadia Comaneci, Romania	Gymnastics	1976–80	5	3	1	9
9	**=Sofia Muratova**, USSR	Gymnastics	1956–60	2	2	4	8
	=Dawn Fraser, Australia	Swimming	1956–64	4	4	0	8
	=Shirley Babashoff, USA	Swimming	1972–76	2	6	0	8
	=Kornelia Ender, East Germany	Swimming	1972–76	4	4	0	8
	=Dara Torres, USA	Swimming	1984–2000	4	0	4	8

* 1896–2004 inclusive

Larissa Latynina holds the record for total medals won by any athlete in any sport in Olympic history. Vera Cáslavská (1968), along with Daniela Silivas of Romania (1988), are the only gymnasts to obtain medals in all six events at one Olympics. Gymnastics and swimming dominate the medal table, with canoeist Birgit Fischer-Schmidt outstanding not only among women competitors but as the holder of the most Olympic canoeing medals of all time.

↑ Spitz splash
Although Mark Spitz has won 11 medals, his overall total has been exceeded by seven other Olympic athletes.

← Redgrave's record
Britain's Steve Redgrave is a member of the élite pantheon of Olympic athletes who have won five consecutive golds.

Winter Olympics

top 10 WINTER OLYMPICS MEDAL-WINNING COUNTRIES

COUNTRY	(GOLD)	MEDALS* (SILVER)	(BRONZE)	(TOTAL)
1 USSR/Unified Team/Russia	113	82	78	273
2 Norway	94	93	73	260
3 USA*	70	70	51	191
4 Germany/West Germany	68	67	52	187
5 Austria	41	57	65	163
6 Finland	41	51	49	141
7 East Germany	39	37	35	111
8 Sweden	36	28	38	102
9 Switzerland	32	33	36	101
10 Canada	30	28	37	95

* Up to and including the 2002 Salt Lake City Games; includes medals won for figure skating and ice hockey in the Summer Games prior to the launch of the Winter Olympics in 1924

First Fact American athlete Edward "Eddie" Eagan (1897–1967) is the first and – to date – the only person to win gold medals in both Summer and Winter Olympic Games. In 1920 he beat Sverre Sörsdal of Norway in the light-heavyweight boxing final at the Antwerp Olympics. He failed to win a medal at the 1924 Olympics and did not take part in the 1928 Games, but at the 1932 Lake Placid Winter Olympics he was a member of the winning four-man bobsleigh team for the USA .

➲ Calgary commemoration
The cross-country skier was one of a series of ten silver $20 coins issued by Canada to commemorate the 1988 Winter Olympics.

top 10 WINTER OLYMPICS GOLD MEDALLISTS

	MEDALLIST / COUNTRY	SPORT	GOLD MEDALS*
1	Bjørn Dählie, Norway	Cross-country skiing	8
2 =	Lyubov Egorova, UT#/Russia	Cross-country skiing	6
=	Lydia Skoblikova, USSR	Speed skating	6
4 =	Bonnie Blair, USA	Speed skating	5
=	Eric Heiden, USA	Speed skating	5
=	Larissa Lazutina, UT#/Russia	Cross-country skiing	5
=	Clas Thunberg, Norway	Speed skating	5
=	Ole Einar Bjøerndalen, Norway	Biathlon	5
9 =	Ivar Ballangrud, Norway	Speed skating	4
=	Lee-Kyung Chun, South Korea	Short track speed skating	4
=	Yevgeny Grishin, USSR	Speed skating	4
=	Sixten Jernberg, Sweden	Cross-country skiing	4
=	Johann Olav Koss, Norway	Speed skating	4
=	Galina Kulakova, USSR	Cross-country skiing	4
=	Matti Nykänen, Finland	Ski jumping	4
=	Claudia Pechstein, Germany	Speed skating	4
=	Raisa Smetanina, UT#/Russia	Cross-country skiing	4
=	Gunde Svan, Sweden	Cross-country skiing	4
=	Alexander Tikhonov, USSR	Biathlon	4
=	Thomas Wassberg, Sweden	Cross-country skiing	4
=	Nikolai Zimyatov, USSR	Cross-country skiing	4

* All events up to and including the 2002 Salt Lake City Games
# UT = Unified Team, Commonwealth of Independent States, 1992

top 10 WINTER OLYMPICS **MEDAL WINNERS**

	MEDALLIST / COUNTRY	SPORT	YEARS	(GOLD)	MEDALS* (SILVER)	(BRONZE)	(TOTAL)
1	**Bjørn Dählie**, Norway	Cross-country skiing	1992–98	8	4	0	12
2	**Raisa Smetanina**, USSR	Cross-country skiing	1976–92	4	5	1	10
3 =	**Sixten Jernberg**, Sweden	Cross-country skiing	1956–64	4	3	2	9
=	**Lyubov Egorova**, UT#/Russia	Cross-country skiing	1992–94	6	3	0	9
=	**Stefania Belmondo**, Italy	Cross-country skiing	1992–2002	2	3	4	9
=	**Larisa Lazutina**, UT#/Russia	Cross-country skiing	1992–2002	5	3	1	9
7 =	**Galina Kulakova**, USSR	Cross-country skiing	1968–80	4	2	2	8
=	**Karin Kania (née Enke)**, East Germany	Speed skating	1980–88	3	4	1	8
=	**Gunda Neimann-Stirnemann**, East Germany/Germany	Speed skating	1992–98	3	4	1	8
10 =	**Clas Thunberg**, Norway	Speed skating	1924–28	5	1	1	7
=	**Ivar Ballangrud**, Norway	Speed skating	1928–36	4	2	1	7
=	**Veikko Hakulinen**, Finland	Cross-country skiing	1952–60	3	3	1	7
=	**Eero Mäntyranta**, Finland	Cross-country skiing	1960–68	3	2	2	7
=	**Andrea Ehrig (née Mitscherlich; formerly Schöne)**, East Germany	Speed skating	1976–88	1	5	1	7
=	**Marja-Liisa Kirvesniemi (née Hämäläinen)**, Finland	Cross-country skiing	1980–98	3	0	4	7
=	**Bogdan Musiol**, East Germany/Germany	Bobsledding	1986–92	1	5	1	7
=	**Elena Välbe**, UT#/Russia	Cross-country skiing	1992–98	3	0	4	7
=	**Kjetil Andre Aamoldt**, Norway	Alpine skiing	1992–2002	3	2	2	7
=	**Rico Gross**, Germany	Biathlon	1992–2002	3	2	2	7
=	**Claudia Pechstein**, Germany	Speed skating	1992–2002	4	1	2	7

* All events up to and including the 2002 Salt Lake City Games
\# UT = Unified Team, Commonwealth of Independent States, 1992

Prior to Bjørn Dählie's Olympic achievements, Russia's Raisa Smetanina was the all-time Winter Olympics medallist. Born on 29 February 1952, she appeared in five Olympics for the Soviet Union and the Unified Team in 1992. Her first medal was silver in the 5-km Cross Country at Innsbruck in 1976. She came away from those Games with two golds and a silver, won silver and gold in 1980, two silvers in 1984, a bronze and silver in 1988, and her 10th and last medal, a gold, in the 4 x 5-km Relay in 1992. Considered the greatest cross-country skier of all time, Bjørn Dählie (born 1967) gained more golds and more medals than any other Winter Games competitor in three Olympics and might have gone on to further wins in Salt Lake City in 2002 had his career not been cut short by injury.

➲ **Small wonder**
Despite her diminutive 1.55 m (5 ft) height, Italian skier Stefania Belmondo won Olympic medals in four Games.

top 10 SUMMER OLYMPICS
MEDAL-WINNING
COUNTRIES

	COUNTRY	(GOLD)	MEDALS* (SILVER)	(BRONZE)	(TOTAL)
1	USA	907	697	615	2,219
2	USSR/Unified Team/Russia	525	436	409	1,370
3	Germany/West Germany	229	258	298	785
4	Great Britain	189	242	237	668
5	France	199	202	230	631
6	Italy	189	154	168	511
7	Sweden	140	157	179	476
8	Hungary	158	141	161	460
9	East Germany	159	150	136	445
10	Australia	119	126	154	399

* 1896–2004 inclusive

There have been 25 Summer Olympics since the 1896 Games in Athens (including the 1906 Intercalated Games, also held in Athens). The USSR first entered the Olympic Games in 1952, but boycotted the 1984 Games. The USA boycotted the 1980 Games. James Connolly of the USA became the first Olympic champion in 1896 when he took the hop, step, and jump (now triple jump) first prize which, in those days, was a silver medal. Runners-up used to receive bronze medals and 3rd-placed athletes were not rewarded for their efforts. However, all Olympic records consider the 1st, 2nd, and 3rd athletes in 1896 to have received gold, silver, and bronze medals.

➔ Olympic victors
The USA and USSR/Russia have dominated the Summer Olympics: US athlete Jesse Owens (above) won four gold medals at the 1936 Berlin Olympics, Russian rower Nikolai Spinev (top right) and US athlete Shawn Crawford (bottom right) were both gold medal winners at the 2004 Athens Games, while 17-year-old Soviet gymnast Olga Korbut (bottom left) was a triple gold and silver medal-winner at the 1972 Munich Olympics.

⬅ Munich medals
US swimmer Mark Spitz won an unprecedented seven of his country's total of 33 gold medals at the 1972 Munich Olympics.

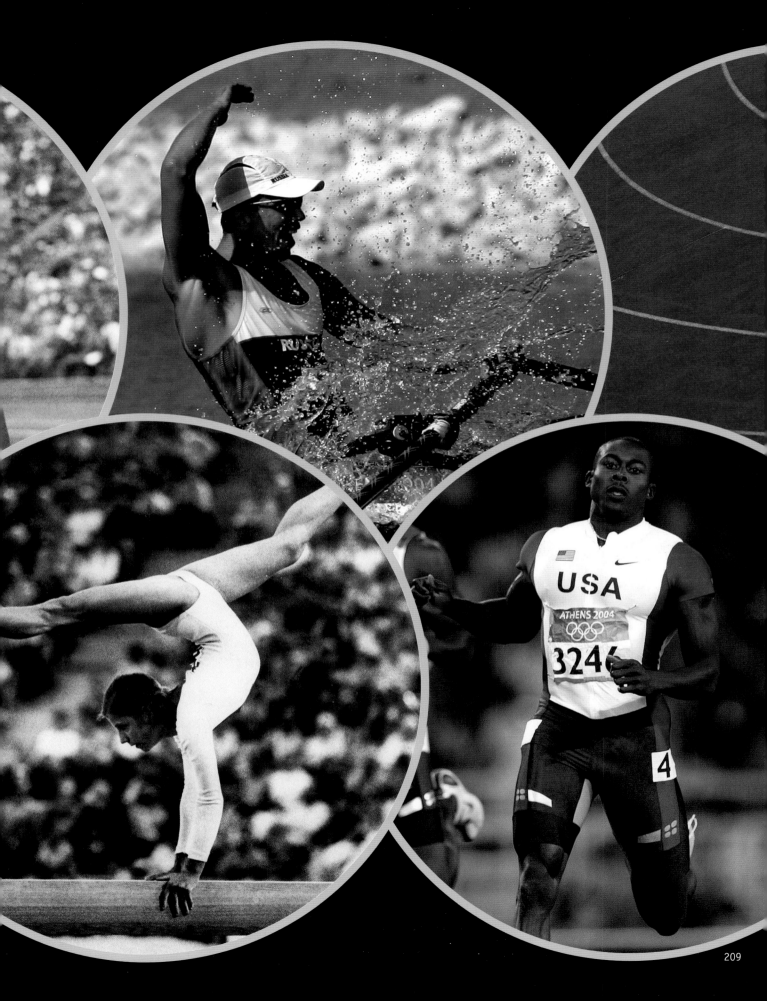

American Football

top 10 CAREER TOUCHDOWNS

	PLAYER	YEARS	TOUCHDOWNS*
1	Jerry Rice	1985–2004	207
2	Emmitt Smith	1990–2004	175
3	Marcus Allen	1982–97	144
4	Marshall Faulk	1994–2004	135
5	Cris Carter	1987–2002	130
6	Jim Brown	1957–65	126
7	Walter Payton	1975–87	125
8	John Riggins	1971–85	116
9	Lenny Moore	1956–67	111
10	Barry Sanders	1989–98	109

* As at end of 2004 season

Source: National Football League

A wide receiver, Jerry Rice also holds Super Bowl records in touchdowns, receptions, and receiving yards, winning three Super Bowls with the San Francisco 49ers (1989, 1990, 1995). He only once topped the NFL scoring list, in 1987, with 130 points.

top 10 NFL POINT-SCORERS

	PLAYER	YEARS	POINTS*
1	Gary Anderson	1982–2004	2,448
2	Morten Andersen	1982–2004	2,358
3	George Blanda	1949–75	2,002
4	Norm Johnson	1982–99	1,736
5	Nick Lowery	1980–96	1,711
6	Jan Stenerud	1980–85	1,699
7	Eddie Murray	1980–2000	1,594
8	Al Del Greco	1984–2000	1,584
9	John Carney	1988–2004	1,537
10	Matt Stover	1991–2004	1,481

* As at end of 2004 season

Source: National Football League

Born in 1959, Gary Anderson started his career with the Pittsburgh Steelers in 1982 before playing two seasons with the Philadelphia Eagles in 1995–96. He had a year with the San Francisco 49ers in 1997, moved on to the Minnesota Vikings in 1998, and then to the Tennessee Titans in 2003. He broke George Blanda's points record in 2000. Anderson came out of retirement in 2003 and again in 2004 to help out the Titans.

First Fact

At the end of the 1932 season, the Chicago Bears were tied with the Portsmouth (Ohio) Spartans, and a play-off was arranged to decide the league champions. On 18 December heavy snow made it impossible to play on Chicago's Wrigley Field so the game was moved indoors to Chicago Stadium, an indoor arena just vacated by a circus. As the field for this first-ever indoor NFL game was 80 yards shorter than a normal playing area, with walls at each end, the goal posts had to be repositioned and new rules invented. A crowd of 11,198 saw the Bears win 9-0.

↩ Marshall law

St. Louis Rams running back Marshall Faulk (born 1973) set the NFL record for yards from scrimmage with 1,381 rushing and 1,048 receiving.

top 10 BIGGEST **WINNING MARGINS** IN THE SUPER BOWL

	WINNERS	RUNNERS-UP	YEAR	SCORE	MARGIN
1	San Francisco 49ers	Denver Broncos	1990	55–10	45
2	Chicago Bears	New England Patriots	1986	46–10	36
3	Dallas Cowboys	Buffalo Bills	1993	52–17	35
4	Washington Redskins	Denver Broncos	1988	42–10	32
5	Los Angeles Raiders	Washington Redskins	1984	38–9	29
6	=Baltimore Ravens	New York Giants	2001	34–7	27
	=Tampa Bay Buccaneers	Oakland Raiders	2003	48–21	27
8	Green Bay Packers	Kansas City Chiefs	1967	35–10	25
9	San Francisco 49ers	San Diego Chargers	1995	49–26	23
10	San Francisco 49ers	Miami Dolphins	1985	38–16	22

Source: National Football League

The closest Super Bowl was in 1991 when the New York Giants beat the Buffalo Bills 20–19. Scott Norwood missed a 47-yard field goal eight seconds from the end of time to deprive the Bills of their first-ever Super Bowl win.

top 10 **NFL COACHES** WITH THE MOST WINS

	COACH	GAMES WON*
1	Don Shula	347
2	George Halas	324
3	Tom Landry	270
4	Curly Lambeau	229
5	Chuck Noll	209
6	Dan Reeves	201
7	Chuck Knox	193
8	Marty Schottenheimer	182
9	Paul Brown#	170
10	Bud Grant	168

* Regular and post-season games

A further 52 wins that came in the AAFC are not recognized by the NFL

Source: National Football League

top 10 **MOST SUCCESSFUL** SUPER BOWL TEAMS

	TEAM	SUPER BOWL GAMES (WINS)	(RUNNERS-UP)	(POINTS*)
1	Dallas Cowboys	5	3	13
2	=Pittsburgh Steelers	4	1	10
	=San Francisco 49ers	5	0	10
4	=Denver Broncos	2	4	8
	=New England Patriots	3	2	8
	=Oakland / Los Angeles Raiders	3	2	8
	=Washington Redskins	3	2	8
8	=Green Bay Packers	3	1	7
	=Miami Dolphins	2	3	7
10	New York Giants	2	1	5

* Based on two points for a Super Bowl win, and one for runner-up; up to and including 2005 Super Bowl

Source: National Football League

top 10 **OLDEST** NFL TEAMS*

	PRESENT NAME / NAME DURING FIRST SEASON	FIRST SEASON
1	=Arizona Cardinals / Chicago Cardinals	1920
	=Chicago Bears / Decatur Staleys	1920
3	Green Bay Packers / Green Bay Packers	1921
4	New York Giants / New York Giants	1925
5	Detroit Lions / Portsmouth OH Spartans	1930
6	Washington Redskins / Boston Braves	1932
7	=Philadelphia Eagles / Philadelphia Eagles	1933
	=Pittsburgh Steelers / Pittsburgh Pirates	1933
9	St. Louis Rams / Cleveland Rams	1937
10	=Cleveland Browns / Cleveland Browns	1946
	=San Francisco 49ers / San Francisco 49ers	1946

* Current teams only; based on first season in the League

➲ **Ahead of the game**
Among the first NFL teams, the NY Giants have gained two and the Washington Redskins three Super Bowl victories.

Track Athletics

top 10 COUNTRIES WITH THE **MOST TRACK ATHLETICS MEDALS** AT THE 2004 ATHENS OLYMPIC GAMES

	COUNTRY	(GOLD)	MEDALS (SILVER)	(BRONZE)	(TOTAL)
1	USA	6	7	5	18
2	Russia	1	6	2	9
3	= Ethiopia	2	2	3	7
	= Kenya	1	4	2	7
5	Jamaica	2	1	2	5
6	Australia	–	1	3	4
7	= Great Britain	3	–	–	3
	= Morocco	2	1	–	3
9	= Bahrain	1	–	1	2
	= China	2	–	–	2
	= France	–	–	2	2
	= Greece	2	–	–	2
	= Italy	2	–	–	2
	= Nigeria	–	–	2	2
	= Portugal	–	1	1	2
	= Romania	–	1	1	2
	= Ukraine	–	1	1	2

top 10 **FASTEST MILERS** EVER*

	ATHLETE / COUNTRY	YEAR	TIME (MIN:SEC)
1	**Hicham El Guerrouj**, Morocco	1999	3:43.13
2	**Noah Ngeny**, Kenya	1999	3:43.40
3	**Noureddine Morceli**, Algeria	1993	3:44.39
4	**Steve Cram**, GB	1985	3:46.32
5	**Daniel Komen**, Kenya	1997	3:46.38
6	**Vénuste Niyongabo**, Burundi	1997	3:46.70
7	**Saïd Aouita**, Morocco	1987	3:46.76
8	**Bernard Lagat**, Kenya	2001	3:47.28
9	**Sebastian Coe**, GB	1981	3:47.33
10	**Laban Rotich**, Kenya	1997	3:47.65

* Outdoor records as at 1 Jan 2005; fastest time by each athlete only included

top 10 **FASTEST WOMEN** EVER*

	ATHLETE / COUNTRY	YEAR	TIME (SEC)
1	**Florence Griffith Joyner**, USA	1988	10.49
2	**Marion Jones**, USA	1998	10.65
3	**Christine Arron**, France	1998	10.73
4	**Merlene Ottey**, Jamaica	1996	10.74
5	**Evelyn Ashford**, USA	1984	10.76
6	= **Irina Privalova**, Russia	1994	10.77
	= **Ivet Lalova**, Bulgaria	2004	10.77
8	**Dawn Sowell**, USA	1989	10.78
9	= **Xuemei Li**, China	1997	10.79
	= **Inger Miller**, USA	1999	10.79

* Based on fastest time for the 100 metres as at 1 Jan 2005; fastest time by each athlete only included

At the quarter-finals of the US Olympic trials on 16 July 1988, Florence Griffith Joyner (1959–98), nicknamed "Flo Jo", set a women's record that has never been beaten. Her mysterious death at the age of 38 fuelled rumours that her achievement had been assisted by performance-enhancing drugs.

↩ Hayes makes it
Joanna Hayes (b. 1976) wins the 100-metre hurdles at the 2004 Olympics to set a new Olympic record of 12.37 seconds and add to the USA's track tally of six golds.

ATHENS 2004 ⊕⊕⊕⊕⊕

the 10 LATEST TRACK WORLD RECORDS

	ATHLETE / COUNTRY / EVENT	WINNING TIME (HR:MIN:SEC)	DATE
1	**Saif Saaeed Shaheen**, Qatar Men's 3,000 m steeplechase	7:53:63	3 Sept 2004
2	**Denis Nizhegorodov**, Russia Men's 50 km walk	3:35:29	13 June 2004
3	**Elvan Abeylegesse**, Turkey Women's 5,000 m	14:24.68	11 June 2004
4	**Kenenisa Bekele**, Ethiopia Men's 10,000 m	26:20.31	8 June 2004
5	**Kenenisa Bekele**, Ethiopia Men's 5,000 m	12:37.35	31 May 2004
6	**Paul Tergat**, Kenya Men's marathon	2:04:55	28 Sept 2003
7	**Jefferson Pérez**, Ecuador Men's 20 km walk	1:17:21	23 Aug 2003
8	**Yuliya Pechonkina**, Russia Women's 400 m hurdles	52.34	8 Aug 2003
9	**Paula Radcliffe**, GB Women's marathon	2:15:25	13 Apr 2003
10	**Tim Montgomery**, USA Men's 100 m	9.78	14 Sept 2002

➊ Long-distance runners
Kenenisa Bekele leads fellow Ethiopian Sileshi Sihine to set a new 10,000 metre record at the 2004 Olympics.

top 10 FASTEST MEN EVER*

	ATHLETE / COUNTRY	YEAR	TIME (SEC)
1	**Tim Montgomery**, USA	2002	9.78
2	**Maurice Greene**, USA	1999	9.79
3	=**Donovan Bailey**, Canada	1996	9.84
	=**Bruny Surin**, Canada	1999	9.84
5	=**Leroy Burrell**, USA	1994	9.85
	=**Justin Gatlin**, USA	2004	9.85
7	=**Carl Lewis**, USA	1991	9.86
	=**Frank Fredericks**, Namibia	1996	9.86
	=**Ato Boldon**, Trinidad	1998	9.86
	=**Francis Obikwelu**, Portugal	2004	9.86

* Based on fastest time for the 100 metres as at 1 Jan 2005; fastest time by each athlete only included

Some would argue that Michael Johnson (USA) should be in this category with his remarkable 200 metre record of 19.32 seconds in 1996 (equivalent to a 100 metre time of 9.66 seconds), but his best 100 metre time is only 10.09 seconds.

Field Athletics

top 10 **LONGEST-STANDING** OUTDOOR FIELD ATHLETICS WORLD RECORDS (FEMALE)

ATHLETE / COUNTRY	EVENT	DATE SET	DATE BROKEN	DURATION (YRS	MTHS	DAYS)
1 **Natalya Lisovskaya**, USSR	Shot put	7 June 1987	*	17	6	24
2 **Stefka Kostadinova**, Bulgaria	High jump	30 Aug 1987	*	17	4	1
3 **Galina Chistyakova**, Russia	Long jump	11 June 1988	*	16	6	21
4 **Gabriele Reinsch**, Germany	Discus	9 July 1988	*	16	5	23
5 **Jackie Joyner-Kersee**, USA	Heptathlon	24 Sept 1988	*	16	3	8
6 **Gisela Mauermayer**, Germany	Shot put	15 July 1934	4 Aug 1948	14	0	20
7 **Gisela Mauermayer**	Discus	11 July 1936	8 Aug 1948	12	0	28
8 **Kinue Hitomi**, Japan	Long jump	20 May 1928	30 July 1939	11	2	10
9 **Francina Blankers-Koen**, Netherlands	Long jump	19 Sept 1943	20 Feb 1954	11	5	1
10 **Iolanda Balas**, Romania	High jump	16 July 1961	4 Sept 1971	10	1	19

* As at 1 Jan 2005

top 10 **LONGEST-STANDING** OUTDOOR FIELD ATHLETICS WORLD RECORDS (MALE)

ATHLETE / COUNTRY	EVENT	DATE SET	DATE BROKEN	DURATION (YRS	MTHS	DAYS)
1 **Jesse Owens**, USA	Long jump	25 May 1935	12 Aug 1960	25	2	18
2 **Patrick Ryan**, USA	Hammer	17 Aug 1913	27 Aug 1938	25	0	10
3 **Bob Beamon**, USA	Long jump	18 Oct 1968	30 Aug 1991	22	10	12
4 **Daniel Ahearn**, USA	Triple jump	30 May 1911	27 Oct 1931	20	4	28
5 **Peter O'Connor**, GB	Long jump	5 Aug 1901	23 July 1921	19	11	13
6 **Ralph Rose**, USA	Shot put	21 Aug 1909	6 May 1928	18	8	15
7 **Jürgen Schult**, Germany	Discus	6 June 1986	*	18	6	25
8 **Yuriy Syedikh**, Russia	Hammer	30 Aug 1986	*	18	4	2
9 **Naoto Tajima**, Japan	Triple jump	6 Aug 1936	30 Sept 1951	15	1	24
10 **Cornelius Warmerdam**, USA	Pole vault	23 May 1942	27 Apr 1957	14	11	4

* As at 1 Jan 2005

top 10 LONGEST-STANDING CURRENT OLYMPIC FIELD ATHLETICS RECORDS

	ATHLETE / COUNTRY	EVENT	WINNING DISTANCE OR SCORE	DATE
1	**Bob Beamon**, USA	Men's long jump	8.90 m	18 Oct 1968
2	**Ilona Slupianek**, East Germany	Women's shot	22.41 m	24 July 1980
3	**Ulf Timmermann**, East Germany	Men's shot	22.47 m	23 Sept 1988
4	**Jackie Joyner-Kersee**, USA	Women's heptathlon	7,291 points	24 Sept 1988
5	**Sergey Litvinov**, USSR	Men's hammer	84.80 m	26 Sept 1988
6 =	**Martina Hellmann**, East Germany	Women's discus	72.30 m	29 Sept 1988
=	**Jackie Joyner-Kersee**	Women's long jump	7.40 m	29 Sept 1988
8	**Inessa Kravets**, Ukraine	Women's triple jump	15.33 m	4 Aug 1996
9	**Kenny Harrison**, USA	Men's triple jump	18.09 m	27 July 1996
10	**Charles Austin**, USA	Men's high jump	2.39 m	28 July 1996

Bob Beamon's record-breaking jump in 1968 is regarded as one of the greatest achievements in athletics. He was aided by Mexico City's rarefied atmosphere, but to add a staggering 55 cm (22½ in) to the old world record, and win the competition by 71 cm (28 in) was no mean feat. Beamon's jump of 8.90 m (29 ft 2½ in) was the first beyond both 8.53 and 8.84 m (28 and 29 ft). The next jump to exceed 8.53 m (28 ft) in the Olympics was not until 1980, 12 years after Beamon's leap.

top 10 COUNTRIES WITH THE MOST FIELD ATHLETICS MEDALS AT THE 2004 ATHENS OLYMPIC GAMES

	COUNTRY	(G)	(S)	(B)	(TOTAL)
1	**Russia**	5	3	5	13
2	**USA**	2	5	–	7
3	**Cuba**	2	1	1	4
4 =	**Greece**	–	2	1	3
=	**Sweden**	3	–	–	3
6	**Bulgaria**	–	1	1	2
7	**Czech Republic**	1	–	1	2
8	**Germany**	–	2	–	2
9	**Lithuania**	1	1	–	2
10	**Ukraine**	1	–	1	2
	Great Britain	–	–	1	1

the 10 MOST RECENT FIELD ATHLETICS WORLD RECORDS*

	ATHLETE / COUNTRY	EVENT	WINNING DISTANCE OR SCORE	DATE
1	**Yelena Isinbayeva**, Russia	Women's pole vault	4.92 m	3 Sept 2004
2	**Osleidys Menéndez**, Cuba	Women's javelin throw	71.54 m	1 July 2001
3	**Roman Sebrle**, Czech Republic	Men's decathlon	9,026 points	27 May 2001
4	**Mihaela Melinte**, Romania	Women's hammer throw	76.07 m	29 Aug 1999
5	**Jan Zelezny**, Czech Republic	Men's javelin throw	98.48 m	25 May 1996
6	**Inessa Kravets**, Ukraine	Women's triple jump	15.50 m	10 Aug 1995
7	**Jonathan Edwards**, GB	Men's triple jump	18.29 m	7 Aug 1995
8	**Sergey Bubka**, Ukraine	Men's pole vault	6.14 m	31 July 1994
9	**Javier Sotomayor**, Cuba	Men's high jump	2.45 m	27 July 1993
10	**Mike Powell**, USA	Men's long jump	8.95 m	30 Aug 1991

*As at 1 Jan 2005

Russian and pole
In 2004 in Brussels, Belgium, Yelena Isinbayeva (b. 1982) beat her own gold medal-winning Olympic height of 4.91 m to set a new world women's pole vault record.

Cricket

top 10 ENGLAND RUN-MAKERS IN TEST CRICKET

	BATSMAN	YEARS	INNINGS	RUNS*
1	Graham Gooch	1975–95	215	8,900
2	Alec Stewart	1989–2003	235	8,463
3	David Gower	1978–92	204	8,231
4	Geoff Boycott	1964–82	193	8,114
5	Mike Atherton	1989–2001	212	7,728
6	Colin Cowdrey	1954–75	188	7,624
7	Wally Hammond	1927–47	140	7,249
8	Sir Leonard Hutton	1937–55	138	6,971
9	Ken Barrington	1955–68	131	6,806
10	Graham Thorpe	1993–2004	177	6,636

* As at 31 Mar 2005

Graham Gooch (b.1953) played for Essex, making his Test debut in 1975 and succeeding John Emburey as Captain in 1988. As well as his record Test run total, achieved in 118 Tests, he is the only England batsman to score over 1,000 runs during an English season (1,058 against New Zealand and India in 1990).

top 10 WICKET-TAKERS IN TEST CRICKET

	BOWLER / COUNTRY	YEARS	TESTS	WICKETS*
1	Shane Warne, Australia	1992–2005	123	583
2	Muttiah Muralitharan, Sri Lanka	1992–2004	91	532
3	Courtney Walsh, West Indies	1984–2001	132	519
4	Glenn McGrath, Australia	1993–2005	109	499
5	Anil Kumble, India	1990–2005	95	461
6	Kapil Dev, India	1978–94	131	434
7	Richard Hadlee, New Zealand	1973–90	86	431
8	Wasim Akram, Pakistan	1985–2002	104	414
9	Curtly Ambrose, West Indies	1988–2000	98	405
10	Ian Botham, England	1977–92	102	383

* As at 31 Mar 2005

TOP 10 HIGHEST INDIVIDUAL TEST INNINGS

	BATSMAN	MATCH	VENUE	YEAR	RUNS*
1	Brian Lara	West Indies v England	St. John's	2003–04	400#
2	Matthew Hayden	Australia v Zimbabwe	Perth	2003–04	380
3	Brian Lara	West Indies v England	St. John's	1993–94	375
4	Gary Sobers	West Indies v Pakistan	Kingston	1957–58	365#
5	Len Hutton	England v Australia	The Oval	1938	364
6	Sanath Jayasuriya	Sri Lanka v India	Colombo	1997–98	340
7	Hanif Mohammad	Pakistan v West Indies	Bridgetown	1957–58	337
8	Walter Hammond	England v New Zealand	Auckland	1932–33	336#
9	=Don Bradman	Australia v England	Leeds	1930	334
	=Mark Taylor#	Australia v Pakistan	Peshawar	1998–99	334#

* As at 31 Mar 2005
# Not out

First Fact The first cricketer to score a century in a Test match was the legendary player W. G. (William Gilbert) Grace (1848–1915). On 6 September 1880 he batted in the first ever Test in England, against Australia at Kennington Oval, where he scored 152 of England's total of 420 runs. Grace partnered his brother E. M. (Edward Mills) Grace (1841–1911), who scored 36. Their younger brother G. F. (George Frederick) Grace (1850–80) also played, but was out for a duck – and tragically died of pneumonia two weeks later, at the age of just 29.

Len Hutton's Test record of 364 in 1938 seemed unbeatable until Gary Sobers came along and broke it by one run nearly 20 years later. His record also looked invincible until Brian Lara smashed it with a 375 in 1993–94 but the West Indian's record stood for a "mere" 10 years until October 2003, when Matthew Hayden of Australia scored 380 on the second day of the first Test against Zimbabwe at Perth.

top 10 RUN-MAKERS IN TEST CRICKET

	BATSMAN / COUNTRY	YEARS	TESTS	RUNS*
1	Allan Border, Australia	1978–94	156	11,174
2	Steve Waugh, Australia	1985–2004	168	10,927
3	Sachin Tendulkar, India	1989–2005	123	10,134
4	Sunil Gavaskar, India	1971–87	125	10,122
5	Brian Lara, West Indies	1990–2004	112	10,094
6	Graham Gooch, England	1975–95	118	8,900
7	Javed Miandad, Pakistan	1976–94	124	8,832
8	Viv Richards, West Indies	1974–91	121	8,540
9	Alec Stewart, England	1989–2004	133	8,463
10	David Gower, England	1978–92	117	8,231

* As at 31 Mar 2005

Allan Border (b. 1955), Captain of Australia in 1984–85 and 1993–94, achieved a number of records in addition to his run-scoring. He played in 153 consecutive Test matches, scored more 50s (63) and more of over 50 (93) than any player, achieved the most catches as a fielder (154), and was the first player to score 150 in both innings in a Test match (in Pakistan in 1980).

top 10 RUN-MAKERS IN FIRST CLASS CRICKET

	BATSMAN	(YEARS)	TOTAL (INNINGS)	HIGHEST (SCORE)	(RUNS)*
1	Jack Hobbs	1905–34	1,325	365[#]	61,760
2	Frank Woolley	1906–38	1,530	305[#]	58,959
3	Patsy Hendren	1907–37	1,300	301[#]	57,611
4	Philip Mead	1905–36	1,340	280[#]	55,061
5	W. G. Grace	1865–1908	1,478	344	54,211
6	Herbert Sutcliffe	1919–45	1,098	313	50,670
7	Walter Hammond	1920–51	1,005	336	50,551
8	Geoff Boycott	1962–86	1,014	261[#]	48,426
9	Tom Graveney	1948–72	1,223	258	47,793
10	Graham Gooch	1973–2000	990	333	44,846

* As at 31 Mar 2005

[#] Not out

Sir John Berry "Jack" Hobbs made his cricketing debut for Surrey in 1905. Not only is he the most prolific scorer in First Class cricket, his total of 199 centuries is a record. He was knighted in 1953 and after retiring bought a sports shop in Fleet Street.

top 10 RUN-MAKERS IN ONE DAY INTERNATIONALS

	BATSMAN / COUNTRY	INNINGS	RUNS*
1	Sachin Tendulkar, India	335	13,503
2	Inzamam-ul-Haq, Pakistan	314	10,684
3	Sourav Ganguly, India	269	9,945
4	Sanath Jayasuriya, Sri Lanka	325	9,924
5	Mohammad Azharuddin, India	308	9,378
6	Aravinda de Silva, Sri Lanka	296	9,284
7	Brian Lara, West Indies	244	9,280
8	Saeed Anwar, Pakistan	244	8,823
9	Desmond Haynes, West Indies	237	8,648
10	Mark Waugh, Australia	236	8,500

* As at 31 Mar 2005

Born in 1973, Sachin Tendulkar made his One Day International debut at Gujranwala against Pakistan in 1989–90 at the age of 16, facing the bowling of Wasim Akram and Waqar Younis. He also made his test debut at 16. Standing at just 1.62 m (5 ft 4 in), he has played First Class cricket for Bombay, Yorkshire, and his home country of India. His highest One Day score is 186 not out.

top 10 WICKET-TAKERS IN ONE DAY INTERNATIONALS

	BOWLER	COUNTRY	MATCHES	WICKETS*
1	Wasim Akram	Pakistan	356	502
2	Waqar Younis	Pakistan	262	416
3	Muttiah Muralitharan	Sri Lanka	238	369
4 =	Anil Kumble	India	260	323
=	Chaminda Vaas	Sri Lanka	250	323
6 =	Glenn McGrath	Australia	205	315
=	Javagal Srinath	India	229	315
8	Shaun Pollock	South Africa	228	313
9	Shane Warne	Australia	194	293
10	Saqlain Mushtaq	Pakistan	169	288

* As at 31 Mar 2005

Considered the finest bowler of his generation, Wasim Akram (b. 1966) captained his country and contributed to Pakistan's notable success in One-Day Internationals, including its victory in the World Series in Australia in 1994. During his One-Day career, in addition to his wicket-taking record, he scored 3,717 runs, while in his Test career he took 414 Test wickets, a record for a Pakistan player.

Basketball

top 10 OLYMPIC BASKETBALL COUNTRIES*

| | COUNTRY | MEDALS | | | |
		(G)	(S)	(B)	(TOTAL)
1	USA	17	2	3	22
2	USSR/Unified Team/Russia	5	4	5	14
3	Yugoslavia	1	5	2	8
4	Brazil	0	1	4	5
5	=Australia	0	2	1	3
	=Lithuania	0	0	3	3
7	=Bulgaria	0	1	1	2
	=China	0	1	1	2
	=France	0	2	0	2
	=Italy	0	2	0	2
	=Uruguay	0	0	2	2

* Based on total of gold, silver, and bronze medals won in the men's and women's competitions

A demonstration sport at the 1904 Olympics, basketball made its official debut at Berlin in 1936, when it was played outdoors. Dr. James Naismith, the Canadian inventor of the game, presented the medals to the winning US team. The USA went on to dominate the medals table, with Teresa Edwards (USA) the only person to have won five Olympic medals for basketball. She won gold in 1984, 1992, 1996, and 2000, and bronze in 1988.

top 10 TEAMS WITH THE MOST NBA TITLES

	TEAM*	YEARS	TITLES
1	Boston Celtics	1957–86	16
2	Minneapolis Lakers / Los Angeles Lakers	1949–2002	14
3	Chicago Bulls	1991–98	6
4	=Detroit Pistons	1989–2004	3
	=Philadelphia Warriors / Golden State Warriors	1947–75	3
	=Syracuse Nationals / Philadelphia 76ers	1955–83	3
7	=Baltimore Bullets / Washington Bullets	1948–78	2
	=Houston Rockets	1994–95	2
	=New York Knicks	1970–72	2
	=San Antonio Spurs	1999–2003	2

* Teams separated by / indicate change of franchise and mean they have won the championship under both names

Source: National Basketball Association

Basketball is one of the few sports that can trace its exact origins. It was invented by Dr. James Naismith at Springfield, Massachusetts, in 1891. Professional basketball in the USA dates back to 1898, but the National Basketball Association (NBA) was not formed until 1949, when the National Basketball League and Basketball Association of America merged. The NBA consists of 27 teams split into Eastern and Western Conferences. At the end of an 82-game regular season, the top eight teams in each Conference play off and the two Conference champions meet in a best-of-seven final for the NBA Championship.

top 10 BIGGEST NBA ARENAS

	ARENA / LOCATION	TEAM	CAPACITY
1	Palace of Auburn Hills, Auburn Hills, Michigan	Detroit Pistons	22,076
2	United Center, Chicago, Illinois	Chicago Bulls	21,711
3	MCI Center, Washington, DC	Washington Wizards	20,674
4	Gund Arena, Cleveland, Ohio	Cleveland Cavaliers	20,562
5	First Union Center, Philadelphia, Pennsylvania	Philadelphia 76ers	20,444
6	Continental Airlines Arena, East Rutherford, New Jersey	New Jersey Nets	20,049
7	Rose Garden, Portland, Oregon	Portland Trail Blazers	19,980
8	Delta Center, Salt Lake City, Utah	Utah Jazz	19,911
9	Air Canada Centre, Toronto, Canada	Toronto Raptors	19,800
10	Madison Square Garden, New York City New York	New York Knicks	19,763

Source: National Basketball Association

The Palace of Auburn Hills in a Detroit, Michigan, suburb is the new home the Detroit Pistons, who previously played at the Pontiac Silverdome. On 19 November 2004 it became notorious for a serious brawl that led to the suspension of a number of NBA players.

top 10 CURRENT NBA PLAYERS WITH THE **HIGHEST POINTS AVERAGE**

	PLAYER	GAMES PLAYED	POINTS SCORED	POINTS AVERAGE*
1	Allen Iverson	610	16,738	30.7
2	Shaquille O'Neal	882	23,583	26.7
3	LeBron James	159	3,829	24.1
4	Vince Carter	526	10,989	23.9
5	Paul Pierce	521	12,086	23.0
6	Tim Duncan	586	13,204	22.5
7	Kobe Bryant	627	14,034	22.4
9	Tracy McGrady	565	12,423	22.0
8	Chris Webber	686	14,945	21.8
10	Dirk Nowitzki	522	11,106	21.3

* Regular season games only; as at end of 2004–05 season

Source: National Basketball Association

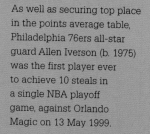

⊙ Sixers star

As well as securing top place in the points average table, Philadelphia 76ers all-star guard Allen Iverson (b. 1975) was the first player ever to achieve 10 steals in a single NBA playoff game, against Orlando Magic on 13 May 1999.

top 10 NBA **POINT-SCORERS**

	PLAYER	YEARS	TOTAL POINTS*
1	Kareem Abdul-Jabbar	1969–89	38,387
2	Karl Malone	1985–2004	36,928
3	Michael Jordan	1984–2003	32,292
4	Wilt Chamberlain	1959–73	31,419
5	Moses Malone	1976–95	27,409
6	Elvin Hayes	1968–84	27,313
7	Hakeem Olajuwon	1984–2002	26,946
8	Oscar Robertson	1960–74	26,710
9	Dominique Wilkins	1982–99	26,668
10	John Havlicek	1962–78	26,395

* Regular season games only; as at end of 2004–05 season

Source: National Basketball Association

If points from the ABA were also considered, then Kareem Abdul-Jabbar would still be No.1, with the same total. The greatest point-scorer in NBA history, he was born as Lew Alcindor but adopted a new name on converting to the Islamic faith in 1969. The next year he turned professional, playing for Milwaukee. His career spanned 20 seasons before he retired at the end of the 1989 season.

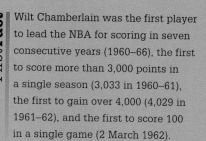

First Fact Wilt Chamberlain was the first player to lead the NBA for scoring in seven consecutive years (1960–66), the first to score more than 3,000 points in a single season (3,033 in 1960–61), the first to gain over 4,000 (4,029 in 1961–62), and the first to score 100 in a single game (2 March 1962).

Boxing

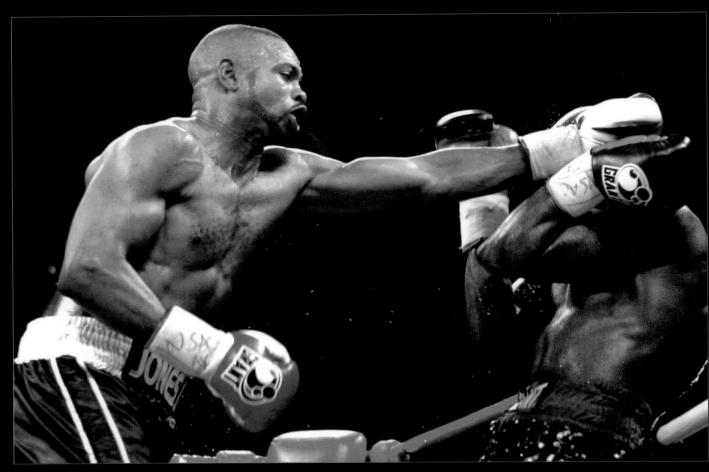

⬆ **Triple triumph** In 2003 Roy Jones Jr. won his third world title – and appeared in *The Matrix Reloaded.*

the 10 LATEST BOXERS TO WIN **THREE OR MORE WORLD TITLES**

BOXER / COUNTRY	TITLES WON	DATES*
1 **"Sugar" Shane Mosley**, USA	Junior Middleweight, WBC Welterweight, IBF Lightweight	Aug 1997–Sept 2003
2 **James Toney**, USA	IBF Cruiserweight, IBF Super Middleweight, IBF Middleweight	May 1991–Apr 2003
3 **Roy Jones Jr.**, USA	WBA Heavyweight, IBF/WBA/WBC Light Heavyweight, IBF Middleweight	May 1993–Mar 2003
4 **Johnny Tapia**, USA	IBF Featherweight, WBA Bantamweight, IBF Junior Bantamweight	July 1997–Apr 2002
5 **Oscar De La Hoya**, USA	WBA/WBC Junior Middleweight, WBC Welterweight, WBC Junior Welterweight, IBF Lightweight	May 1995–June 2001
6 **Felix Trinidad**, USA (Puerto Rico)	IBF/WBA Middleweight, IBF/WBA Junior Middleweight, IBF/WBC Welterweight	May 1993–May 2001
7 **Leo Gamez**, Venezuela	WBA Junior Bantamweight, WBA Flyweight, WBA Junior Flyweight	Aug 1993–Oct 2000
8 **Julio Cesar Chavez**, Mexico	IBF/WBC Junior Welterweight, WBC/WBA Lightweight, WBC Junior Lightweight	Sept 1984–May 1994
9 **Thomas Hearns**, USA	WBA/WBC Light Heavyweight, Middleweight, Junior Middleweight, WBA Welterweight	Aug 1980–May 1991
10 **Roberto Duran**, Panama	WBC Middleweight, Welterweight, WBA Junior Middleweight, Lightweight	May 1972–Feb 1989

* Dates between which first and last titles won

top 10 LONGEST-REIGNING WORLD HEAVYWEIGHT CHAMPIONS

	BOXER / COUNTRY	RECOGNITION	DATES	DURATION (YRS)	(MTHS)
1	Joe Louis, USA	World	1937–49*	11	8
2	Larry Holmes, USA	WBC, IBF	1978–85#	8	3
3	William Harrison "Jack" Dempsey, USA	World	1919–26	7	2
4	John Arthur "Jack" Johnson, USA	World	1908–15	6	3
5	James Jackson Jeffries, USA	World	1899–1905	5	10
6	James John Corbett, USA	World	1892–1897	4	6
7	Lennox Lewis, UK	WBC, WBA, IBF	1997–2001†	4	2
8	Jess Willard, USA	World	1915–19	4	1
9	Brian Nielsen, Denmark	IBO	1996–99*	3	8
10	Rocky Marciano, USA	World	1952–56*	3	7

* Retired / relinquished title

\# Relinquished WBC title on 11 Dec 1983 to assume title of the newly established IBF

† WBC from 7 Feb 1997; IBF, IBO, WBA, and WBC 13 Nov 1999–29 Apr 2000, when WBA title relinquished; IBF, IBO, and WBC 29 Apr 2000–22 Apr 2001

The first boxing board to be established was the World Boxing Association (WBA) in 1921, originally founded as the National Boxing Association (NBA). In 1963, the World Boxing Council (WBC) was established, followed in 1983 by the International Boxing Federation (IBF), and in 1988 by the World Boxing Organization (WBO). Finally, in 1991, the International Boxing Organization (IBO) was founded.

top 10 OLDEST BOXING WORLD HEAVYWEIGHT CHAMPIONS*

	BOXER / COUNTRY	RECOGNITION	DATE OF WIN	(YRS)	AGE MTHS	DAYS)
1	George Foreman#, USA	IBF, WBA	5 Nov 1994	46	9	14
2	Evander Holyfield#, USA	WBA	12 Aug 2000	37	9	13
3	Corrie Sanders, South Africa	WBO	8 Mar 2003	37	7	1
4	Jersey Joe Walcott, USA	Universal	18 July 1951	37	6	5
5	Muhammad Ali#, USA	WBA	15 Sept 1978	36	7	29
6	Lennox Lewis#, UK	IBF, IBO, WBC	17 Nov 2001	36	2	15
7	Roy Jones Jr., USA	WBA	1 Mar 2003	34	1	13
8	Bob Fitzsimmons, USA	Universal	17 Mar 1897	33	9	24
9	Frank Bruno, USA	WBC	2 Sept 1995	33	9	16
10	Trevor Berbick, Jamaica	WBC	22 Mar 1986	33	7	21

* Based on age at date when world title won or regained; only latest titles listed

\# Age at date of regaining title

top 10 LATEST UNDISPUTED WORLD HEAVYWEIGHT BOXING CHAMPIONS

	BOXER / COUNTRY	YEAR
1	Lennox Lewis, UK	1999
2	Riddick Bowe, USA	1992
3	Evander Holyfield, USA	1990
4	James "Buster" Douglas, USA	1990
5	Mike Tyson, USA	1987
6	Leon Spinks, USA	1978
7	Muhammad Ali, USA	1974
8	George Foreman, USA	1973
9	Joe Frazier, USA	1970
10	Muhammad Ali, USA	1967

"Undisputed" champions are those who are recognized by the main governing bodies at the time of winning their world title. The current main governing bodies are: the World Boxing Council (WBC), World Boxing Association (WBA), International Boxing Federation (IBF), and World Boxing Organization (WBO). Champions not recognized by all the major bodies of the day may coexist with these, so at any one time there may be more than one "world champion" in each weight division.

➲ Veteran victory
Corrie Sanders (born. 1967) achieved a decisive second-round knockout to become heavyweight champion, despite his advanced (for a boxer) age of 37.

Cycling

top 10 OLDEST CYCLING CLASSIC RACES

	RACE	FIRST HELD
1	**Liège–Bastogne–Liège**	1892
2	**Paris–Brussels**	1893
3 =	**Paris–Roubaix**	1896
=	**Paris–Tours***	1896
5	**Tour de France**	1903
6	**Tour of Lombardy**	1905
7	**Giro d'Italia (Tour of Italy)**	1906
8	**Milan–San Remo**	1907
9	**Tour of Flanders**	1913
10	**Grand Prix des Nations**	1932

* Known as the Blois–Chaville 1974–1987

The oldest-ever classic was the Bordeaux to Paris race, inaugurated in 1891. The longest continuous race in the world, it covered around 600 km (373 miles) non-stop, lasting around 16 hours. The riders were paced for part of the journey. Pacing ceased in 1986 and the race was discontinued two years later.

◀ Steady Eddy
Belgian champion Eddy Merckx (b. 1945) is considered one of the greatest cyclists of all time. His attempt to win a record sixth Tour de France was thwarted when he was attacked and injured by a spectator.

top 10 CYCLISTS WITH THE MOST WINS IN THE THREE MAJOR TOURS

	CYCLIST / COUNTRY	YEARS	TOUR	GIRO	VUELTA	TOTAL
1	**Eddy Merckx**, Belgium	1968–74	5	5	1	11
2	**Bernard Hinault**, France	1978–85	5	3	2	10
3	**Jacques Anquetil**, France	1957–64	5	2	1	8
4 =	**Fausto Coppi**, Italy	1940–53	2	5	0	7
=	**Miguel Induráin**, Spain	1991–95	5	2	0	7
6	**Lance Armstrong**, USA	1999–2004	6	0	0	6
7 =	**Gino Bartali**, Italy	1938–48	2	3	0	5
=	**Alfredo Binda**, Italy	1925–33	0	5	0	5
=	**Felice Gimondi**, Italy	1965–76	1	3	1	5
10	**Tony Rominger**, Switzerland	1992–95	0	1	3	4

The three major tours are: the Tour de France, launched in 1903 and won by Maurice Garin, France; the Tour of Italy (Giro d'Italia) first contested in 1909 and won by Luigi Ganna, Italy; and the Tour of Spain (Vuelta de España), first held in 1935 and won by Gustave Deloor, Belgium. Eddy Merckx won a record 33 stages of the Tour de France in 1969–75.

top 10 **FASTEST AVERAGE WINNING SPEEDS** IN THE TOUR DE FRANCE

CYCLIST / COUNTRY	YEAR	AVERAGE SPEED (KM/H)	(MPH)
1 **Lance Armstrong**, USA	2003	40.956	25.448
2 **Lance Armstrong**	2004	40.553	25.198
3 **Lance Armstrong**	1999	40.276	25.026
4 **Lance Armstrong**	2001	40.070	24.898
5 **Marco Pantani**, Italy	1998	39.983	24.844
6 **Lance Armstrong**	2002	39.919	24.804
7 **Lance Armstrong**	2000	39.570	24.587
8 **Miguel Indurain**, Spain	1992	39.504	24.546
9 **Jan Ullrich**, Germany	1997	39.237	24.380
10 **Bjarne Rijs**, Denmark	1996	39.227	24.374

The Tour de France consists of some 20 stages and covers a distance of up to 4,000 km (2,485 miles), over a three-week period, so achieving these *average* speeds represents an extraordinary feat of skill and endurance.

top 10 **OLYMPIC CYCLING** COUNTRIES

COUNTRY	MEDALS (GOLD)	(SILVER)	(BRONZE)	(TOTAL)
1 **France**	37	22	24	83
2 **Italy**	35	15	7	57
3 **Germany/West Germany**	16	19	20	55
4 **Great Britain**	12	23	19	54
5 **USA**	13	15	19	47
6 **Australia**	13	15	13	41
7 **Netherlands**	14	16	8	38
8 **USSR/Unified Team/Russia**	15	8	12	35
9 **Belgium**	6	8	10	24
10 **Denmark**	6	7	8	21

France has maintained its dominance of Olympic cycling events since the first modern Games in 1896, when the first ever gold medal winner was Léon Flameng. He cycled round a 333.3-m track 300 times to win the 100-km race. Flameng also won silver in the 10,000-m race and bronze in the 2,000-m.

First Fact The first Tour de France took place in 1903. Originally a publicity event for *L'Auto* newspaper, it took in six stages and covered a total distance of 2,428 km (1,508 miles) with 60 competitors taking part. It was won by Maurice Garin (France) at an average speed of 25.679 km/h (15.956 mph).

➲ Tour de Lance
After winning the Tour de France on a record six occasions, American cyclist Lance Armstrong (b. 1971) moved to new sponsors Discovery Channel and confirmed his intention to aim for a seventh victory in 2005.

Skateboarding

top 10 SKATEBOARDERS WITH THE MOST MEDALS IN THE X GAMES

	SKATER / COUNTRY	YEARS	(GOLD)	MEDALS* (SILVER)	(BRONZE)	(TOTAL)
1 =	Tony Hawk, USA	1995–2003	9	3	3	15
=	Andy Macdonald, USA	1996–2003	8	5	2	15
3 =	Rodil de Araujo Jr., Brazil	1996–2003	6	4	–	10
=	Bucky Lasek, USA	1998–2004	6	4	–	10
5	Bob Burnquist, Brazil	1998–2003	3	3	3	9
6	Rune Glifberg, Denmark	1995–2004	–	2	6	8
7 =	Chris Senn, USA	1997–2001	3	1	2	6
=	Pierre-Luc Gagnon, Canada	2002–04	2	4	–	6
=	Eric Koston, USA	2000–03	3	1	2	6
10 =	Neal Hendrix, USA	1995–2003	–	2	2	4
=	Mike Crum, USA	1999–2003	–	2	2	4
=	Kerry Getz, USA	2000–01	1	2	1	4

* Medals won at the X Games 1–10 and 2003 Global X Games; includes Vert, Street, and Park, doubles and best trick

top 10 VERT SKATERS, 2004 (MALE)

	SKATER / COUNTRY	WCS WORLD RANKING POINTS, 2004
1	Sandro Dias, Brazil	6,000
2	Neal Hendrix, USA	4,375
3	Andy Macdonald, USA	4,350
4	Lincoln Ueda, Brazil	4,275
5	Rune Glifberg, Denmark	4,150
6	Rodrigo Menezes, Brazil	4,025
7	Mike Crum, USA	3,925
8	Bob Burnquist, Brazil	2,900
9	Jake Brown, Australia	2,875
10	Juergen Horrwarth, Germany	2,725

Source: World Cup Skateboarding (WCS)

top 10 VERT SKATERS, 2004 (FEMALE)

	SKATER / COUNTRY	WCS WORLD RANKING POINTS, 2004*
1	Cara-Beth Burnside, USA	2,900
2	Lyn-Z Adams Hawkins, USA	2,700
3	Mimi Knoop, USA	2,500
4	Holly Lyons, USA	2,200
5	Tina Neff, Germany	1,450
6	Catherine Ashley, USA	1,300
7	Ciara d'Agostino, USA	1,200
8	Heidi Fitzgerald, USA	700
9	Julia Bauer, USA	650
10	Starr Quinn, USA	600

* Total of points won in the Slam City Jam, Beach Games, and Vans Triple Crowns Finals

Source: World Cup Skateboarding (WCS)

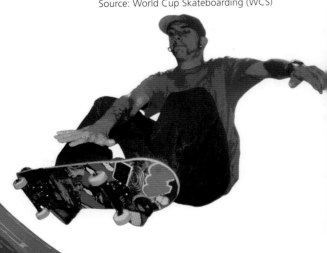

○ Star turn

Through his innovative and often unique tricks and his appearances in bestselling video games, Tony Hawk (b. 1968) has established himself as the world's best-known skateboarder.

top 10 STREET SKATERS, 2004 (MALE)

SKATER / COUNTRY	WCS WORLD RANKING POINTS, 2004
1 Rodil de Araujo Jr., Brazil	6,600
2 Ryan Sheckler, USA	4,150
3 Greg Lutzka, USA	3,770
4 Ronnie Creager, USA	3,705
5 Austen Seaholm, USA	3,540
6 Paul Machnau, Canada	3,475
7 Wagner Ramos, Brazil	3,375
8 Kyle Berard, USA	3,230
9 Bastien Salabanzi, France	3,125
10 Dayne Brummet, USA	3,110

Source: World Cup Skateboarding (WCS)

Ranking is arrived at by adding the points from a skater's four best results at North American WCS Points Events together with their best three results from WCS Points Events in Europe, Australia, Asia, and South America. Skaters have to take part in the World Championships in Dortmund, Germany, to win the No. 1 ranking.

top 10 STREET SKATERS, 2004 (FEMALE)

SKATER / COUNTRY	WCS WORLD RANKING POINTS, 2004*
1 Elissa Steamer, USA	4,000
2 Vanessa Torres, USA	3,800
3 Lyn-Z Adams Hawkins, USA	3,100
4 Patiane Freitas, Brazil	2,850
5 Lauren Perkins, USA	2,450
6 Alison Matasi, Canada	2,250
7 =Amy Caron, USA	2,000
=Jessica Krause, USA	2,000
9 Lauren Mollica, USA	1,775
10 Elizabeth Nitu, USA	1,700

* Total of points won in the Gallaz Skate Jam, Gravity Games, Vans Triple Crowns, and Canadian Open events

Source: World Cup Skateboarding (WCS)

Golf

top 10 **LOWEST** FOUR ROUND **WINNING** TOTALS IN MAJOR CHAMPIONSHIPS

	PLAYER / COUNTRY	VENUE	YEAR	TOTAL*
1	**David Toms**, USA	Atlanta, Georgia#	2001	265
2	**Phil Mickelson**, USA	Atlanta, Georgia#	2001	266
3	=**Greg Norman**, Australia	Royal St. George's, Sandwich†	1993	267
	=**Steve Elkington**, Australia	Riviera, California#	1995	267
	=**Colin Montgomerie**, UK	Riviera, California#	1995	267
6	=**Tom Watson**, USA	Turnberry†	1977	268
	=**Nick Price**, Zimbabwe	Turnberry†	1994	268
	=**Steve Lowery**, USA	Atlanta, Georgia#	2001	268
9	=**Jack Nicklaus**, USA	Turnberry†	1977	269
	=**Nick Faldo**, UK	Royal St. George's, Sandwich†	1993	269
	=**Jesper Parnevik**, Sweden	Turnberry†	1994	269
	=**Nick Price**, Zimbabwe	Southern Hills, Tulsa#	1994	269
	=**Davis Love III**, USA	Winged Foot, New York#	1997	269
	=**Tiger Woods**, USA	St. Andrews†	2000	269

* As at 1 Jan 2005
# US PGA Championship
† British Open Championship

The lowest four round totals in the other two Majors are: US Masters: 270 by Tiger Woods, US at Augusta, Georgia, 1997; US Open: 272 by Jack Nicklaus, US at Baltusrol, 1980; 272 by Lee Janzen, US at Baltusrol, 1993; and 272 by Tiger Woods, US at Pebble Beach, 2000.

⬆ **On the ball**
Vijay Singh stands second to Tiger Woods for career winnings but in 2004 Singh knocked Woods from the top of the World Golf Rankings.

top 10 **BIGGEST WINNING** MARGINS IN THE MAJORS

	PLAYER / COUNTRY	YEAR	TOURNAMENT	VENUE	WINNING MARGIN
1	**Tiger Woods**, USA	2000	US Open	Pebble beach	15
2	**Tom Morris Sr.**, UK	1862	British Open	Prestwick	13
3	=**Tom Morris Jr.**, UK	1870	British Open	Prestwick	12
	=**Tiger Woods**, USA	1997	US Masters	Augusta	12
5	**Willie Smith**, USA	1899	US Open	Baltimore	11
6	=**Jim Barnes**, USA	1921	US Open	Columbia	9
	=**Jack Nicklaus**, USA	1965	US Masters	Augusta	9
8	=**J.H. Taylor**, UK	1900	British Open	St. Andrews	8
	=**James Braid**, UK	1908	British Open	Prestwick	8
	=**J.H. Taylor**, UK	1913	British Open	Hoylake	8
	=**Ray Floyd**, USA	1976	US Masters	Augusta	8
	=**Tiger Woods**, USA	2000	British Open	St. Andrews	8

The biggest winning margin in the other Major – the US PGA Championship – was in 1980 when Jack Nicklaus won by seven strokes from Andy Bean at Oak Hill.

top 10 MONEY-WINNING GOLFERS

PLAYER / COUNTRY	CAREER WINNINGS* ($)
1 Tiger Woods, USA	45,142,737
2 Vijay Singh, Fiji	36,760,089
3 Phil Mickelson, USA	29,557,928
4 Davis Love III, USA	29,207,838
5 Ernie Els, South Africa	24,466,992
6 Jim Furyk, USA	19,731,382
7 Nick Price, Zimbabwe	19,715,533
8 David Toms, USA	18,942,915
9 Scott Hoch, USA	18,455,984
10 Justin Leonard, USA	17,639,781

* As at 1 Jan 2005

Tiger Woods' winnings from his profession place him at the top of this list, while his total earnings from endorsements of everything from golfing equipment to motor vehicles have made him the world's richest sportsman.

top 10 BRITISH AND EUROPEAN PLAYERS WITH THE MOST WINS IN THE RYDER CUP

PLAYER / COUNTRY	WINS
1 Nick Faldo, UK	23
2 Bernhard Langer, Germany	21
3 Severiano Ballesteros, Spain	20
4 Colin Montgomerie, UK	19
5 José Maria Olazábal, Spain	15
6 = Peter Oosterhuis, UK	14
= Ian Woosnam, UK	14
8 = Bernard Gallacher, UK	13
= Tony Jacklin, UK	13
10 Neil Coles, UK	12

* Up to and including 2004 Ryder Cup

First contested between the USA and Britain, the Ryder Cup was extended to include Ireland in 1973 and Europe since 1979. The European team has won on six occasions, with one draw in 1989.

top 10 PLAYERS TO WIN THE MOST MAJORS

PLAYER / COUNTRY	BRITISH OPEN	US OPEN	US MASTERS	US PGA	TOTAL*
1 Jack Nicklaus, USA	3	4	6	5	18
2 Walter Hagen, USA	4	2	0	5	11
3 = Ben Hogan, USA	1	4	2	2	9
= Gary Player, South Africa	3	1	3	2	9
5 = Tom Watson, USA	5	1	2	0	8
= Tiger Woods, USA	1	2	3	2	8
7 = Bobby Jones, USA	3	4	0	0	7
= Arnold Palmer, USA	2	1	4	0	7
= Gene Sarazen, USA	1	2	1	3	7
= Sam Snead, USA	1	0	3	3	7
= Harry Vardon, UK	6	1	0	0	7

* As at 1 Jan 2005

The oldest major tournament is the British Open, first played at Prestwick in 1860 and won by Willie Park. The first US Open was at the Newport Club, Rhode Island, held in 1895 and won by Horace Rawlins, playing over his home course. The US PGA Championship was first held at the Siwanoy Club, New York, where Jim Barnes beat Jock Hutchison by one hole in the match-play final. It did not become a stroke-play event until 1958. The youngest of the four majors is the Masters, played over the beautiful Augusta National course in Georgia. Entry is by invitation only and the first winner was Horton Smith. No man has won all four Majors in one year. Ben Hogan, in 1953, won three of the four, but did not compete in the PGA Championship. Bobby Jones achieved a unique Grand Slam in 1930 by winning the British Open and US Open, as well as winning the amateur titles in both countries.

Horse Sports

top 10 JOCKEYS IN A FLAT RACING SEASON

	JOCKEY	YEAR	WINS		JOCKEY	YEAR	WINS
1	Gordon Richards	1947	269	6	Frankie Dettori	1994	233
2	Gordon Richards	1949	261	7	Fred Archer	1883	232
3	Gordon Richards	1933	259	8	Gordon Richards	1952	231
4	Fred Archer	1885	246	9	Fred Archer	1878	229
5	Fred Archer	1884	241	10	Gordon Richards	1951	227

Richards rode over 200 winners in a season 12 times, while Archer did so on eight occasions. The only other men to reach double centuries are Tommy Loates (1893), Pat Eddery (1990), Michael Roberts (1992), and Kieren Fallon (1997, 1998, 1999, and 2003).

top 10 FASTEST TIMES IN THE MELBOURNE CUP

	HORSE	YEAR	TIME (MIN:SECS)		HORSE	YEAR	TIME (MIN:SECS)
1	Kingston Rule	1990	3:16.30	7	Saintly	1996	3:18.80
2	Media Puzzle	2002	3:16.97	8 =	Kiwi	1983	3:18.90
3	Tawriffic	1989	3:17.10	=	Black Knight	1984	3:18.90
4	Might and Power	1997	3:18.30	=	Empire Rose	1988	3:18.90
5	Gold and Black	1977	3:18.40	=	Let's Elope	1991	3:18.90
6	Brew	2000	3:18.68				

Held at the Flemington Park racetrack in Victoria, the Melbourne Cup was inaugurated in 1861 and takes place on the first Tuesday in November, when most of Australia comes to a standstill at 3.20 pm to listen to the race. More than 200,000 spectators attend the meeting. Originally held over two miles, it went metric in 1972 and is now run over 3,200 metres – 18.7 metres shorter than the original distance. The fastest time over two miles was 3 minutes 19.1 seconds by *Rain Lover* in 1968.

top 10 NATIONAL HUNT JOCKEYS WITH THE MOST WINS

	JOCKEY	YEARS	WINS*		JOCKEY	YEARS	WINS*
1	Tony McCoy	1994–2004	2,150	6	Mick Fitzgerald	1988–2005	1,072
2	Richard Dunwoody	1983–99	1,699	7	Stan Mellor	1952–72	1,035
3	Peter Scudamore	1978–95	1,678	8	Adrian Maguire	1991–2002	1,024
4	Richard Johnson	1994–2005	1,232	9	Peter Niven	1984–2002	1,002
5	John Francome	1970–85	1,138	10	Fred Winter	1939–64	923

* As at 1 Jan 2005

Peter Niven and Adrian Maguire both passed the 1,000 winner mark in 2001 and by coincidence they are the only two members of the "1,000" club never to have won the National Hunt Jockey's title. Niven is the first Scot to ride 1,000 National Hunt winners. Tony McCoy became the first man to ride 2,000 National Hunt winners on *Magical Balliwick* at Wincanton on 17th January 2004.

top 10 JOCKEYS WITH THE MOST BREEDERS' CUP WINS

	JOCKEY	YEARS	WINS		JOCKEY	YEARS	WINS
1	Jerry Bailey	1991–2003	14	=	Laffit Pincay Jr.	1985–93	7
2	Pat Day	1984–2001	12	=	Jose Santos	1986–2002	7
3	Mike Smith	1992–2002	10	=	Pat Valenzuela	1986–2003	7
4	Chris McCarron	1985–2001	9	10 =	Corey Nakatani	1996–2004	6
5	Gary Stevens	1990–2000	8	=	John Velazquez	1998–2004	6
6	= Eddie Delahoussaye	1984–93	7				

Source: The Breeders' Cup

Held at a different venue each year, the Breeders' Cup is an end-of-season gathering with seven races run during the day, with the season's best thoroughbreds competing in each category. Staged in October or November, there is $13 million prize money on offer with $4 million going to the winner of the day's senior race, the Classic. Churchill Downs is the most-used venue, with five Breeders' Cups since the first in 1984.

top 10 OLYMPIC EQUESTRIAN MEDAL-WINNING NATIONS*

	COUNTRY	GOLD	SILVER	BRONZE	TOTAL		COUNTRY	GOLD	SILVER	BRONZE	TOTAL
1	Germany/West Germany	35	19	21	75	6	Italy	7	9	7	23
2	US	9	19	18	46	7	Switzerland	4	10	7	21
3	Sweden	17	8	14	39	8	Netherlands	9	9	2	20
4	France	12	12	11	35	9	USSR/UnifiedTeam/Russia	6	5	4	15
5	Great Britain	6	9	10	25	10	Belgium	4	2	5	11

* Combined total of medals won for Show Jumping, Three Day Eventing, and Dressage; including the discontinued events of high jump and long jump (1900), and the individual and team figures event (1920)

Football

top 10 TRANSFER FEES BETWEEN ENGLISH CLUBS

	PLAYER	FROM	TO	YEAR	FEE (£)
1	Rio Ferdinand	Leeds United	Manchester United	2002	29,100,000
2	Wayne Rooney	Everton	Manchester United	2004	20,000,000
3	Rio Ferdinand	West Ham United	Leeds United	2000	18,000,000
4	Damien Duff	Blackburn Rovers	Chelsea	2003	17,000,000
5	Alan Shearer	Blackburn Rovers	Newcastle United	1996	15,000,000
6	Louis Saha	Fulham	Manchester United	2004	12,820,000
7	Dwight Yorke	Aston Villa	Manchester United	1998	12,600,000
8	Juan Veron	Manchester United	Chelsea	2003	12,500,000
9 =	Emile Heskey	Leicester City	Liverpool	2000	11,000,000
=	Robbie Fowler	Liverpool	Leeds United	2001	11,000,000
=	Frank Lampard	West Ham United	Chelsea	2001	11,000,000

Transfer fees appear to have spiralled in recent years, but it was a similar story in 1979 when Trevor Francis became Britain's first million-pound footballer. In 1962, Manchester United made Denis Law Britain's first £100,000 player when they bought him from the Italian club Torino. The first four-figure transfer fee came in 1905, when Middlesbrough paid Sunderland £1,000 for Alf Common, and the first £100 deal was clinched in 1892 when Aston Villa bought Willie Groves from West Bromwich.

When Bill Nicholson signed Jimmy Greaves for Spurs from Milan in 1961 he paid £99,999, but would not pay the other £1 because he did not want Greaves to have to carry the burden of being "Britain's first £100,000 footballer".

top 10 PREMIERSHIP GOALSCORERS

	PLAYER	CLUB(S)	GOALS*
1	Alan Shearer	Blackburn Rovers/Manchester United / Newcastle United	243
2	Andy Cole	Newcastle United/Manchester United/Blackburn Rovers	163
3	Les Ferdinand	Queen's Park Rangers/Newcastle United/Tottenham Hotspur/ West Ham United/Leicester City	149
4	Robbie Fowler	Liverpool/Leeds United/Manchester City	143
5	Teddy Sheringham	Nottingham Forest/Tottenham Hotspur/Manchester United/Portsmouth	139
6	Dwight Yorke	Aston Villa/Manchester United/Blackburn Rovers/Birmingham City	120
7	Michael Owen	Liverpool	118
8	Ian Wright#	Arsenal	113
9	Thierry Henry	Arsenal	112
10	Dion Dublin	Manchester United/Coventry City/Aston Villa/Leicester City	111

* As at end of the 2003–04 season

Retired

Although he started his career at Southampton, Alan Shearer never played for them in the Premiership. Shearer's first Premiership goal was for Blackburn Rovers on the opening day of the 1992–93 season, when he scored two against Crystal Palace. Despite missing half of the season through injury he still managed to score 16 goals. In April 1988 he scored a hat-trick for Southampton against Arsenal, and in doing so became the youngest scorer of a hat-trick in the top flight, at the age of 17 years and 240 days.

top 10 **CLUBS** WITH THE MOST FA CUP WINS

	TEAM	YEARS	TOTAL
1	Manchester United	1909–2004	11
2	Arsenal	1930–2003	9
3	Tottenham Hotspur	1901–91	8
4	Aston Villa	1887–1957	7
5 =	Blackburn Rovers	1884–1928	6
=	Newcastle United	1910–55	6
=	Liverpool	1965–2001	6
8 =	The Wanderers	1872–78	5
=	West Bromwich Albion	1888–1968	5
=	Everton	1906–95	5

The first ever FA Cup Final was played in 1872 at the Kennington Oval cricket ground with a crowd of about 2,000, when the Wanderers beat the Royal Engineers 1–0. Matches were played at Wembley (except for the 1970 replay, which took place at Old Trafford) from 1923, when Bolton Wanderers met West Ham United in front of a record crowd of 126,047, until the ground's closure in 2001 when the Millennium Stadium in Cardiff became the new home of English football.

top 10 **CLUBS** WITH THE MOST FOOTBALL LEAGUE TITLES

	CLUB	PERIOD	FL TITLES
1	Liverpool	1901–1990	18
2	Manchester United	1908–2003	15
3	Arsenal	1931–2004	13
4	Everton	1891–1987	9
5	Aston Villa	1894–1981	7
6	Sunderland	1892–1936	6
7 =	Sheffield Wednesday*	1903–30	4
=	Newcastle United	1905–27	4
9 =	Blackburn Rovers	1912–95	3
=	Huddersfield Town	1924–26	3
=	Wolverhampton Wanderers	1954–59	3
=	Leeds United	1969–92	3

* Previously The Wednesday

Running text fill to go here please running text fill to go here please. Running text fill to go here please running text fill to go here please. Running text fill to go here please running text fill to go here please.

top 10 **GOALSCORERS** IN A PREMIERSHIP SEASON

	PLAYER	CLUB	SEASON	GOALS*
1 =	Andy Cole	Newcastle United	1993–94	34
=	Alan Shearer	Blackburn Rovers	1994–95	34
3 =	Alan Shearer	Blackburn Rovers	1993–94	31
=	Alan Shearer	Blackburn Rovers	1995–96	31
5 =	Kevin Phillips	Sunderland	1999–2000	30
=	Thierry Henry	Arsenal	2003–04	30
7	Robbie Fowler	Liverpool	1995–96	28
8 =	Chris Sutton	Norwich City	1993–94	25
=	Matt Le Tissier	Southampton	1993–94	25
=	Robbie Fowler	Liverpool	1994–95	25
=	Les Ferdinand	Newcastle United	1995–96	25
=	Alan Shearer	Newcastle United	1996–97	25
=	Ruud van Nistelrooij	Manchester United	2002–03	25

* As at end 2003–04 season

top 10 **CLUBS** TO HAVE WON THE **MOST MATCHES** IN THE PREMIERSHIP

	TEAM	WINS*
1	Manchester United	292
2	Arsenal	244
3	Liverpool	223
4	Chelsea	203
5	Newcastle United	191
6	Leeds United	189
7	Aston Villa	181
8 =	Southampton	164
=	Tottenham Hotspur	164
10	Blackburn Rovers	162

* As at end of the 2003–04 season; all except Newcastle United (426) and Blackburn Rovers (392) have played 468 Premiership matches

International Soccer

top 10 GOALSCORERS IN INTERNATIONAL FOOTBALL

	PLAYER	COUNTRY	YEARS	GOALS*
1	Ali Daei	Iran	1993–2004	103
2	Ferenc Puskás	Hungary/Spain	1945–56	84
3	Pelé	Brazil	1957–71	77
4	Sándor Kocsis	Hungary	1948–56	75
5	Gerd Müller	West Germany	1966–74	68
6	Majed Abdullah	Saudi Arabia	1978–94	67
7	= Hossam Hassan	Egypt	1985–2004	63
	= Jassem Al-Houwaidi	Kuwait	1992–2002	63
	= Kiatisuk Senamuang	Thailand	1993–2004	63
10	Imre Schlosser	Hungary	1906–27	59

* As at 29 Jan 2005

Source: Roberto Mamrud, Karel Stokkermans, and RSSSF 1998/2005

If amateur appearances were included, Vivian Woodward (England) would figure on the list at No. 5 because he scored 73 goals for both the full and amateur England sides in 1903–14. The only two players on this list to win World Cup Winners' medals are Pelé and Gerd Müller. Between them, they scored 26 World Cup goals, with Müller's 14 making a record.

⬆ ZZ at the top
Despite securing the biggest transfer fee in football history, Zinedine Zidane has announced his retirement after the 2006–07 season.

top 10 TRANSFERS IN WORLD FOOTBALL

	PLAYER / COUNTRY	FROM	TO	YEAR	FEE (£)*
1	Zinedine Zidane, France	Juventus, Italy	Real Madrid, Spain	2001	45,620,000
2	Luis Figo, Portugal	Barcelona, Spain	Real Madrid, Spain	2000	37,000,000
3	Hernán Crespo, Argentina	Parma, Italy	Lazio, Italy	2000	35,500,000
4	Gianluigi Buffon, Italy	Parma, Italy	Juventus, Italy	2001	32,600,000
5	Christian Vieri, Italy	Lazio, Italy	Inter Milan, Italy	1999	32,000,000
6	Rio Ferdinand, UK	Leeds United, England	Manchester United, England	2002	29,100,000
7	Gaizka Mendieta, Spain	Valencia, Spain	Lazio, Italy	2001	29,000,000
8	Ronaldo, Brazil	Inter Milan, Italy	Real Madrid, Spain	2002	28,490,000
9	Juan Sebastian Veron, Argentina	Lazio, Italy	Manchester United, England	2001	28,100,000
10	Rui Costa, Portugal	Fiorentina, Italy	AC Milan, Italy	2001	28,000,000

* Figures vary slightly from source to source, depending on whether local taxes, agents' fees, and player's commission are included

The world's first £100,000 player was Omar Sivori, when he moved to Juventus (Italy) from Río de la Plata (Argentina) in 1957; the world's first £1 million player was Giuseppe Savoldi, when he moved from Bologna (Italy) to Napoli (Italy) in 1975; the world's first £10 million player was Gianluigi Lentini, when he moved from Torino (Italy) to AC Milan (Italy) in June 1992; and the first to be transferred for £20 million was the Brazilian Denilson, when he moved from São Paolo (Brazil) to Real Betis (Spain) in 1998.

top 10 PLAYERS WITH THE MOST INTERNATIONAL CAPS

	PLAYER	COUNTRY	YEARS	CAPS*
1	Claudio Suárez	Mexico	1992–2004	172
2	Mohamed Al-Deayea	Saudi Arabia	1990–2004	170
3	= Adnan Kh. Al-Talyania	United Arab Republic	1984–97	164
	= Cobi Jones	USA	1992–2004	164
5	Hossam Hassan	Egypt	1985–2004	163
6	Lothar Matthäus	West Germany/Germany	1980–2000	150
7	Sami Al-Jaber	Saudi Arabia	1992–2002	144
8	= Mohammed Al-Khilaiwi	Saudi Arabia	1990–2001	143
	= Thomas Ravelli	Sweden	1981–97	143
10	Marko Kristal	Estonia	1992–2004	142

* As at 29 Jan 2005

Source: Roberto Mamrud, Karel Stokkermans, and RSSSF 1998/2005

The first to amass 100 international caps was William Ambrose Wright, who played for England 104 times between 1947 and 1959. Mexican Claudio Suárez tops the table of male footballers, but US women's soccer player Kristine Marie Lilly has gained 294 caps.

top 10 COUNTRIES IN THE WORLD CUP

	COUNTRY	PLAYED	WON	DRAWN	LOST	FOR	AGAINST	POINTS*
1	Brazil	80	53	14	13	173	78	120
2	Germany/West Germany	78	45	17	16	162	103	107
3	Italy	66	38	16	12	105	62	92
4	Argentina	57	29	10	18	100	69	68
5	England	45	20	13	12	62	42	53
6	France	41	21	6	14	86	58	48
7	Spain	40	16	10	14	61	48	42
8	Yugoslavia	37	16	8	13	60	46	40
9	Uruguay	37	15	8	14	61	52	38
10	= Netherlands	32	14	9	9	56	36	37
	= Sweden	38	14	9	15	66	60	37

* Based on two points for a win and one point for a draw; matches resolved on penalties are classed as a draw

Brazil has qualified for every World Cup since the first in 1930, coming third in 1938, second in 1950 at home (the only time Brazil has hosted the event), and winning the tournament on the first of five occasions in 1958, when they defeated host nation Sweden 5–2. Brazil's other wins were in 1962, 1970, 1994, and 2002.

top 10 ENGLAND PLAYERS WITH THE MOST CAPS

	PLAYER / YEARS	INTERNATIONAL GOALS	CAPS*
1	Peter Shilton 1970–90	0	125
2	Bobby Moore 1962–73	2	108
3	Bobby Charlton 1958–70	49	106
4	Billy Wright 1946–59	3	105
5	Bryan Robson 1980–91	26	90
6	Kenny Sansom 1979–88	1	86
7	Ray Wilkins 1976–86	3	84
8	= Gary Lineker 1984–92	48	80
	= David Beckham 1996–2005	16	80
10	= John Barnes 1983–95	11	79

* As at 30 Mar 2005

Bobby Charlton's 49 goals scored for England in international matches stands as the all-time record, with Gary Lineker's 48 just behind. Jimmy Greaves's 44-goal tally is even more remarkable, since they were achieved in just 57 matches, while Nat Lofthouse's 30 goals produced from 33 games and Tommy Lawton's 22 from 23 only just miss an average of one goal per game. Peter Shilton made his senior debut for Leicester City in May 1966, and four years later he made his England debut against East Germany. Had Ray Clemence not also been at his peak at the same time, Shilton would surely have added more to his tally of 125 caps.

Motor Sports

top 10 DRIVERS WITH THE MOST FORMULA ONE WORLD TITLES

	DRIVER / COUNTRY	WORLD TITLE YEARS	RACES WON	WORLD TITLES
1	**Michael Schumacher**, Germany	1994–2004	83	7
2	**Juan Manuel Fangio**, Argentina	1951–57	24	5
3	**Alain Prost**, France	1985–93	51	4
4	= **Jack Brabbham**, Australia	1959–60	14	3
	= **Jackie Stewart**, UK	1969–71	27	3
	= **Niki Lauda**, Austria	1975–84	25	3
	= **Nelson Piquet**, Brazil	1981–87	23	3
	= **Ayrton Senna**, Brazil	1988–91	41	3
9	= **Alberto Ascari**, Italy	1952–53	13	2
	= **Graham Hill**, UK	1962–68	14	2
	= **Jim Clark**, UK	1963–65	25	2
	= **Emerson Fittipaldi**, Brazil	1972–74	14	2

top 10 FORMULA ONE DRIVERS WITH THE MOST GRAND PRIX WINS

	DRIVER / COUNTRY	CAREER	WINS*
1	**Michael Schumacher**, Germany	1991–2004	83
2	**Alain Prost**, France	1980–93	51
3	**Ayrton Senna**, Brazil	1984–94	41
4	**Nigel Mansell**, UK	1980–95	31
5	**Jackie Stewart**, UK	1965–73	27
6	= **Jim Clark**, UK	1960–68	25
	= **Niki Lauda**, Austria	1971–85	25
8	**Juan Manuel Fangio**, Argentina	1950–58	24
9	**Nelson Piquet**, Brazil	1978–91	23
10	**Damon Hill**, UK	1992–99	22

* As at end of 2004 season

Michael Schumacher's first Formula One drive was for Jordan in the 1991 Belgian Grand Prix. His first win was also in Belgium, a year later with Benetton. It was also at Belgium, in a Ferrari in 2001, that he overtook Alain Prost's record of 51 wins.

➔ Ahead of the race
Michael Schumacher has attained a level of statistical success in Formula One that is unlikely ever to be overtaken.

top 10 CONSTRUCTORS WITH THE MOST FORMULA ONE WORLD TITLES

	CONSTRUCTOR / COUNTRY	YEARS	TITLES*
1	**Ferrari**, Italy	1961–2004	14
2	**Williams**, UK	1980–97	9
3	**McLaren**, UK	1974–98	8
4	**Lotus**, UK	1963–78	7
5 =	**Brabham**, UK	1966–67	2
=	**Cooper**, UK	1959–60	2
7 =	**Benetton**, Italy	1995	1
=	**BRM**, UK	1962	1
=	**Matra**, France	1969	1
=	**Tyrrell**, UK	1971	1
=	**Vanwall**, UK	1958	1

* As at end of 2004 season

top 10 CARS WITH THE MOST WINS IN THE RALLY OF GREAT BRITAIN*

	CAR	YEARS	WINS
1 =	**Ford Escort**	1972–79	8
=	**Subaru Impreza**	1994–2004	8
3	**Saab 96**	1960–71	5
4 =	**Lancia Delta**	1985–91	4
=	**Toyota Celica**	1990–96	4
6 =	**Audi Quattro**	1981–83	3
=	**Peugeot 205**	1984–2001	3
8 =	**Jaguar SS100**	1937–38	2
=	**Jaguar XK120**	1951–53	2
=	**Volvo PV544**	1963–64	2
=	**Lancia Fulvia**	1969–70	2

* Known as the RAC Rally until 1997

top 10 FASTEST LE MANS 24-HOUR RACES

	DRIVERS / COUNTRIES	CAR	YEAR	WINNERS' AVERAGE SPEED (KM/H)	(MPH)
1	**Helmut Marko** (Austria), **Gijs van Lennep** (Holland)	Porsche 917K	1971	222.304	138.133
2	**Jan Lammers** (Holland), **Johnny Dumfries**, **Andy Wallace** (UK)	Jaguar XJR-9LM	1988	221.665	137.737
3	**Jochen Mass**, **Manuel Reuter** (West Germany), **Stanley Dickens** (Sweden)	Sauber Mercedes C9	1989	219.990	136.696
4	**Dan Gurney**, **A. J. Foyt** (USA)	Ford GT Mk4	1967	218.038	135.483
5	**Seiji Ara** (Japan), **Rinaldo Capello** (Italy), **Tom Kristensen** (Denmark)	Audi R8	2004	215.418	133.885
6	**Rinaldo Capello** (Italy), **Tom Kristensen** (Denmark), **Emanuele Pirro** (Italy)	Bentley Speed 8	2003	214.418	133.233
7	**Geoff Brabham** (Australia), **Christophe Bouchot**, **Eric Hélary** (France)	Peugeot 905B	1993	213.358	132.574
8	**Frank Biella** (Germany), **Tom Kristensen** (Denmark), **Emanuele Pirro** (Italy)	Audi V8	2002	213.068	132.394
9	**Klaus Ludwig**, **Louis Krages** ("John Winter") (West Germany), **Paulo Barilla** (Italy)	Porsche 956B	1985	212.021	131.744
10	**Chris Amon**, **Bruce McLaren** (New Zealand)	Ford GT Mk2	1966	210.795	130.983

The *24 heures du Mans*, or Le Mans 24-hour Race, has been staged on the circuit at Le Mans, France, since 1923, when the average speed was 92.065 km/h (57.205 mph). Driven by a team of two or three drivers, the car that covers the greatest distance in 24 hours wins the race.

Motorcycling

top 10 RIDERS WITH THE MOST WORLD 500CC TITLES

	RIDER / COUNTRY	CAREER	TITLES*
1	**Giacomo Agostini**, Italy	1964–77	8
2	**Mick Doohan**, Australia	1989–99	5 #
3	= **John Surtees**, UK	1952–60	4
	= **Mike Hailwood**, UK	1958–67	4
	= **Geoff Duke**, UK	1950–59	4
	= **Eddie Lawson**, USA	1983–92	4 #
	= **Valentino Rossi**, Italy	1996–2004	4
8	= **Kenny Roberts**, USA	1974–83	3 #
	= **Wayne Rainey**, USA	1984–93	3 #
10	= **Umberto Masetti**, Italy	1949–58	2 #
	= **Phil Read**, UK	1961–76	2
	= **Barry Sheene**, UK	1970–84	2 #
	= **Freddie Spencer**, USA	1980–93	2

* As at end of 2004 season

\# The rider's only world titles

⊙ High five

Despite a series of accidents, Mick Doohan won an unprecedented five consecutive world titles in 1994–98.

top 10 FASTEST ISLE OF MAN SENIOR TTS

	RIDER* / BIKE	YEAR	AVERAGE SPEED (KM/H)	(MPH)
1	**David Jefferies**, Suzuki	2002	200.74	124.73
2	**Adrian Archibald**, Suzuki	2003	200.40	124.53
3	**Adrian Archibald**, Suzuki	2004	199.25	123.81
4	**David Jefferies**, Yamaha	2000	196.25	121.95
5	**Steve Hislop**, Norton	1992	195.18	121.28
6	**David Jefferies**, Yamaha	1999	195.16	121.27
7	**Steve Hislop**, Honda	1991	194.87	121.09
8	**Ian Simpson**, Honda	1998	192.78	119.79
9	**Philip McCallen**, Honda	1996	192.73	119.76
10	**Steve Hislop**, Honda	1994	191.91	119.25

* All from Great Britain and Northern Ireland

The first 100-mph race took place in 1960, when John Surtees won at an average speed of 164.86 km/h (102.44 mph). The first 100-mph lap had been achieved in 1957 by Bob McIntyre riding a Gilera.

top 10 RIDERS WITH THE MOST RACE WINS IN A YEAR

	RIDER / COUNTRY	CLASS (CC)	YEAR	WINS*
1	**Mick Doohan**, Australia	500	1997	12
2	= **Giacomo Agostini**, Italy	500	1972	11
	= **Valentino Rossi**, Italy	125	1997	11
	= **Daijiro Kato**, Japan	250	2001	11
	= **Valentino Rossi**	500	2001	11
	= **Valentino Rossi**	MotoGP	2002	11
7	= **Mike Hailwood**, UK	250	1966	10
	= **Giacomo Agostini**	500	1968	10
	= **Giacomo Agostini**	500	1969	10
	= **Giacomo Agostini**	500	1970	10
	= **Anton Mang**, Germany	250	1987	10
	= **Fausto Gresini**, Italy	125	1987	10

* As at end of 2004 season

top 10 RIDERS IN THE 2004 MOTOGP WORLD CHAMPIONSHIP

	RIDER / COUNTRY	MOTOGP WORLD CHAMPIONSHIP POINTS
1	**Valentino Rossi**, Italy	304
2	**Sete Gibernau**, Spain	257
3	**Max Biaggi**, Italy	217
4	**Alex Barros**, Brazil	165
5	**Colin Edwards**, USA	157
6	**Makoto Tamada**, Japan	150
7	=**Carlos Checa**, Spain	117
	=**Nicky Hayden**, USA	117
	=**Loris Capirossi**, Italy	117
10	**Shinya Nakano**, Japan	83

World Championship points are awarded to riders who finish in the top 15 positions. The winner receives the maximum 25 points, runner-up 20, third 16, fourth 13, fifth 11, and then one point less for each of the next finishers, down to a single point for the fifteenth rider.

⬤ **Sete of his pants**
Newcomer Sete Giberneau took four first places in the 2004 season, but just missed out on his fifth first place to previous MotoGP champion Valentino Rossi.

top 10 RIDERS WITH THE MOST GRAND PRIX RACE WINS

	RIDER / COUNTRY	YEARS	WINS*
1	**Giacomo Agostini**, Italy	1965–76	122
2	**Angel Nieto**, Spain	1969–85	90
3	**Mike Hailwood**, UK	1959–67	76
4	**Valentino Rossi**, Italy	1996–2004	68
5	**Mick Doohan**, Australia	1990–98	54
6	**Phil Read**, UK	1961–75	52
7	**Jim Redman**, Southern Rhodesia	1961–66	45
8	=**Anton Mang**, West Germany	1976–88	42
	=**Max Biaggi**, Italy	1992–2004	42
10	**Carlo Ubbiali**, Italy	1949–60	39

* As at end of 2004 season

The UK's Barry Sheene won 23 races during his career and is the only man to win Grand Prix races at 50 and 500cc.

Rugby

top 10 BIGGEST WINS IN RUGBY UNION FULL INTERNATIONALS

	TEAMS (WINNER FIRST)	COMPETITION	DATE	SCORE	WINNING MARGIN
1	Japan v Taiwan	World Cup Qualifier	7 Jul 2002	155–3	152
2	Hong Kong v Singapore	World Cup Qualifier	27 Oct 1994	164–13	151
3	England v Romania	International	17 Nov 2001	134–0	134
4	Japan v Thailand	International	4 Nov 1996	141–10	131
5 =	Japan v Taiwan	World Cup qualifier	27 Oct 1998	134–6	128
=	New Zealand v Japan	World Cup	4 Jun 1995	145–17	128
7	Zimbabwe v Botswana	International	7 Sep 1996	130–10	120
8	Tonga v Korea	World Cup Qualifier	22 Mar 2003	119–0	119
9	Japan v Taiwan	World Cup Qualifier	21 Jul 2002	120–3	117
10 =	Japan v Sri Lanka	International	16 Dec 1998	116-0	116
=	Namibia v Madagascar	World Cup Qualifier	15 Jun 2002	116–0	116

As at 1 Jan 2005

In three consecutive World Cup qualifying matches between 30 June and 21 July 2002 Taiwan lost to Korea 119-7, and twice to Japan 155-3 and 120-3. Toru Kurihara scored a total of 81 points in the latter two matches for Japan. Taiwan's only points in the record-breaking match was a penalty from Chi-Chung Chen.

top 10 POINTS-SCORERS IN RUGBY UNION MAJOR INTERNATIONALS

	PLAYER / COUNTRY	YEARS	POINTS*
1	Neil Jenkins, Wales/British Lions	1991–2002	1,090
2	Diego Dominguez, Italy/Argentina	1989–2003	1,010
3	Andrew Mehrtens, New Zealand	1995–2004	967
4	Michael Lynagh, Australia	1984–95	911
5	Matthew Burke, Australia	1993–2004	878
6	Jonny Wilkinson, England/British Lions	1998–2003	853
7	Gavin Hastings, Scotland/British Lions	1986–95	733
8	Grant Fox, New Zealand	1985–93	645
9	Hugo Porta, Argentina	1971–90	590
10	Nicky Little, Fiji	1976–2003	574

* As at 1 Jan 2005

top 10 MOST-CAPPED RUGBY UNION PLAYERS

	PLAYER / COUNTRY	YEARS	CAPS*
1	Jason Leonard, England/British Lions	1990–2004	119
2	Philippe Sella, France	1982–95	111
3	George Gregan, Australia	1994–2004	105
4	David Campese, Australia	1982–96	101
5	Fabien Pelous, France	1995–2004	95
6	Serge Blanco, France	1980–91	93
7 =	Sean Fitzpatrick, New Zealand	1987–97	92
=	Martin Johnson, England/British Lions	1993–2003	92
=	Gareth Llewellyn, Wales	1989–2004	92
10 =	Rory Underwood, England/British Lions	1984–96	91
=	Neil Jenkins, Wales/British Lions	1991–2002	91

* As at 1 January 2005

Nicknamed "The Ginger Monster", Neil Jenkins became Rugby Union's most prolific points-scorer in the World Cup match against Samoa at Cardiff's Millennium Stadium on 14 October 1999. He scored 16 points and took his tally to 925, breaking the record of 911 set four years earlier by Australian Michael Lynagh. Sadly for Jenkins, who was also earning his 72nd cap, the game ended in a shock 38-31 defeat by the Samoans. Gavin Hastings made his Scotland debut, alongside brother Scott, in the 1986

Jason Leonard broke Philippe Sella's world record as the most capped player when he appeared for England in the 2003 World Cup semi-final against France. Add to that his five caps for the Lions and his final tally rose to 118 by the end of the tournament. Born in 1968, Leonard played the game over two decades and after three Lions tours and four World Cups he got his just rewards in 2003 as a member of the victorious England team in Australia. He started his career with his home-town team

top 10 SCORES IN THE 2003 WORLD CUP

	WINNERS / LOSER	ROUND	SCORE
1	Australia v Namibia	Pool A	111–13
2	England v Uruguay	Pool C	111–13
3	New Zealand v Tonga	Pool D	91–7
4	Australia v Romania	Pool A	90–8
5	England v Georgia	Pool C	84–6
6	South Africa v Uruguay	Pool C	72–6
7	New Zealand v Italy	Pool D	70–7
8	New Zealand v Canada	Pool D	68–6
9	Argentina v Namibia	Pool A	67–14
10	Ireland v Namibia	Pool A	64–7

The highest scoring match in Pool B was France's 61–18 win over Fiji.

The 2003 Rugby World Cup tournament ended in the most dramatic fashion. England's star Jonny Wilkinson delivered a drop-goal in the last minute of extra-time to give England a historic win and the Northern Hemisphere its first ever World Champion side.

the 10 BRITISH LIONS' BIGGEST TEST WINS

	OPPONENTS / VENUE	TEST / YEAR	SCORE
1	Australia, Brisbane	2nd Test 1966	31–0
2	Australia, Brisbane	1st Test 2001	29–13
3	South Africa, Pretoria	2nd Test 1974	28–9
4	South Africa, Port Elizabeth	3rd Test 1974	26–9
5	South Africa, Cape Town	1st Test 1997	26–16
6	= Australia, Sydney	2nd Test 1950	24–3
	= Australia, Sydney	2nd Test 1959	24–3
8	South Africa, Johannesburg	1st Test 1955	23–22
9	South Africa, Port Elizabeth	3rd Test 1938	21–16
10	New Zealand, Wellington	2nd Test 1993	20–7

This Top 10 is based on the greatest number of points scored by the Lions, not the greatest margin of victory, their record for which is their 31–0 win over Australia in 1966. After this remarkable win, the British Lions continued on an enormously

top 10 TRY-SCORERS IN A BRITISH SUPER LEAGUE SEASON

	PLAYER / TEAM	YEARS	TRIES
1	Danny Maguir, Leeds Rhinos	2004	29
2	Paul Newlove, St. Helens	1996	28
3	Kris Radlinski, Wigan Warriors	2001	27
4	= Matt Daylight, Gateshead Thunder	1999	25
	= Toa Kohe-Love, Warrington Wolves	1999	25
6	= Jason Robinson, Wigan	1996	24
	= Anthony Sullivan, St. Helens	1999	24
	= Dennis Moran, London Broncos	2003	24
9	= Francis Cummins, Leeds Rhinos	1999	23
	= Greg Fleming, London Broncos	1999	23
	= Graham Appo, Warrington Wolves	2003	23

Running text to go in here please running text to go in here please. Running text to go in here please running text to go in here please. Running text to go in here please running text to go in here please. Running text to go in here please running text to go in here please.Running text to go in here please running text to go in here please.Running text to go in here please running text to go in here please.Running text to go in here please running text to go in here please.

the 10 LATEST WINNERS OF THE LANCE TODD TROPHY

	PLAYER	MATCH
2004	Sean Long	St. Helens v Wigan Warriors
2003	Gary Connolly	Leeds Rhinos v Bradford Bulls
2002	Kris Radlinski	Wigan Warriors v St. Helens
2001	Sean Long	St. Helens v Bradford
2000	Henry Paul	Bradford v Leeds
1999	Leroy Rivett	Leeds v London
1998	Mark Aston	Sheffield v Wigan
1997	Tommy Martyn	St. Helens v Bradford
1996	Robbie Paul	Bradford v St. Helen
1995	Jason Robinson	Wigan v Leeds

The Lance Todd trophy is one of Rugby League's most prestigious awards and is awarded to the Man of the Match in the Challenge Cup Final. The winner of the trophy is decided by the members of the Rugby League Writers Association and is presented after the Challenge Cup final. The trophy is named in memory of former player and coach Lance Todd. The New Zealand tourist played for Wigan and was a renowned coach with Salford before his death in a road accident following a game at Oldham.

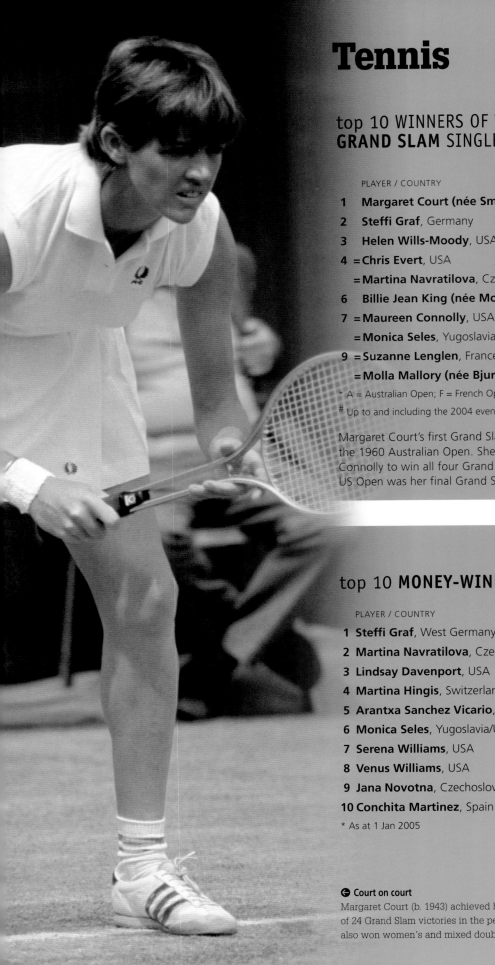

Tennis

top 10 WINNERS OF WOMEN'S GRAND SLAM SINGLES TITLES

PLAYER / COUNTRY	(A)	(F)	(W)	(US)	(TOTAL#)
1 Margaret Court (née Smith), Australia	11	5	3	5	24
2 Steffi Graf, Germany	4	6	7	5	22
3 Helen Wills-Moody, USA	0	4	8	7	19
4 =Chris Evert, USA	2	7	3	6	18
=Martina Navratilova, Czechoslovakia/USA	3	2	9	4	18
6 Billie Jean King (née Moffitt), USA	1	1	6	4	12
7 =Maureen Connolly, USA	1	2	3	3	9
=Monica Seles, Yugoslavia/USA	4	3	0	2	9
9 =Suzanne Lenglen, France	0	2	6	0	8
=Molla Mallory (née Bjurstedt), USA	0	0	0	8	8

The GRAND SLAM column header spans (A), (F), (W), (US).

* A = Australian Open; F = French Open; W = Wimbledon; US = US Open

Up to and including the 2004 events

Margaret Court's first Grand Slam singles title was on home soil when she won the 1960 Australian Open. She became only the second woman after Maureen Connolly to win all four Grand Slam events in one year in 1970. The 1973 US Open was her final Grand Slam singles title.

top 10 MONEY-WINNING TENNIS PLAYERS (WOMEN)

PLAYER / COUNTRY	WINNINGS ($)*
1 Steffi Graf, West Germany/Germany	21,895,277
2 Martina Navratilova, Czechoslovakia/USA	21,194,804
3 Lindsay Davenport, USA	18,694,975
4 Martina Hingis, Switzerland	18,344,660
5 Arantxa Sanchez Vicario, Spain	16,935,625
6 Monica Seles, Yugoslavia/USA	14,891,762
7 Serena Williams, USA	14,798,661
8 Venus Williams, USA	14,503,591
9 Jana Novotna, Czechoslovakia	11,249,134
10 Conchita Martinez, Spain	11,009,539

* As at 1 Jan 2005

← Court on court
Margaret Court (b. 1943) achieved her record total of 24 Grand Slam victories in the period 1960–73 and also won women's and mixed doubles at all four events.

top 10 WINNERS OF MEN'S GRAND SLAM SINGLES TITLES

	PLAYER / COUNTRY	(A)	(F)	(W)	(US)	(TOTAL#)
1	Pete Sampras, USA	2	0	7	5	14
2	Roy Emerson, Australia	6	2	2	2	12
3	=Björn Borg, Sweden	0	6	5	0	11
	=Rod Laver, Australia	3	2	4	2	11
5	Bill Tilden, USA	0	0	3	7	10
6	=Andre Agassi, USA	4	1	1	2	8
	=Jimmy Connors, USA	1	0	2	5	8
	=Ivan Lendl, Czechoslovakia/USA	2	3	0	3	8
	=Fred Perry, Great Britain	1	1	3	3	8
	=Ken Rosewall, Australia	4	2	0	2	8

The GRAND SLAM* header spans columns (A), (F), (W), (US), (TOTAL#).

* A = Australian Open; F = French Open; W = Wimbledon; US = US Open
# Up to and including the 2004 events

Australia's Roy Emerson had held the record for the most Grand Slam singles titles since 1968, but Pete Sampras equalled his record of 12 wins when he won Wimbledon in 1999 and the following year; when he beat Pat Rafter to retain his title, it was his 13th and record-breaking title.

top 10 MONEY-WINNING TENNIS PLAYERS (MEN)

	PLAYER / COUNTRY	WINNINGS ($)*
1	Pete Sampras, USA	43,280,489
2	Andre Agassi, USA	29,366,679
3	Boris Becker, West Germany/Germany	25,080,956
4	Yevgeny Kafelnikov, Russia	23,883,797
5	Ivan Lendl, Czechoslovakia/USA	21,262,417
6	Stefan Edberg, Sweden	20,630,941
7	Goran Ivanisevic, Croatia	19,876,579
8	Michael Chang, USA	19,145,632
9	Gustavo Kuerten, Brazil	14,609,954
10	Lleyton Hewitt, Australia	14,502,450

* As at 1 Jan 2005

◑ Net profit
Andre Agassi has more than matched his tennis earnings with income from endorsements of sportswear, mobile phones, and other products, establishing him as the world's wealthiest tennis star.

Water Sports

Golden boy
400-metre record-holder Ian Thorpe won three golds at the 2000 Olympics when he was just 17, and two at the 2004 Games – more gold wins than any other Australian.

top 10 OLYMPIC MEDAL-WINNING SWIMMERS (WOMEN)

SWIMMER / COUNTRY	(GOLD)	MEDALS (SILVER)	(BRONZE)	(TOTAL)
1 Jenny Thompson, USA	8	3	1	12
2 Franziska van Almsick, Germany	0	4	6	10
3 = Shirley Babashoff, USA	2	6	0	8
= Kornelia Ender, Germany	4	4	0	8
= Dawn Fraser, Australia	4	4	0	8
= Susie O'Neill, Australia	2	4	2	8
= Dara Torres, USA	4	0	4	8
= Inge de Bruijn, Netherlands	4	2	2	8
9 = Dagmar Hase, Germany	1	5	1	7
= Krisztina Egerszegi, Hungary	5	1	1	7

List-leader Jenny Thompson (b. 1973) competed in individual and relay events in four consecutive Olympics (1994–2004) to amass her unrivalled collection of both golds and medals overall. Her closest rival Franziska van Almsick won her first Olympic medal in 1992 at the age of just 14.

top 10 OLYMPIC MEDAL-WINNING SWIMMERS (MEN)

SWIMMER / COUNTRY	(GOLD)	MEDALS (SILVER)	(BRONZE)	(TOTAL)
1 = Matt Biondi, USA	8	2	1	11
= Mark Spitz, USA	9	1	1	11
3 Gary Hall Jr., USA	5	3	2	10
4 = Alexander Popov Unified Team/Russia	4	5	0	9
= Ian Thorpe, Australia	5	3	1	9
6 = Roland Matthes, Germany	4	2	2	8
= Michael Phelps, USA	6	0	2	8
8 = Zoltán Halmay, Hungary	2	4	1	7
= Tom Jager, USA	5	1	1	7
= Peter van den Hoogenband, Netherlands	3	2	2	7

* 1896–2004 excluding the 1906 Intercalated Games

Matt Biondi and Mark Spitz tie in first place, but the latter's achievement (and greater tally of golds) is all the more remarkable since he won a record seven at the same games (Munich, 1972), setting a new world record in each event.

top 10 LONGEST-STANDING CURRENT OLYMPIC SWIMMING RECORDS

	SWIMMER / COUNTRY / EVENT	TIME (MIN:SEC)	DATE WHEN RECORD SET
1	**Heike Friedrich**, East Germany Women's 200 m freestyle	1:57.65	21 Sept 1988
2	**Janet Evans**, USA Women's 400 m freestyle	4:03.85	22 Sept 1988
3	**Alexander Popov**, Unified Team Men's 50 m freestyle	0:21.91	30 July 1992
4	**Krisztina Egerszegi**, Hungary Women's 200 m backstroke	2:07.06	31 July 1992
5 =	**Yana Klochkova**, Ukraine Women's 400 m individual medley	4:33.59	16 Sept 2000
=	**Ian Thorpe**, Australia Men's 400 m freestyle	3:40.59	16 Sept 2000
7	**Inge de Bruijn**, Netherlands Women's 100 m butterfly	0:56.61	17 Sept 2000
8 =	**Australia**, Australia Men's 4 x 200 m freestyle relay	7:07.05	19 Sept 2000
=	**Pieter van den Hoogenband**, Netherlands Men's 100 m freestyle	0:47.84	19 Sept 2000
=	**Yana Klochkova**, Ukraine Women's 200 m individual medley	2:10.68	19 Sept 2000

The 200 m freestyle event was first competed at the Mexico Olympic in 1968, when it was won by Debbie Meyer (USA), establishing an Olympic record of 2 minutes 10.5 seconds. This was steadily trimmed to below 2 minutes, with Heike Friedrich's 1988 win at Seoul remaining unbeaten in all four subsequent Games.

top 10 OLYMPIC SAILING* COUNTRIES

	COUNTRY	MEDALS (G)	(S)	(B)	(TOTAL)
1	USA	18	22	18	58
2	Great Britain	23	14	10	47
3	France	16	11	14	41
4	Sweden	9	12	11	32
5	Norway	17	11	3	31
6 =	Denmark	11	8	6	25
=	Netherlands	7	9	9	25
8	Germany/ West Germany	6	6	7	19
9	Australia	5	3	8	16
10 =	New Zealand	6	4	5	15
=	Spain	10	4	1	15
=	USSR/Unified Team/Russia	4	6	5	15

* Previously named Olympic yachting

As a result of poor weather conditions, the sailing events scheduled for the first modern Olympics (Athens, 1896) were cancelled, but have been included since 1900. The USA did not win its first gold medals until the Los Angeles Games of 1932, but has gone on to take the lead in the overall medal table.

the 10 LATEST WINNERS OF THE AMERICA'S CUP

YEAR	WINNING BOAT / SKIPPER / COUNTRY	CHALLENGER / COUNTRY	SCORE
2003	**Alinghi**, Russell Coutts, Switzerland	Team New Zealand, New Zealand	5–0
2000	**Black Magic**, Russell Coutts, New Zealand	Prada Luna Rossa, Italy	5–0
1995	**Black Magic**, Russell Coutts, New Zealand	Young America, USA	5–0
1992	**America3**, Bill Koch, USA	Il Moro di Venezia, Italy	4–1
1988	**Stars and Stripes**, Dennis Conner, USA	New Zealand, New Zealand	2–0
1987	**Stars and Stripes**, Dennis Conner, USA	Kookaburra III, Australia	4–0
1983	**Australia II**, John Bertrand, Australia	Liberty, USA	4–3
1980	**Freedom**, Dennis Conner, USA	Australia, Australia	4–1
1977	**Courageous**, Ted Turner, USA	Australia, Australia	4–0
1974	**Courageous**, Ted Hood, USA	Southern Cross, Australia	4–0

The 132-year US domination of the America's Cup came to an end at 5.21 am on 26th September 1983, when 37-year-old John Bertrand skippered *Australia II* to victory with a revolutionary boat designed by Ben Lexcen and owned by Alan Bond.

Winter Sports

top 10 SNOWBOARDERS WITH THE MOST FIS WORLD CHAMPIONSHIP MEDALS

	SNOWBOARDER / COUNTRY	YEARS	(GOLD)	MEDALS (SILVER)	(BRONZE)	(TOTAL)
1	Nicolas Huet, France	1999–2005	2	1	2	5
2 =	Mike Jacoby, USA	1996–97	1	2	–	3
=	Helmut Pramstaller, Austria	1996–97	1	–	2	3
=	Jasey-Jay Anderson, Canada	2001–05	3	–	–	3
=	Antti Autti, Finland	2003–05	2	–	1	3
6 =	Bernd Kroschewski, Germany	1997	1	–	1	2
=	Markus Hurme, Finland	1997–2001	–	1	1	2
=	Anton Pogue, USA	1997–2001	–	–	2	2
=	Markus Ebner, Germany	1999–2001	1	1	–	2
=	Stefan Kaltschuetz, Austria	1999–2001	–	1	1	2
=	Mathieu Bozzetto, France	1999–2003	–	2	–	2
=	Dejan Kosir, Slovenia	2001–03	1	1	–	2
=	Kim Christiansen, Norway	2001–05	1	–	1	2
=	Simon Schoch, Switzerland	2003	–	1	1	2
=	Seth Wescott, USA	2003–05	1	1	–	2

Source: Fédération Internationale de Ski (FIS)

top 10 OLYMPIC FIGURE SKATING COUNTRIES

	COUNTRY	TOTAL MEDALS*
1	USSR/Unified Team/Russia	45
2	USA	42
3	Austria	20
4	Canada	19
5	Great Britain	15
6	France	12
7	Germany/West Germany	11
8 =	East Germany	10
=	Sweden	10
10 =	Norway	6
=	Hungary	6

* Gold, silver, and bronze medals; up to and including 2002 Winter Olympic Games

Figure skating was part of the Summer Olympics in 1908 and 1920, becoming part of the Winter programme in 1924.

🔙 Snow business
World champion snowboarder Jasey-Jay Anderson is Canada's best hope for gold at the 2006 Winter Olympics.

top 10 SKIERS WITH THE MOST ALPINE WORLD CUP TITLES

	SKIER / COUNTRY	YEARS	(OA)	(S)	(GS)	TITLES*(SG)	(DH)	(C)	(TOTAL)
1	Ingemar Stenmark, Sweden	1976–84	3	8	7	–	–	–	18
2	Annemarie Moser-Pröll, Austria	1971–79	6	–	3	–	7	1	17
3	=Marc Girardelli, Luxembourg	1984–95	5	3	1	–	2	4	15
	=Pirmin Zurbriggen, Switzerland	1984–90	4	–	3	4	2	2	15
5	=Vreni Schneider, Switzerland	1986–95	3	6	5	–	–	–	14
	=Hermann Maier, Austria	1998–2005	4	–	2	6	2	–	14
7	Katja Seizinger, Germany	1992–98	2	–	–	5	4	–	11
8	=Gustavo Thoeni, Italy	1971–74	4	2	3	–	–	–	9
	=Phil Mahre, USA	1981–83	3	1	2	–	–	3	9
	=Erika Hess, Switzerland	1981–84	2	5	1	–	–	1	9
	=Alberto Tomba, Italy	1988–95	1	4	4	–	–	–	9
	=Renate Goetschl, Germany	1997–2000	–	–	1	1	5	2	9

* OA = Overall; S = Slalom; GS = Giant slalom; SG = Super-giant slalom; DH = Downhill; C = Combined

The Alpine Skiing World Cup was launched as an annual event in 1967, with the addition of the super-giant slalom in 1986. Points are awarded for performances over a series of selected races during the winter months. As well as her 17 titles, Annemarie Moser-Pröll won a record 62 individual events in the period 1970–79, and went on to win gold for the Downhill event in the 1980 Olympic Games, when she achieved a record speed for women in the event of 99.598 km/h (61.887 mph).

top 10 SKIERS WITH THE MOST WORLD AND OLYMPIC NORDIC TITLES

	SKIER / COUNTRY	YEARS	TITLES*(ON)	(WC)	(TOTAL)
1	Bjørn Dæhlie, Norway	1991–98	8	5	13
2	Yelena Välbe, USSR/UT/Russia	1989–98	3	9	12
3	Larissa Lazutina, UT/Russia	1992–99	5	5	10
4	Gunde Svan, Sweden	1984–91	4	5	9
5	=Galina Kulakova, USSR	1968–76	4	3	7
	=Lyubov Yegorova, UT/Russia	1992–94	6	1	7
7	=Sixten Jernberg, Sweden	1956–64	4	2	6
	=Bente Skari (née Martinsen), Norway	1999–2003	1	5	6
9	=Birger Ruud, Norway	1931–37	2	3	5
	=Veikko Hakulinen, Finland	1952–60	3	2	5
	=Eero Mäntyränta, Finland	1960–68	3	2	5
	=Raisa Smetanina, USSR	1976–88	4	1	5
	=Vladimir Smirnov, USSR/UT/ Kazakhstan	1988–98	1	4	5
	=Stefania Belmondo, Italy	1993–2002	1	4	5

* ON = Olympic Nordic gold medal; WC = World Championship gold medal

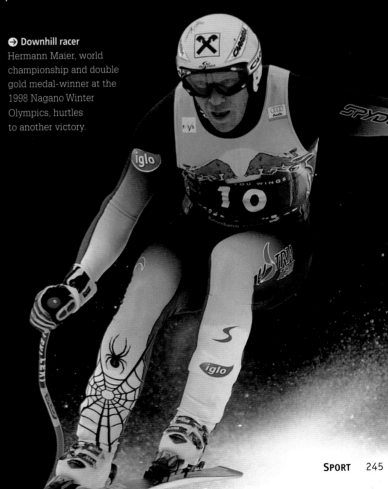

➔ Downhill racer
Hermann Maier, world championship and double gold medal-winner at the 1998 Nagano Winter Olympics, hurtles to another victory.

Further Information

THE UNIVERSE & THE EARTH

Asteroids
http://neo.jpl.nasa.gov/
NASA's Near Earth Object Program

Astronautics
http://www.astronautix.com/
Spaceflight news and reference

Comets
http://www.cometography.com/
Comet catalogue and descriptions

Elements
http://www.webelements.com/
A guide to all the elements in the periodic table

Islands
http://islands.unep.ch/isldir.htm
Information on the world's islands

NASA
http://www.nasa.gov/home/index.html
The main website for the American space programme

Oceans
http://www.oceansatlas.org/index.jsp
The UN's resource on oceanographic issues

Planets
http://www.nineplanets.org/
A multimedia tour of the Solar System

Mountains
http://peaklist.org/
Lists of the world's tallest mountains

Space
http://www.space.com/
Reports on events in space exploration

LIFE ON EARTH

Animals
http://animaldiversity.ummz.umich.edu/site/index.html
A wealth of animal data

Birds
http://www.bsc-eoc.org/avibase/avibase.jsp
A database on the world's birds

Conservation
http://iucn.org/
The leading nature conservation site

Endangered
http://www.cites.org/
Lists of endangered species of flora and fauna

Environment
http://www.unep.ch/
The UN's Earthwatch and other programmes

Fish
http://www.fishbase.org/home.htm
Global information on fishes

Food and Agriculture Organization
http://www.fao.org/
Statistics from the UN's FAO website

Forests, UK
http://www.forestry.gov.uk/
The website of the Forestry Commission

Insects
http://ufbir.ifas.ufl.edu/
The University of Florida Book of Insect Records

Pets
http://petsforum.com/
Information about cats, dogs, and other pets

THE HUMAN WORLD

Crime, international
http://www.interpol.int/
Interpol's crime statistics

Crime, UK
http://www.homeoffice.gov.uk/
Home Office crime and prison population figures

Death penalty
http://web.amnesty.org/pages/deathpenalty-statistics-eng
Facts ands statistics from Amnesty International

Leaders
http://www.terra.es/personal2/monolith/home.htm
Facts about world leaders since 1945

Names
http://www.behindthename.com/
Most popular names lists and other information

Parliaments
http://www.ipu.org/
Women in parliaments, etc from the Inter-Parliamentary Union

Religions
http://www.worldchristiandatabase.org/wcd/
World religion data

Royalty
http://www.royal.gov.uk/
The official site of the British Monarchy, with histories

Rulers
http://rulers.org/
A database of the world's rulers and political leaders

World Health Organization
http://www.who.int/en/
World health information and advice

TOWN & COUNTRY

Bridges
http://www.struct.kth.se/research/bridges/Bridges.htm
The longest bridges listed by type

Countries
http://www.theodora.com/wfb/
Country data, rankings, etc

Country and city populations
http://www.citypopulation.de/cities.html
A searchable world guide to the world's countries and major cities

Country data
http://www.odci.gov/cia/publications/factbook/
The CIA World Factbook

Country population
http://www.un.org/esa/population/unpop.htm
The UN's worldwide data on population issues

Development
http://www.worldbank.org/
Development and other statistics from around the world

Population
http://www.census.gov/
US and international population statistics

Skyscrapers
http://www.emporis.com/en/bu/sk/
The Emporis database of high-rise buildings

Tunnels
http://home.no.net/lotsberg/
A database of the longest rail, road, and canal tunnels

UK statistics
http://www.statistics.gov.uk/
The home of official UK figures on population, etc

CULTURE & LEARNING

The Art Newspaper
http://www.theartnewspaper.com/
News and views on the art world

The Bookseller
http://www.thebookseller.com/
The organ of the British book trade

The British Library
http://www.bl.uk/
The route to the catalogues and exhibitions in the national library

Education
http://www.dfes.gov.uk/statistics/
Official statistics relating to education in the UK

Languages of the world
http://www.ethnologue.com/
Online reference work on the world's 6,912 languages

Languages online
http://global-reach.biz/globstats/index.php3
Facts and figures on online languages

The Man Booker Prize
http://www.bookerprize.co.uk/
Britain's most prestigious literary prize

Nobel Prizes
http://www.nobel.se/
A searchable database of all Nobel Prizewinners

UK museums & galleries
http://www.24hourmuseum.org.uk/
A guide to exhibitions and events at the UK

UNESCO
http://www.unesco.org/
Comparative international statistics on education and culture

MUSIC & MUSICIANS

All Music Guide
http://www.allmusic.com/
A comprehensive guide to all genres of music

Billboard
http://www.billboard.com/
US music news and charts data

The Brit Awards
http://www.brits.co.uk/
The official website for the popular music awards

The British Phonographic Industry Ltd
http://www.bpi.co.uk/
Searchable database of gold discs and other certified awards

Grammy Awards
http://www.naras.org/
The official site for the famous US music awards

Launch
http://uk.launch.yahoo.com/index.html
UK music charts and news from Yahoo

MTV
http://www.mtv.co.uk/
The online site for the MTV UK music channel

New Musical Express
http://www.nme.com/
The online version of the popular music magazine

Official UK Charts Company
http://www.theofficialcharts.com/
Weekly and historical music charts

VH1
http://www.vh1.com/
Online UK music news

STAGE & SCREEN

Academy Awards
http://www.oscars.org/academyawards/
The official "Oscars" website

BBC
http://www.bbc.co.uk/
Gateway to BBC TV and radio, with a powerful Internet search engine

Empire Online
http://www.empireonline.co.uk/
The website of the UK film magazine

Film Distributors' Association
http://www.launchingfilms.com/
Trade site for UK film releases and statistics

Golden Globe Awards
http://hfpa.org/html/
Hollywood Foreign Press Association's Golden Globes site

Internet Movie Database
http://www.imdb.com/
The best of the publicly accessible film websites; IMDbPro is available to subscribers

London Theatre Guide
http://www.londontheatre.co.uk/
A comprehensive guide to West End theatre productions

Screen Daily
http://www.screendaily.com/
Daily news from the film world at the website of UK weekly *Screen International*

Variety
http://www.variety.com/
Extensive entertainment information (extra features available to subscribers)

Yahoo! Movies
http://movies.yahoo.com/
Charts plus features, trailers, and links to the latest film releases

COMMERCIAL WORLD

The Economist
http://www.economist.com/
Global economic and political news

Energy
http://www.bp.com/
The *BP Statistical Review of World Energy*

Environmental Sustainability Index
http://www.ciesin.columbia.edu/indicators/ESI/
Data on the planet's future

Forbes magazine
http://www.forbes.com/
"Rich lists" and other rankings and business information

Gold
http://www.gold.org/
The website of the World Gold Council

Health & Safety, UK
http://www.hse.gov.uk/
Information and statistics on workplace safety and accidents

International Labour Organization
http://www.ilo.org/
Facts and figures on the world's workers

Organisation for Economic Co-operation and Development
http://www.oecd.org/
World economic and social statistics

United Nations Development Programme
http://www.undp.org/
Country GDPs and other development data

The World Bank
http://www.worldbank.org/
World development, trade, and labour statistics

TRANSPORT & TOURISM

Air disasters
http://www.airdisaster.com/
Reports on aviation disasters

Association of Leading Visitor Attractions
http://www.alva.org.uk/
Information and visitor statistics on the UK's top tourist attractions

Imperial War Museum
http://www.iwm.org.uk/
The website of the UK's major military collection

Metros
http://www.lrta.org/world/worldind.html
A guide to the world's light railways and tram systems

Railways
http://www.railwaygazette.com/
The world's railway business in depth from *Railway Gazette International*

Road transport
http://www.irfnet.org/
Facts and figures from the International Road Federation

Shipwrecks
http://users.accesscomm.ca/shipwreck/
A huge database of the world's wrecked and lost ships

Statistics on Tourism & Research
http://www.staruk.org.uk/
UK tourism stats from Star UK

Tourism Offices Worldwide Directory
http://www.towd.com/
Contact details for tourism offices around the world

World Tourism Organisation
http://www.world-tourism.org/
The world's principal travel and tourism organization

SPORT & LEISURE

Athletics
www.britishathletics.info/
British athletics news and rankings

Cricket
http://www.cricinfo.com/
Cricinfo, launched in 1993, now merged with the online version of *Wisden*

FIFA
http://www.fifa.com
The official website of FIFA, the world governing body of soccer

Football
www.football-league.co.uk
The official site of the Football League

Formula One
http://www.eia.doe.gov/
The official F1 website

Olympics
www.olympic.org/uk/games/index_uk.asp
The official Olympics website

Premier League
http://www.premierleague.com
The official web site of soccer's Premier League

Rugby
http://www.itsrugby.com/
Comprehensive rugby site

Skiing
http://www.fis-ski.com/
Fédération Internationales de Ski
The world governing body of skiing and snowboarding

International Rugby Board
http://www.irb.com
The official website of the IRB

Index

Acknowledgments

Special research: Ian Morrison (sport);
Dafydd Rees (USA); Louise Reip

Alexander Ash; Caroline Ash; Nicholas Ash;
Emma Beatty; Roland Bert; Peter Bond; Nicolas
Brasch; Thomas Brinkoff; Richard Chapman;
Pete Compton; Luke Crampton; Philip Eden;
Christopher Forbes; Russell E. Gough; Robert
Grant; Bob Gulden; Angela Hayes; Duncan
Hislop; Andreas Hörstemeier; Richard Hurley;
Todd M. Johnson; Larry Kilman; Dr. Benjamin
Lucas; Roberto Mamrud; Chris Mead; Sylvia
Morris; Roberto Ortiz de Zarate; Matthew
Paton; Tony Pattison; Christiaan Rees; Linda
Rees; Kathy Rooney; John Seech; Robert Senior;
Karel Stockkermans; Mitchell Symons; Natacha
Vassiltchikov; Lucy T. Verma

Academy of Motion Picture Arts and Sciences –
Oscar statuette is the registered trademark
and copyrighted property of the Academy
of Motion Picture Arts and Sciences
Ad Age Global
Airports Council International
Air Transport Users Council
American Association of Port Authorities
Amnesty International
Amusement Business
Art Loss Register
The Art Newspaper
Art Sales Index
Association of Leading Visitor Attractions
Atlantic Oceanographic and Meteorological
Laboratory/National Oceanic and
Atmospheric Administration
Audit Bureau of Circulations Ltd.
BBC Radio 1
BBC Radio 4
Bloomsbury English Dictionary
BP Statistical Review of World Energy 2004
The BRIT Awards
British Council
British Library
British Museum
British Video Association
Broadcasters Audience Research Board Ltd.
Business Week
Cameron Mackintosh Ltd.
Canada Geological Society
Center for the Study of Global Christianity,
Gordon-Conwell Theological Seminary
Central Intelligence Agency
Christie's
Commission for Distilled Spirits
CricInfo
CRC Handbook of Chemistry and Physics

Criminal Statistics England & Wales
De Beers
Department for Environment, Food
and Rural Affairs
The Economist
Energy Information Administration
Entertainment and Leisure Software
Publishers Association
Euromonitor
Europa
Fédération Internationale de Football Association
Fédération Internationale de Ski
Feline Advisory Bureau/Felix
Food and Agriculture Organization of the
United Nations
Forbes
Forestry Commission
Gemstone Publishing, Inc.
Gold Fields Mineral Services
Health and Safety Executive
HM Treasury
Home Accident Surveillance System
Home Office
Initiative Global Adex 2004
Interbrand
International Agency for Research on Cancer
International Civil Aviation Organization
International Coffee Organisation
International Game Fish Association
The International Institute for Strategic Studies,
The Military Balance 2004–2005
International Labour Organization
International Obesity Task Force
International Olympic Committee
International Shark Attack File/American
Elasmobranch Society/Florida Museum
of Natural History
International Tea Committee Ltd.
International Telecommunication Union
Internet World Stats
Interpol
Joint United Nations Programme on
HIV/AIDS (UNAIDS)
Leisure Accident Surveillance System
Lloyds Register-Fairplay Ltd.
MRIB
MTV Video Music Awards (VMA)
Music Information Database
National Academy of Recording Arts and
Sciences, USA (Grammy Awards)
National Aeronautics and Space Administration
(NASA), USA
National Basketball Association (USA)
National Football League (USA)
New South Wales Registry of Births, Deaths
and Marriages in Australia

Niagara Falls Museum
Nielsen BookScan
Nielsen/NetRatings
Office for National Statistics
The Official UK Charts Company
Organisation for Economic Co-operation
and Development
Organisation Internationale des Constructeurs
d'Automobiles
The Overstreet Comic Book Price Guide
Pet Food Manufacturers' Association
Power & Motoryacht
P.W. Productions
Radio Joint Audience Research Ltd.
Railway Gazette International
River Systems of the World
Royal Astronomical Society
Royal Opera House, Covent Garden
RSSSF
Sarah Mitchell Partnership
Screen Digest
Screen International
Shakespeare Centre
Society of London Theatre(Olivier Awards)
Society of Motor Manufacturers and Traders Ltd.
Sotheby's
Stores
Times University Guides
TNS Infosys
Tour de France
The Tree Register of the British Isles
United Nations
United Nations Educational, Scientific
and Cultural Organization
United Nations Population Division
United World Chart, mediatraffic
US Census Bureau
US Geological Survey
US Social Security Administration
Variety
Victorian Registry of Births, Deaths
and Marriages in Australia
volcanolive.com
WebElements
Whitbread Book Awards
World Association of Newspapers
World Atlas of Coral Reefs
World Bank
World Cup Skateboarding
World Economic Forum
World Gold Council
World Health Organization
World of Learning
World Tourism Organizationa

PUBLISHER'S ACKNOWLEDGMENTS

Dorling Kindersley would like to thank the following for their contributions: Design: Rebecca Painter, Mandy Earey

PACKAGER'S ACKNOWLEDGMENTS

The Bridgewater Book Company would like to thank Alison Bolus, Ursula Caffrey, Sarah Doughty, Nicky Gyopari, and Sara Harper for their editorial assistance, and Emily Wilkinson, Richard Peters, Lyndsey Godden and Chris Morris for their design work.

Picture Credits

The publisher would like to thank the following for their kind permission to reproduce their photographs:
(Abbreviations key: t = top, b = bottom, r = right, l = left, c = centre)

AKG-IMAGES: 68tl

CORBIS: 10t Eye Ubiquitous, 12bl Gianni Dagli Orti, 12/13 Bettmann, 15 Denis Scott, 24 Doug Wilson, 29 Tom Bean, 31 Historical Picture Archive, 36 W. Perry Conway, 37r David A. Northcott, 39m Steve Austin; Papilio, 43r George D. Lepp, 44t Dex Images, 48 Enzo & Paolo Ragazzini, 53 ER Productions, 57 Baci, 58 Peter Johnson, 59 John Van Hasselt/Sygma, 60 Kate Brooks, 62 Frank Trapper, 63 Tess Peni/Austral International/Sygma, 66 Bettmann, 67 Reuters, 68 Bl Stapleton Collection, 69tr Miyajima Shigeki/Sygma, 69br, 71 Bettmann, 74 Hulton-Deutsch Collection, 75 Michael St Maur Sheil, 76r Chris Helgren/Reuters, 83 Macduff Everton, 83 inset Steve Bein, 84/85 Bob Krist, 86/87 Nik Wheeler, 88 Roy Corral, 90 Simon Kwong/Reuters, 91 Imagemore Co.Ltd., 97r Carl and Ann Purcell, 98 Reuters, 104 Ron Watts, 105 Dean Conger, 106 Francis G Mayer, 110b Reuters, 111t Reuters, 112l Underwood and Underwood, 113t +113b Bettmann, 114 Roger Ressmeyer, 115 Neal Preston, 116 Steve Azzara, 117b Bettmann, 118 David Bergman, 119 Rune Hellestad, 121 David Bergman, 122 Robert Eric/Sygma, 125t Derick A. Thomas; Dat's Jazz, 125b Gary Hershorn/Reuters, 126 Reuters, 127 Reuters, 130 Roger Ressmeyer, 141 Trapper Frank/Corbis Sygma, 142 Bettmann, 143 Merie W. Wallace/ Warner Bros/Bureau L.A.Collections, 144 Merie W. Wallace/ Warner Bros/Bureau L.A.Collections, 148 Tracy Bennett/Paramount Pictures/ Bureau L.A,150 Neal Preston, 152 Warner Bro.Picture/Bureau L.A. Collection, 156 © Walt Disney Pictures/Pixar Animation/Bureau L.A.Collections, 157 DreamWorks Animation/Bureau L.A.Collections, 158/9 Jeffrey L.Rotman, 161 Jack Dabaghian/Reuters, 163 Fred Prouser/Reuters, 166 Wally McNanee, 167 Tom & Dee Ann McCarthy, 168 Reuters, 169b Charles Jean Marc/Sygma, 171 Russell Boyce/Reuters, 173 Hulton-Deutsch Collection, 175 Claro Cortes IV/Reuters, 176t Shaun Best/Reuters, 176b Eriko Sugita/Reuters, 177 Steve Raymer, 187 Neil Rabinowitz, 190 Hulton-Deutsch Collection, 191 Tom Wagner/Saba, 193 Michael S. Yamashita, 194 Jason Hawkes, 198 Nik Wheeler, 199 Jonathan Blair, 200 William Manning, 204 Ruzniewski J.Y/Sygma, 205 Bettmann, 206b Reuters, 208/9T Hulton-Deutsch Collection, 209t Kin Cheung/Reuters, 209bl Bettmann, 209br Eddy Lemaistre/For Picture, 210 Reuters, 212 Dylan Martinez/Reuters, 213 Gary Hershorn/Reuters, 214 Reuters, 219 Leo Dennis/NewSport, 220 Steve Marcus/Reuters, 221b Reuters, 222 Corbis TempSport, 223 ERIC GAILLARD/Reuters, 225 Matt A Brown/X Games IV, 226 tr Ellen Ozier/Reuters, 229 Reuters, 232t

Reuters, 234 Victor Fraile/Reuters, 236 Reuters, 237 David W Cerny, 240 Bettmann, 241 Duomo, 242 Reuters, 244b Andy Clark/Reuters, 245 Leonhard Foeger/Reuters

DK: 10/11 Mike Dunning, 11 Harry Taylor courtesy of the Natural History Museum, 14bl Luciano Corbella, 14br Julian Baum, 20bl +t+b, Jerry Young, 20ml Dave King, 20m, 23t, 25 mr+tr Richard Bronson, 31 inset Michael Moran, 32/33, 34b Colin Keates, 34t Richard Lewis, 35 Jeremy Hunt, 37t Tom Shepard/Oxford ScientificFilms, 38l Jerry Young, 38r Cyril Laubschel, 39t Dave King, 40t Frank Greenaway courtesy The Natural History Museum, 40b Colin Keates courtesy The Natural History Museum, 41bl Jerry Young 41tl Colin Keates, 41tr Rob Reichenfeld, 41mr Geoff Dann, 44bl, 45t Max Gibbs, 45 tm + bl Dave King, 45br Paul Bricknell, 46l, 46m Gordon Clayton, 46b Cyril Laubschel, 46r Bill Ling, 48/9b Matthew Ward, 49tl Peter Chadwick,49l Matthew Ward, 49r Neil Fletcher and Matthew Ward, 52, 60b Lisa Stock, 61 Guy Rycart, 70 Francesca Yorke, 71 background Sallie Alane Reason, 80t, 82 Martin Cropper, 97t, 112 Scott Pitts, 113, 134b Demetrio Carrasco 155tr, 174 Alan Keohane, 178, 178br, 180l Trish Grant, 180r Guy Rycart, 206r Coin design © courtesy of the Royal Canadian Mint/Image de pièce © courtoisie de la Monnaie royale canadienne, 208 Clive, 211b both Sebastian Quigly, 215t John Garrett, 230/231, 243t Andy Crawford, 243b James Stevenson and Tina Chambers courtesy of the National Maritime Museum

ENVIROMISSION LTD.: 93all

GETTY-IMAGES: 43l Jonathan and Angela /Taxi

PHIL/CDC: 56

REXFEATURES: 112/113, 120 Giovanni Canitano, 123 ROO, 128 Walt Disney/Everett, 135 Brian Rasic 137 KUS, 138 Warner Bros./Everett, 139 Lions Gate/Everett, 140 Universal/Everett, 151 New Line/Everett, 154 Walt Disney/Everett, 155 Universal/Everett, 162 Dreamworks/Everett, 170b Nick Cornish,

NASA: 14T JPL, 16/17 all, 18, 19, 21, 22 Jeff Schmaltz/Modis/GSFC, 30, 39bl

U.S.Air Force: 77

VINTAGE MAGAZINE CO: 102/103,103

WHO/P.Virot: 54/55 all

FILMS
128 Sweet Home Alabama © Disney Enterprises Inc.
129 The Motorcycle Diaries © South Fork Pictures
136 Gone with the Wind © SELZNICK/MGM
137 Spiderman II © MARVEL/SONY PICTURES
138t Troy © Warner Bros.
139 Farenheit © Lions Gate Films
140 Ray © Universal Pictures
145 Ben Hur © MGM
147 Lord of the Rings © New Line Productions,Inc.
149 The Aviator © Warner Bros/Miramax
151 Lord of the Rings: © New Line Productions,Inc.
153 Master and Commander,The Far Side of the World © 20th Century Fox/Universal
155 Meet The Fockers © Universal Pictures
156 The Incredibles © Disney Enterprises Inc.
157 Shark Tale © DreamWorks Animation
162 Shrek © DreamWorks Animation

For further information see: **www.dkimages.com**